Berlitz HANDBOOK

VIETNAM

SO-ABA-733

Contents

Top **25** attractions

1 **Halong Bay Cruise** Visit the World Heritage bay where dragons emerge from the deep as limestone cliffs *(see p.22, 119)*

2 **Hue Imperial City** Explore this resplendent Forbidden City on the banks of the Perfume River *(see p.137)*

3 **Exploring Hanoi's Old Quarter** Spend a day wandering the ancient streets of Vietnam's most atmospheric city *(see p.72)*

4 **Kiteboarding in Mui Ne** In the air, riding the surf or on the beach at this watersports capital. *(see p.176)*

5 **Cuc Phuong National Park** Lush jungles inhabited by some of the world's rarest primates *(see p.123)*

6 **Sa Pa's hill-tribe villages** Visit exotic ethnic groups amid breath-taking mountain scenery *(see p.103)*

7 **Ruou can** Sampling the finest mountain spirits is one of the highlights of a visit to a hill-tribe village *(see p.31)*

8 **Biking in Dalat** A great way to experience the hill town and its French colonial architecture *(see p.185)*

9 **Cu Chi Tunnels** Crawl through the extraordinary network of subterranean passages (see p.219)

10 **Diving at Nha Trang** Vietnam's favourite party town is blessed with accessible coral reefs (see p.50)

11 **Mekong Delta boat trips** Take the scenic route to the floating markets (see p.28)

12 **Tam Coc and Ngo Dong River** Drift through spellbinding scenery on a tranquil river (see p.26, 123)

13 **Whale worship in Phan Thiet** Temples house whale skeletons venerated by fishermen (see p.177)

15 **Hiking in Cat Tien National Park** Night safaris, crocodile lakes and jungle hikes galore *(see p.189)*

14 **Craft Villages** Discover the small settlements around Hanoi through the crafts they produce *(see p.83)*

16 **Street food** From fruit to grilled meats, all is available in Vietnam's street markets *(see p.36, 285)*

17 **Phu Quoc and the Con Dao Archipelago** Coconut groves, sandy beaches and coral reefs, still relatively undeveloped *(see p.242)*

18 **My Son** Wander among ancient Cham temple ruins, reflecting on more than 1,000 years of history *(see p.154)*

19 **China Beach and Marble Mountain** Serene temples next door to Vietnam's premier surf beach *(see p.148–9)*

20 **Modern Saigon** Catch a view from the 68th floor, shop in luxury malls then go clubbing until late in this booming metropolis *(see p.200)*

21 **Ben Thanh Market** Haggle like a local over fresh produce, clothing and much more *(see p.209)*

22 **Hanoi museums and Ho Chi Minh Mausoleum** Gen up on the country's past *(see p.71–79)*

23 **Hoi An** An atmospheric trading port with unique architecture, great shopping and dining *(see p.150)*

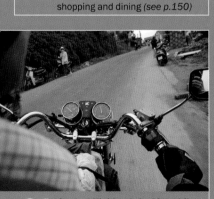

24 **Central Highlands by Motorbike** An exciting road trip through a little-known area *(see p.192)*

25 **Hue Imperial Tombs** Journey up the Perfume River to visit the Nguyen kings' tombs *(see p.144)*

Vietnam fact file

Vietnam squeezes a wide diversity of landscapes into its relatively compact area. High green mountains dominate the northern and western border areas, covered in forests and coffee plantations. Sandy beaches line the eastern sea, flanked at either end by extensive flooded deltas. Ethnic Vietnamese, Chinese and Khmer inhabit the coastal port cities, beaches and deltas, and sizeable populations of ethnic minorities live in the rugged highlands.

BASICS
Population: 90 million
Area: 331,210 sq km
(127,880 sq miles)
Official language: Vietnamese
State religion: Atheist
Capital city: Hanoi
President: Nguyen Minh Triet

National anthem: 'Tien quan ca'
(The Song of the Marching Troops)
National symbols: yellow five-pointed star on red field, Communist hammer and sickle

National sports/art forms: football (soccer), water puppets, lacquer, silk embroidery, pottery, weaving
National airline: Vietnam Airlines

CURRENCY
Vietnamese dong (VND)
The following figures are approximate:
£1 = VND32,700
€1 = VND28,850
US$1 = VND20,600

TIME ZONE
GMT +7 (no daylight saving time)

In July:
    New York: 1am
    London: 6am
    Hanoi: noon
    Sydney: 3pm
    Auckland: 5pm
In January:
    New York: 12am
    London: 5am
    Hanoi: noon
    Sydney: 4pm
    Auckland: 6pm

IMPORTANT TELEPHONE NUMBERS
Country code: +84
International calls: 00 + country code + number
Police: 113
Ambulance: 114
Fire: 115

AGE RESTRICTIONS
Driving: 18
Drinking: none
Age of consent: 18
Smoking: unsuccessful efforts have been made to ban smoking indoors

ELECTRICITY
The voltage is generally 220V, 50 cycles, but sometimes 110V, 50 cycles is used. Sockets are mostly two round pins, but some use flat pins

OPENING HOURS
Banks: Mon–Sat 8–11.30am and 1.30–4.30pm
Shops: daily 9am–8 or 9pm; some close 11.30am–1.30 or 2pm
Restaurants: lunch is usually 11.30am–1pm, but many places are open later. Dinner is traditionally 5–7pm but restaurants are often open until 9pm or later
Museums: often closed on Monday.
Offices: usually closed on Sunday; some may also be closed on Saturday

POSTAL SERVICE
Opening hours for post offices
(buu dien): daily 7–11.30am and 1.30–9pm
Postboxes: inside post offices only
Standard post: variable per location
Airmail: variable per location

Trip planner

WHEN TO GO

Climate
Southern Vietnam has two seasons: wet and dry. The rains arrive in May and last until November. During these months it tends to rain fiercely for about one hour a day (but some days not at all), normally in the afternoon or early evening. Late February to late April are the hottest months, with temperatures nudging up to 34°C (93°F) and accompanied by high humidity levels. December to February is relatively cool and dry.

In the north, the summer months from May to September are hot and humid, with a good deal of rain. Winter, from late December to early March, can be grey, drizzly and is often cool. The transitional seasons in March/April and October/December are good times to visit.

A quiet moment in Hoi An

Public holidays	
1 January	New Year's Day
January/February	*Tet* (the three days following the full moon)
3 February	Founding of the Vietnamese Communist Party
Variable April	Hung Kings Holiday
30 April	Liberation Day
1 May	International Labour Day
19 May	Ho Chi Minh's Birthday
June	Buddha's Birthday
2 September	National Day/Independence Day

'Tet' is the biggest public holiday, followed by the double holiday of Liberation Day and Labour Day. During 'Tet' the entire country shuts down for about a week. On all other holidays, banks and government departments close, as well as many offices. Most tourist venues and services remain open.

Central Vietnam, from Danang to Nha Trang, has a slightly different climate: the dry season runs from late January to August, the wet from September to December. December to early April is relatively cool.

Bear in mind that the rainy season is not necessarily a bad time to visit. As showers are usually a brief afternoon interlude, they can be planned around. The rains have the added

Sun protection is essential at all times of the year

benefit of initiating the growth of foliage, flowers, and the return of birds, butterflies and other wildlife.

High/low season

Generally, high season is from October through March. The peak is from mid-December through February, at which time prices can nearly double, particularly in beach-resort areas. During the peak season it is essential to have advanced reservations in resort areas such as Mui Ne

and Nha Trang. Conversely, in the low season some hotels, resorts and restaurants may close for a month.

The best and worst times to visit are subjective to some degree. If you are a budget traveller and don't mind a few wet days, come in low season. If you enjoy bustling activity, want the best chance of good beach weather and can afford the extra costs – and particularly want to spend Christmas, New Year or *Tet* in Vietnam – then high season is for you.

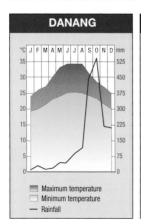

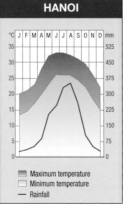

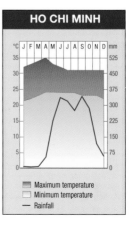

ESSENTIAL EVENTS

The following is a list of the principal festivals through the year in Vietnam. For details on other festivals see the individual Festivals and Events listings at the end of each Places chapter.

January–February

Tet, beginning of the 1st lunar month (varies between mid-January and mid-February). The biggest and most important celebration of the entire year, Tet Nguyen Dan heralds the start of the Vietnamese Lunar New Year. The entire country shuts up shop for a week. There are numerous regional variations of the festival taking place across the country. *See p.238 for more details.*

March–April

Perfume Pagoda Festival, culminates on the 15th day of the 2nd lunar month. A Buddhist festival at this picturesque pagoda southwest of Hanoi *(see p. 84–5)*.

Holiday of the Dead, 5th day of the 3rd lunar month. On this family holiday many people visit the graves of their ancestors to tend them and make offerings of fruit and incense. Paper money (or sometimes paper houses, paper designer clothes or paper stereos), is burnt; the smoke is believed to deliver the items to the deceased in their afterlife.

Whale Festival (Lang Ca Ong), celebrated around the middle of the 3rd lunar month in southern fishing communities where whale worship is practised.

May–June

Phat Dan, 8th day of the 4th lunar month. Buddha's rites of passage are celebrated in pagodas, temples and homes. In some cities there are grand parades with lantern floats and dragon dancing held late in the evening. Pagodas take on a carnival atmosphere, with vegetarian buffets and worshippers making offerings.

Tet Doan Ngo (Summer Solstice Day), 5th day of the 5th lunar month. This

Nguyen Hue street in downtown Ho Chi Minh City becomes a festival of flowers and entertainment for families at *Tet*

Lanterns for sale in Hanoi during Tet Trung Thu, the Mid-Autumn Festival

Tet includes festivities to ensure good health and wellbeing. Offerings are made to spirits, ghosts and the god of death, all to ward off summer epidemics and plagues. Most Vietnamese are aware of this festival but may not actually understand the specifics, as the meaning and symbolism fade from modern culture.

Hue City Festival, nine days in June on even-numbered years. This festival celebrates the cultural heritage of Hue, with music, food, art and performances.

August

Trang Nguyen (Wandering Souls Day), 15th day of the 7th lunar month. This is the second most important Vietnamese festival. Graves are cleaned and offerings are made for the forgotten dead. This is also an important day to tend the roadside altars and altars outside the home, which are often erected for these particular spirits.

September–October

Tet Trung Thu (Mid-Autumn Festival), 15th day of the 8th lunar month. Children parade around with candle-illuminated lanterns, and pastry-covered 'mooncakes' with sweet lotus-seed or red-bean paste are eaten. Evening parades with grand lantern floats pass through the city streets.

Kate Festival, 8th or 9th lunar month. Getting the date right of this Cham festival (often mistakenly called the 'Cham New Year') is difficult because it falls within a unique Cham lunar calendar. It usually takes place in early October. The festival occurs at ancient Cham temples, with feasting, music and processions.

ITINERARIES

Travellers wishing to do justice to the major cities and sights in Vietnam, and to a few of the less popular ones, will require about four to six weeks. In a two-week holiday, if seeing as many of the standard sights as possible is the objective, travellers should plan an itinerary from Hanoi to Ho Chi Minh City (or vice versa), taking in Halong Bay, Hue, Hoi An, Nha Trang and Dalat.

Two weeks of highlights

Days 1–2: **Hanoi.** Fly into Hanoi and spend a couple of leisurely days exploring the attractive old centre.

Days 3–4: **Halong Bay.** Take a tour to this spectacular marine landscape, staying overnight on a traditional junk.

Days 5–6: **Hue.** Travel by overnight train from Hanoi to Hue, Vietnam's old imperial capital. Visit the Forbidden Purple City and the tombs of the Nguyen emperors.

Day 7: **Hoi An.** A short bus ride from Hue, the beautiful old port town of Hoi An is a must-see. Visit ancient Chinese shop-houses and temples.

Days 8–9: **Nha Trang.** Fly from Danang to this southern beach resort. Visit Thap Po Nagar, one of the best-preserved Cham temple sites in Vietnam, and enjoy the nightlife, beaches and scuba diving of Vietnam's favourite party town.

Days 10–11: **Dalat.** Take in the cool mountain air of this lovely hill station in the southern highlands, a three-hour bus ride from Nha Trang .

Days 12–14: **Ho Chi Minh City.** Fly from Dalat to Vietnam's economic

Po Klong Garai Cham Tower at Phan Rang in the region once known as Panduranga

capital and cultural melting pot. Explore the sights of old Saigon, indulge in delectable street food and take a trip out to the remarkable Cu Chi tunnels.

Two weeks in the south

Days 1–2: **Ho Chi Minh City.** Spend three leisurely days acclimatising, sightseeing and sampling the local food and nightlife.

Day 3: **Cu Chi Tunnels and Cao Dai Temple.** A day trip to two very different sights within easy reach of Ho Chi Minh City.

Days 4–5: **Mekong Delta.** Take the bus down to Vinh Long in the heart of the delta, then explore the backwaters by boat. Visit a floating market and fruit orchard.

Days 6–8: **Mui Ne.** Return to Ho Chi Minh City then head east to this up-and-coming beach resort, well loved by watersports enthusiasts.

Days 9–10: **Panduranga tour.** Take an epic two-day journey by car or motorbike, visiting some of the oldest monuments of the Champa Kingdom.

Days 11–12: **Nha Trang.** Continue north to the golden beaches and superb diving of Vietnam's principal resort.

Days 13–14: **Dalat.** Complete the tour with an overnight stay in this delightful mountain town before flying back to Ho Chi Minh City.

Four weeks for adventurers

Days 1–3: **Ho Chi Minh City.** Spend three days acclimatising in Vietnam's steamy southern metropolis.

Days 4–5: **Cat Tien National Park.** Journey north by bus from Ho Chi Minh City to this little-visited reserve for jungle treks amid clouds of butterflies, and a chance to spot rare wildlife.

Days 6–8: **Dalat.** Try abseiling in waterfalls and mountain biking through coffee and tea plantations.

Days 9–10: **Motorbike trip.** Ride north from Dalat through beautiful countryside, see some waterfalls and spend a night at Lak Lake.

Day 11: **Buon Ma Thuot.** Visit the Ethnology Museum and some Ede minority villages in Vietnam's coffee capital.

Days 12–14: **Kon Tum.** Drive north to explore traditional Jarai and Bahnar hill-tribe villages.

Days 15–16: **Ho Chi Minh Trail**. Hop on the motorbike again to explore the infamous route. Arrive in Danang.

Days 17–18: **Danang**. Spend a couple of days relaxing in and around Vietnam's third-largest city, taking a short excursion out to China Beach and the Marble Mountains.

Days 19–22: **Sa Pa**. Fly to Hanoi and board a train to Lao Cai on the Chinese border, from where a short minibus ride takes you to the stunning mountain vistas of Sa Pa. Spend three days exploring the area, visiting hill tribe villages. If the weather is good, hike to the summit of Mt Fansipan.

Days 23–26: **Hanoi**. Return to the capital, explore its fascinating old centre and take a day trip south to the Perfume Pagoda.

Days 27–28: **Halong Bay**. Complete your trip with a tour of the unforgettable scenery of Halong Bay.

Trip planner

BEFORE YOU LEAVE

Visas and entry requirements

Citizens of English-speaking countries are required to purchase a visa before entry. Most visitors apply for a one-month, single-entry tourist visa that costs a minimum of US$25 (depending upon where you arrange it). Multiple-entry tourist visas, valid for 3 months, start at $90.

Nationality	Visa required
UK	✓
US	✓
Canada	✓
Australia	✓
New Zealand	✓
Ireland	✓
South Africa	✓

Apply directly to the Vietnamese embassy or consulate in your home country. For a list, check the Ministry of Foreign Affairs website at www.mofa.gov.vn/en. Alternatively, use a travel agent to obtain your visa, though you will pay a commission charge on top of the visa fee. In addition to the application form, visitors must submit a valid passport and two passport-sized photos. Allow 5–7 working days for approval.

Major tour agents are now able to offer pre-arranged visas for collection when you arrive at the airport. The agent will fax applicants an 'invitation letter' that will need to be presented to immigration on arrival.

The visa period begins on the date specified on the application form.

Embassies and consulates
Embassies in Hanoi
Australia: 8 Dao Tan, Ba Dinh District; tel: 04-3831 7755
Canada: 31 Hung Vuong; tel: 04-3734 5000
Ireland: 8/F, Tower B, Vincom City Towers, 191 Ba Trieu; tel: 04-3974 3291
New Zealand: 63 Ly Thai To; tel: 04-3824 1481

The Chinese border at Lao Cai

South Africa: 3rd Floor, Central Building, 31 Hai Ba Trung; tel: 04-3936 2000
UK: 31 Hai Ba Trung; tel: 04-3936 0500
US: 7 Lang Ha; tel: 04-3831 4590

Consulates in Ho Chi Minh City
Australia: 5B Ton Duc Thang, District 1; tel: 08-3829 6035
Canada: 235 Dong Khoi St, District 1; tel: 08-3827 9899.
New Zealand: 235 Dong Khoi, District 1; tel: 08-3822 6907.
UK: 25 Le Duan, District 1; tel: 08-3829 8433.
US: 4 Le Duan, District 1; tel: 08-3822 9433

Vaccinations
No vaccinations are required, but those against hepatitis and tetanus are strongly recommended.

Booking in advance
Luxury hotels should always be booked in advance.

Tourist information
Vietnam National Administration of Tourism (www.vietnamtourism.com), the official tourism body, is of little use for accurate or up-to-date information. There are no overseas offices.

Maps
The two standard atlases in Vietnam are: 'Viet Nam Travel Atlas – Ban Do Du Lich', and 'Tap Ban Do Giao Thong Duong Bo Viet Nam'.

Books
A Dragon Apparent by Norman Lewis. Travels through Indochina in the declining French empire.
We Were Soldiers Once... and Young by Harold G. Moore and Joseph L. Galloway. A powerful account of a decisive battle in the Vietnam War.
Ho Chi Minh: A Life by William J. Duiker. A readable biography.
Communion: A Culinary Journey Through Vietnam by Kim Fay. In-depth exploration of local cuisine.
The Tale of Kieu by Nguyen Du. The classic epic poem is a foundation of Vietnamese literature.

Websites
General
www.wordhcmc.com
The Word Magazine HCMC
www.wordhanoi.com
The Word Magazine Hanoi
www.newhanoian.com
Reviews of local shops, restaurants and hotels, along with classifieds.
http://tourism.hochiminhcity.gov.vn
Department of Tourism.

Blogs
www.fisheggtree.com
www.ourmaninhanoi.com

Packing list

- Plug adaptor
- Mobile-phone charger
- Torch
- Earplugs
- High-factor sun block, sunglasses, hat
- Pocket alarm
- Universal sink plug
- Small padlocks for securing luggage on overnight train journeys

UNIQUE EXPERIENCES

On the water

Vietnam has some 3,260km (2,025 miles) of coastline, but it's the watery deltas at the northern and southern ends of the country that provide most interest for people seeking to explore by boat. Cruise gently through the orchards and floating markets of the Mekong Delta, or glide between karst cliffs on the calm waters of Halong Bay.

Taking in some of Southeast Asia's most spellbinding scenery from the water is a supremely relaxing and rewarding experience, and there are several such journeys that should be considered when visiting Vietnam.

One of the most magnificent natural splendours in the region, Halong Bay is just 3 hours from Hanoi. This World Heritage Site simply should not be missed. Also within easy reach of Hanoi, the Perfume Pagoda is one of the lesser-known highlights of Vietnam. The boat ride on the Yen River alone is worth the trip, but the hike to the 'most beautiful temple under the southern sky' is the grande finale.

Another possibility is the trip on the Ngo Dong River in Tam Coc, a little further to the south – known as 'Halong Bay on rice paddies'. At the other end of the country, a three-day trip to Vinh Long and Can Tho, in the heart of the Mekong Delta, will immerse the visitor in the romantic ambience of this far-southern region. Meander through small waterways to floating markets and island gardens, and relax in munificent orchards. In Central Vietnam, a cruise down the Perfume River from the ancient city of Hue is the best way to visit the tombs of the Nguyen kings.

A tourist junk in Halong Bay

Halong Bay

Even the most seasoned traveller cannot fail to be mesmerised by **Halong Bay** (Vinh Ha Long), with over 3,000 sheer-sided limestone islands jutting out of the emerald green waters of the Gulf of Bac Bo. In an area covering 1,500 sq km (579 sq miles), sampans, junks, fishing boats – and many tourist vessels – sail past a fairy-tale backdrop of mostly uninhabited karst islands, which harbour a hidden world of grottoes, secluded coves, coral beaches and secret lagoons. Small wonder it was designated a Unesco World Heritage Site in 1994.

It looks like the stuff of legends – as indeed it is. *Ha Long* means 'Descending Dragon', originating from the myth that a celestial dragon once flung itself headlong into the sea, its swishing tail digging deep valleys and crevices in the earth. As it descended into the sea, these filled with water, creating the bay. Another legend relates how the Jade Emperor ordered a dragon to halt an invasion by sea from the north. The dragon spewed out jade and jewels, which, upon hitting the sea, turned into wondrous islands and karst formations, creating a natural fortress against enemy ships.

Legends aside, geologists believe that the ancient limestone seabed that existed here was forced upward and left exposed as the waters receded. Erosion over time formed the karst outcrops, eventually leaving only pinnacles and

Exploring Halong Bay by rowing-boat

caves behind. Similar karst landscapes can be found around Guilin and other parts of southwest China.

Practicalities

The vast majority of visitors to Halong Bay join a group tour, which they arrange through one of the overwhelming number of tour offices

---

Halong Bay tour operators

The best time to visit Halong Bay is during the warmer months, from April to October, as you can swim off the boat and relax on sundecks. However, during the typhoon season, which peaks in September, boats may cancel due to bad weather. Late December to March can be surprisingly cold, often with grey skies and drizzle (the notorious *crachin*).

The tour begins with a 3–4hr road journey (in the morning) from Hanoi to Halong City, where you will board the boat contracted by your tour provider. All tour operators use engine-powered wooden boats, most with private cabins. **Buffalo Tours** (tel: 04-3828 0702; www. buffalotours.com) operates two luxury junks (five to eight cabins) with kayaking options; two- to three-day cruises start from US$159. **Handspan Adventure Travel** (tel: 04-3926 2828; www.handspan. com) offers two- to three-day options on their Aloha junks from US$115, and on the high-end Lagoon Explorer junks with four cabins from US$167. **Exotissimo** (tel: 04-3828 2150; www.exotissimo.com) has a good range of cruising and kayaking options at comparable rates.

in Hanoi *(see panel on page 23)*. It is possible to travel (take a bus, taxi or hire a vehicle) to Halong City independently and charter a boat, however this could end up being more expensive as well as slower. By taking a tour you can verify the quality, safety and other conditions of the boat yourself before you pay. Most tours last the better part of two days and one night, though longer tours are available. It's best to leave your luggage in Hanoi.

A typical tour will include stops at a couple of the caves listed below (there are 15 open to the public), hours of meandering between the karst outcrops, a swing past one of several floating fishing villages, and a swim or two. Longer tours may include a stop on Cat Ba island. Tickets to enter the National Park are either purchased at the Bai Chay Tourist Dock in Halong City or are included in tour packages.

Perhaps the most spectacular cave is on the island closest to Halong City, the vast **Grotto of the Wooden Stakes** (Hang Dau Go), where General Tran Hung Dao amassed hundreds of stakes prior to his 1288 victory. There are three chambers filled with an assortment of stalactites and stalagmites resembling beasts, birds and human forms. On the same island, the **Grotto of the Heavenly Palace** (Hang Thien Cung) has some impressive stalactites and stalagmites, as does **Surprise Grotto** (Hang Sung Sot) on an island further south. *For more on Halong Bay, see p.119–120.*

The Perfume Pagoda

The site of the oddly misnamed **Perfume Pagoda** comprises a group of temples covering an area of 30 sq km (11½ sq miles). Built into the limestone cliffs of the 'Ancient Vestiges of Perfume Grotto' (Dong

Hang Sung Sot, or Surprise Grotto

Tourists embark on the Perfume Pagoda boat trip

Huong Tich), otherwise known as the Perfume Mountains, the earliest temples date from the 15th century. By the early 20th century, there were over 100. This area was the scene of some bitter uprisings against the French colonialists and, as a result, several temples were destroyed during the late 1940s. Fortunately, the area retains much of its natural splendour and is regarded as one of the most beautiful spots in Vietnam. A typical day trip takes a full day, including the 120km (74-mile) return drive southwest of Hanoi, followed by a 3hr return boat ride, and finally a 4km (2½-mile) return hike.

The boat trip

The journey by road south from Hanoi brings travellers to riverside **Yen Vi Village**, where they board a shallow metal-bottomed boat (there are no roads to the Perfume Pagoda). The 90-minute boat trip along the wide, swiftly flowing **Yen River** is as worthwhile as visiting the pagoda itself. Here, fishermen, wade through the crystal waters among the floating graves of their ancestors. As the oarsman steers the boat along the river, relax and take in the mesmerising landscape of jagged limestone hills.

Perfume Pagoda tips

During the first two months after Tet (roughly February/March or March/April, depending on the lunar calendar), the Perfume Pagoda can get very crowded with pilgrims, making for a frustrating (or alternatively, highly interesting) experience. Boats have no cover, so wear sun protection. As there are no places to eat along the way, bring a picnic lunch if your tour package does not include one, plus a torch for the caves.

Huong Tich Grotto

The dreamy landscape has been compared to Guilin in China. An oarswoman, rowing in a physically strenuous fashion, will propel the flat-bottomed boat that will take you to the pagoda. Facing the bow, she pushes the oars forward with her feet, guiding the boat seamlessly through the dark waters. If a Vietnamese interpreter accompanies you on the ride, the oarswoman can point out peaks with such quaint names as the Crouching Elephant, Nun and Rice Tray.

Disembark from the boat at the base of the Huong Tich Mountains for the 2hr hike up to the temple complex and Huong Tich Grotto *(see p.85 for details of the temples)*.

Tam Coc

Prepare for a few hours of idyllic scenery and tranquillity at Tam Coc, as you set off from the wharf in your small sampan, complete with local oarswoman. The boat meanders past jagged limestone rocks jutting out of a landscape of flooded rice paddies merging with Ngo Dong River. As you drift down the river you will pass under three long, low-hanging tunnel caves, the largest complete with numerous beautiful rock formations. These have been bored through the limestone hills over the centuries. Clear lagoons, darting kingfishers and locals scouring for shellfish complete the mesmerising scene: amid the humid heat, the only slap of reality is the hassling by boat crews to purchase local merchandise. The best thing is simply to ignore them (some savvy tour guides even pay the touts not to bother them). On the return, stop at the 13th-century Thai Vi Temple, a short stroll from the banks, where King Tran Nhan Tong retired after his abdication.

The Perfume River

The best way to visit the Nguyen tombs outside of the charming city of Hue is to take a boat up the Perfume River into the countryside south of town. Boat tours will generally last a full day, with lunch usually provided, though be sure to confirm this as there are no restaurants along the way. Most boats are covered, motorised and built to accommodate large-group tours. Stops vary, but commonly include the tombs of Tu Duc, Thieu Tri, Minh Mang, Khai Dinh, Thien Mu Pagoda, and Hon Chen Temple. *For details on the tombs, see p.144–6.* The **Mandarin Café** (24 Tran Cao Van; tel: 054-382 1281; email; mandarin@dng.vnn.vn) is a good place to go to make arrangements.

The Mekong Delta

Ferries have always been an essential part of life along the lower reaches of the Mekong River. For the tourist, travel by boat gives a laid-back, intimate view of this lush tropical region. Highlights include visiting the many orchards and floating markets, as well as the ethnic Khmer Krom and Cham communities. At floating markets, merchants (mostly women) sit in long wooden sampans and sell all manner of goods that you might find at any terrestrial market, including fish and meat, fruit and vegetables, clothing and household wares.

Modes of transport within the delta's labyrinthine waterways range from large wooden canoes with outboard motors, which may carry people, livestock, merchant goods and motorbikes or farm equipment, up to massive barges transporting cars, buses and trucks. Sampans are used by individual families or people bringing their produce to sell at the market. They can be rented (with boatman)

Tam Coc river trip

Traditional transport on a Mekong Delta tour

floor of Cuu Long B Hotel at No.1, 1 Thang 5 Street. Boat trips are fairly expensive, but Cuu Long's English-speaking guides are professional and well-informed. Alternatively, go to the An Binh Boat Station and haggle.

Cai Be Floating Market

The three-hour return ride to **Cai Be Floating Market** is best undertaken in the morning, after a night in Vinh Long. This is a good place to eat breakfast and to buy a picnic lunch. Fresh produce, hand-woven baskets, palm sugar, buffalo horn and coconut utensils, and all kinds of other goods are sold here.

As you leave the dock, you will see people all along the river bank tending to their household chores or washing (women bathe with all their clothes on) and children playing in the water. Many families have small sampans. Look out for the ones with great eyes painted red and black on their prows: these are ocean-going vessels, the tradition being to paint them in this manner so that they can see their way safely to the sea. Depending on the season, you will see rice barges filled with bananas, mangosteens, Java apples or other tropical fruit. It is interesting to see how vegetables, flowers, fish and rice are traded from boats at the floating market. All along the shoreline, fish traps spear the water.

Binh Hoa Phuoc Island

Within easy reach of Vinh Long, with various boat tours available, are the attractive, orchard-covered islands of Binh Hoa Phuoc and Vinh Long. Tours cruise through the backwaters,

by tourists, on request through a tour office or by private arrangement. They do not function as public ferries.

Most visitors (including backpackers) end up seeing the Mekong as part of an organised tour, either three days or five. The itineraries suggested here should take about three days.

Vinh Long

Vinh Long is situated right in the heart of the delta and makes a good base from which to explore. The town sprawls along the southern shore of the Tien Giang, or Upper Mekong River. There are a few architectural remnants from French-colonial times, a market and a handful of hotels but, as with this entire region, the main action is on and around the river.

Secure a boat at **Cuu Long Tourist** (tel: 070-382 3616; www.cuulong-tourist.com), located on the ground through lovely scenery, past fishing villages with stilthouses.

There are many orchards to visit on the islands. Any competent boatman can recommend some. Rambutans, longans – the most important commercial fruit in this area – mangoes and pineapples are all abundant thanks to the delta's rich alluvial soil.

Elephant-ear fish (*ca tai tuong*), the local speciality, is as large as a soup plate and delicately flavoured. Sample some while you are on the island, wrapped in ricepaper with salad, then dipped in a sauce.

The house of a local artist and gardener, Nguyen Thanh Giao, in Binh Hoa Phuoc Village, is open to the public and features a garden filled with bonsai trees and a few hammocks. It makes an idyllic spot for a rest.

Can Tho's floating markets

Some 34km (21 miles) southwest of Vinh Long is the major centre of **Can Tho**, the largest town and effective capital of the delta. Here, Vietnam's substantial ethnic Khmer Krom community begins to make its presence felt. Can Tho is a good place to stay overnight, as the accommodation available is the best in the delta, and good restaurants are plentiful.

Boat trips can be booked with the local tourist office, but a better option is to explore on a small motorboat – for this you will need to enquire along the dock or in guesthouses about chartering a boat.

Most people will want to see one of the famous floating markets: **Cai Rang** is about 5km (3 miles) southeast of the city centre, while **Phong Dien** lies about 20km (12 miles) to the southwest and is a better bet if you want to avoid the crowds. If you are heading back to Ho Chi Minh City, don't stay too late as it takes around three hours to drive back.

Cai Rang Floating Market

Hill tribes

Although the Kinh, or ethnic Vietnamese, are said to make up nearly 87 percent of the population, the government recognises a total of 54 different ethnic groups, each with their own distinct culture and dialect. Most of these, with the exception of the Cham, Khmer and Hoa (ethnic Chinese), inhabit the highland areas of the country.

The traditional cultures of Vietnam's hill tribes are vastly different from those of the ethnic Vietnamese. Yet, as the country develops and communications improve, their unique way of life – costumes, village architecture, languages – is inevitably disappearing through assimilation. For the traveller, visting their villages, often within picturesque highland landscapes, offers a glimpse into a vanishing world.

Collectively, the hill tribes are known by many names. The French called them *Montagnards* (mountain people), and the Vietnamese know them as *nguoi thuong* (highlanders) or *moi* (black savages). The last two are both considered derogatory and the preferred term is now *nguoi dan toc* (ethnic-minority people).

Most of the villages are very friendly and welcoming to tourists. Many are officially designated tourist attractions, but some settlements far from the main roads may be unofficially off-limits, particularly in the provinces of Dak Lak, Gia Lai and Kon Tum, and may require police permission due to political unrest. *See panel on p. 35 for information on off-limits areas.*

Some background

Studies on the origins of the Vietnamese show that the people who settled

Red Dao costume, Ta Phin village

in the Indochinese Peninsula most likely migrated south and southeast from China and Tibet (the Mon-Khmer peoples) and various islands of the south and west Pacific and Indonesia (Malay-Polynesian peoples): scholars have found evidence that vast trade routes existed early on in their settlement, extending east to Taiwan and the Philippines.

The Malay-Polynesians include tribes most closely associated with the Champa Empire, including the Gia Rai, Ede, Raglai, Cho Ru and Rai. The Mon-Khmer dwell further to the north and west, notably including the Bahnar, Sedang, H're, Stieng, M'nong and K'ho.

Many of today's minority groups were displaced by the Kinh Vietnamese as they pushed southward, forcing them into the mountains.

Visiting the minorities: Northern Highlands

The Northern Highlands, bordering Laos and China, are inhabited by a large and colourful array of minorities, many of whom have lived in Vietnam for centuries, while others are more recent arrivals from China, Laos and Thailand, having been displaced by various conflicts in modern times.

The old French hill station at Sa Pa, and Lao Cai, the city at the bottom of the mountain, are the most popular bases from which to visit minority villages (especially those of the Hmong and Dao).

Unlike in the Southern Highlands, where markets tend to be drab and

Drinking *ruou can* rice wine in a Lat village

mundane affairs in city centres, the northern markets present the best opportunities to meet the locals. A number of fascinating but remote weekly markets – located several hours from Sa Pa – offer a glimpse into a more traditional way of life. Local residents still visit these community events in traditional costume, buying and selling their handmade wares and a variety of produce. Can Cau (every Saturday), Coc Ly (every

---

Ruou can

Most hill tribes brew their own unique recipe for rice wine in large ceramic jars. Unlike *ruou gao*, made by the Kinh, *ruou can* is not distilled, so has a rich, sweet flavour, tempered by herbs, roots and grains. *Ruou can* is reserved for special occasions, and always drunk by a group. In most tribes, each person has their own long, bamboo straw, and everybody drinks all at once. Other tribes, such as the K'ho, syphon the alcohol into a bowl

from a single straw, offering the elixir to each person in turn. Drinking *ruou can* is a religious experience for ethnic minorities and surrounded by ceremony and superstition.

Sampling some of this unusual tipple is a highlight of any hill-tribe experience. While *ruou can* is best home-made and experienced in a village, it can also be easily purchased from shops in Dalat and Buon Ma Thuot.

Tuesday) and Muong Hom (every Sunday) are all found near the Chinese border and highly recommended. Colourful, vibrant Bac Ha market starts early on Sunday morning, roughly 80km (50 miles) east of Sa Pa.

Hmong

The Hmong migrated from China in the 18th century. There are many subgroups, their names resulting from the primary colours of their ethnic costume, including Black, Green, Blue, White, Striped and Flower Hmong. The Hmong produce perhaps the most refined handicrafts of any minority group and are particularly renowned for their batik-patterned garments, made by applying wax to certain areas (to retain the original fabric colour) and then dipping the material into indigo dye.

Dao

The Dao, like the Hmong, are well known for their handicrafts, such as batik fabric, blacksmithing, silver jewellery and traditional rifles. The Red Dao women are striking, with their shaved eyebrows and scalps, red turbans and silver jewellery.

Tai (Thai)

The Tai (also spelled Thai, but not to be confused with citizens of Thailand) live close to the Lao and Chinese borders and are easily visited from Lao Cai. They are divided into two groups: Black Thai and White Tai. They arrived in Vietnam nearly 1,000 years ago, but are closely related to the Thai of Thailand in language and culture.

Tay

The Tay live in northeastern Vietnam, along the Chinese border. Like the

Flower Hmong women at Bac Ha market

Thai, they live in large stilt houses made of wooden planks. The Tay are also divided into two subgroups, known as the Pa Di and the Thu Lao. Their ethnic dress is simple: men wear trousers and vests while women wear sarongs, and all items are dyed with indigo. Since 1975, many Tay villages have been relocated to the Southern Highlands and their foothills by the government.

Muong

About two thousand years ago, the Muong and Kinh (ethnic Vietnamese) were probably a single ethnic group. The Kinh moved into the plains, while the Muong remained in the mountains, particularly south of Hanoi, and perpetuated a very different lifestyle. Their society and villages are highly structured – this remains a feudal society where the father in the household has absolute power.

Visiting the minorities: Southern Highlands

Most visitors enter the Southern Highlands in Dalat, via bus from Ho Chi Minh City, Mui Ne or Nha Trang. A more adventurous option, and one that will make for encounters with minority peoples, is to hire a motorbike in Dalat (with a driver if preferred) and ride west to Buon Ma Thuot, or north to Pleiku and Kon Tum. *For more on motorbike tours, see p.192–3.*

Unlike the northern tribes, the southern minorities have, by and large, assimilated with the Vietnamese – at least in terms of clothing and personal appearance. Nonetheless, most of the groups described below continue

Black Hmong boys ride buffalo, near Sa Pa

to live outside of the mainstream of Vietnamese society, and the majority of minority villages in the highland regions are exclusively inhabited by one single minority group.

K'ho

The K'ho live mainly in Lam Dong province, but are also found in

---

Tour operators in Sa Pa

Recommended local tour operators in Sa Pa include: Handspan Adventure Travel (8 Cau May Street; tel: 020-387 2110; www.handspan.com); Topas Adventure Vietnam (24 Muong Hoa Street; tel: 020-387 1331; www. topastravel.vn); and Tulico (Darling Hotel, Thac Bac Street; tel: 020-387 1349; www.tulico-sapa.com.vn).

Many tribes erect a tall bamboo pole decorated with birds, fish and other animal ornaments in front of their *rong* house, and this forms the centrepiece of 'buffalo-stabbing festivals'. These occasions may mark a successful harvest, a wedding, or a gesture to appease the gods in a time of illness or misfortune. A water buffalo, which is a symbol of strength and wealth, is tied to the pole and sacrificed by stabbing it to death. The meat is then distributed among the village. Participants wear traditional costumes, play tribal music and drink *ruou can*.

Making arrangements to see the festivities can be difficult because they do not occur regularly. The best locations are around Buon Ma Thuot, Pleiku and Kon Tum. Ask local tour operators if one will occur during your stay.

neighbouring provinces. Lam Dong's capital, Dalat, means Land of the Lat People (the Lat are a clan of the K'ho). Of all the highland tribes, their ancestral homeland has been most colonised by the majority Kinh population, which has lead to an intensive assimilation of the K'ho into the dominant Vietnamese culture. In more remote areas, there are still a few villages where the K'ho dwell in bamboo stilt houses with thatched roofs. The *gui* (baskets) that they wear on their backs are highly prized due to their fine craftsmanship. K'ho villages are accessible as day trips from Dalat.

Ede

The Ede live mainly in Dak Lak province and were once renowned for their ability to capture and train elephants. The practice now remains only for the entertainment of tourists (there being very few wild elephants left in Vietnam). The Ede live in clapboard longhouses raised off the ground. Villages are accessible around the city of Buon Ma Thuot and at Ban Don (close to Yuk Don National Park).

M'Nong

The M'Nong live throughout the Central Highlands and dwell in longhouses similar to those of the Ede, made of wood or woven grass. Also like the Ede, the M'Nong have a history of training elephants. They also raise livestock and fish in Lak Lake,

Red Dao women

The Ede village of Ako Dhong, with clapboard longhouse in the background

where they welcome visitors on their way from Dalat to Buon Ma Thuot.

Gia Rai

Closest highland ally of the ancient Cham, the Gia Rai (also known as Jarai) have a sophisticated culture and may themselves have built some of the ancient red-brick Cham temples that were once scattered across the highlands and eastern Cambodia. They are best known for the wooden funerary totems that they build around their tombs, featuring men and women engaging in erotic exploits. In traditional Gia Rai societies, the young men build tiny bachelor huts towering above the village on tall bamboo stilts. The Gia Rai live in Gia Lai and Kon Tum provinces, as well as in eastern Cambodia.

Bahnar

The hallmark of the Bahnar is their *rong* (communal lodges), with immense thatched roofs up to 18 metres (60ft) tall and walls made of woven bamboo matting. The roof ridge is often decorated with stylised birds and other symbols. Each village has a *rong* at the centre, surrounded by tightly packed log huts on stilts. The Bahnar have a rich tradition of music and dance that still flourishes. They live in various provinces, but their villages are easiest to visit around Kon Tum City.

Off-limits?

There is no official list of places to which people can and cannot go in Vietnam, but those that wander too far may be arrested at the whim of the local police that finds them. A rule of thumb is that anything more than an hour outside the centre of the three respective provincial capitals, or more than 30mins off the main roads leading in and out of the province, is off-limits, other than the National Park and waterfalls in Dak Lak. Gia Lai province is particularly strict.

Eating out in Vietnam

Savoury, spicy, sweet and sour: Vietnam's characteristic balance of the four tastes in every meal (or even every mouthful) makes for rewarding culinary exploration. Not only are there three distinct regional cuisine traditions, but each city also has its own unique specialties.

Vietnamese cuisine is a banquet of choices that can never be exhausted. At every step of a trip around the country there is something new to explore. The most rewarding experiences often come not from deliberate planning but simply by walking down the road and trying snacks and meals as you find them.

The settings for dining are just as diverse as the food itself. Go for a bowl of *bun bo hue* (Hue beef noodle soup) or *trai cay dia* (fruit salad plate covered in ice, condensed milk and natural syrup) and you'll be sitting on tiny blue or red plastic chairs on a street curb. Motorbikes, bicycles, cyclos and BMWs whizz by, while fruit bats and barn owls swoop overhead... and rats run under the table.

Have lunch at a *com binh danh*, and you'll be served a plate of rice and a selection of vegetable and meat dishes, with a side soup. The most common lunch combination is grilled pork chops on a bed of rice with fish sauce, tomatoes and cucumber, accompanied by sweet-and-sour fish soup. The creatures running under your plastic stool or folding metal chair here are more likely to be dogs and chickens.

Or head to a somewhat more formal outdoor restaurant for *lau hai san* (seafood hotpot). Long banquet-

Bananas in Hanoi's Old Quarter

style tables seat large groups attended by Tiger Beer girls, dressed in tight-fitting uniforms and promoting the popular brew. Empty bottles are stashed in crates under the tables.

Etiquette

Listening to Vietnamese diners happily belch, slurp and smack their lips, and watching them talk with their mouths full and smoke cigarettes between bites, a visitor might conclude that they have no table manners at all. They do, it's just that the issues here are different. Vietnamese diners cherish a lively, boisterous atmosphere, filled with toasts and jokes and conversation, rather than the formal tones of Western restaurants.

Beer is the beverage of choice at group meals and parties. Rice wine is reserved for small gatherings of men, particularly late in the evening. That said, it's still considered slightly impolite for women to drink beer (as it is impolite for them to smoke), and they will often have soft drinks instead.

Note that, while in restaurants, everyone has their own individual glass. In street-food settings, beware: ice-tea glasses are not often washed between customers. Whether hot or ice tea, pour a cup for your neighbours first.

Table scraps can be an awkward issue. Watch your hosts to see how they dispose of them and follow suit. Ideally, there will be a communal bowl to place bones and other inedibles. Sometimes, scraps may be placed on the table beside your plate. At other times, they are just tossed on the floor (this is where the animals under the table come in).

Chopsticks should be placed on the chopstick rest when you are drinking or talking – they should not be waved around, and should never be used to point. When serving yourself, take the portion of food nearest to you, and never, ever stick your chopsticks straight into the rice. This is the arrangement for food offerings to the dead, and is considered to be very bad luck.

Street food in Ho Chi Minh City

It is normal to use one's own chopsticks or spoon to select morsels from the communal bowl, and very polite to select the best bits (again with one's own chopsticks) and place them into one's neighbour's bowl. As a guest, you can expect this treatment throughout a meal.

Highlights: *pho*

Pronounced 'fuh', this noodle soup can be eaten for breakfast or as a late-night snack, although many people consume *pho* for lunch and dinner, too. Discerning Vietnamese will tell you that *pho* tastes best when eaten in the late afternoon or evening, as the broth has been simmering all day long on the stove.

When you order *pho*, steaming hot broth is poured over a bowl of rice noodles topped with chicken or beef, fresh herbs and onion. Sometimes, a raw egg yolk is added, and Vietnamese might also add lime juice, hot peppers, chilli sauce or vinegar to liven things up a little. It is usually served with *quay* – a deep-fried piece of flour dough – and, in the south, a side dish of *rau thom* (fresh herbs, particularly mint).

Some people say that *pho* was devised by Vietnamese who learnt to make *pot-au-feu* for their French employers. The theory goes that the name *pho* actually comes from the French *feu*. The Chinese influence can be seen in the use of noodles, and flavourings such as ginger and star anise in the broth.

Northerners and southerners will argue endlessly over which end of the country has the best *pho*. A Hanoian is likely to complain that a bowl of *pho* in Ho Chi Minh City is too sweet, while someone from Ho Chi Minh City will complain that Hanoi's broth is too bland.

Foundations: fish sauce

It's safe to say that no Vietnamese person can live happily without *nuoc mam* (fish sauce), which is used as an ingredient as well as a dipping sauce. *Nuoc mam* has a pungent aroma and biting saltiness that can take some getting used to, but it's the perfect complement to the subtle flavours of the food. The unmistakeable scent wafts through coastal cities such as Phan Thiet and the island of Phu Quoc, where anchovies can be seen fermenting with salt in large wooden barrels for about six months.

Dishes such as spring rolls or *banh xeo*, a rice-flour pancake studded with shrimp and crunchy bean sprouts, are dipped into a bowl of *nuoc cham*, which is fish sauce mixed with a mixture of lime juice, garlic, sugar and chilli. As with most food, the further

Men eating *pho*

south you are, the spicier and sweeter the *nuoc cham* is likely to be.

There are a few extra-pungent cousins of *nuoc mam* that travellers may encounter. *Man ruoc* (fermented shrimp paste eaten with ricepaper or crackers); *mam nem* (fermented fish paste eaten with rice noodles); and *mam tom* (fermented fish paste eaten with dog meat) are all dipping sauces mixed with sugar, lemon, chilli and garlic.

Private occasions and home cooking

Unlike in the West, it's uncommon for Vietnamese to invite guests into their homes specifically for the purpose of a casual meal only. Usually, such invitations are reserved for a special

Fish sauce from the factory on Phu Quoc

Reading the menu

Communicating with your waiter is much more productive if you know a few simple words *(see also Phrasebook, p.297).*

Preparations	
grilled	*da nuong*
boiled	*da luoc*
steamed	*da hap*
stir-fried	*da chien*
raw	*tuoi song*

Cooking styles	
lemon grass with chilli	*xa ot*
sweet and sour	*chua ngot*
fried with butter	*chien bo*
fish sauce with garlic and lemon	*mam dam*
caramelised in clay pot	*kho to*
vegetarian	*an chay*

hot	*nong*
cold	*lanh*

Ingredients	
vegetables	*rau cu*
egg noodle	*smi tom*
rice noodles	*bun gao*
pork	*thit heo*
chicken	*thit ga*
fish	*ca*
beef	*thit bo*
duck	*thit vit*
seafood	*hai san*
peanuts	*dau phung*
cashews	*hat dieu*
soy sauce	*nuoc tuong (xi dau)*
salt	*muoi*
pepper	*tieu*
chilli sauce	*mam ot*
salt and chilli	*muoi ot*

occasion, such as *dam cuoi* (weddings) and *dam gio* (annual feasts held on the death anniversaries of family members). If, however, you happen to be in someone's home around mealtime, you are sure to be invited.

Vietnamese home cooking requires steamed white rice at every meal. There is always at least one meat dish. This may be stewed or caramelised pork and quail eggs, or marinated and fried fish. Side dishes include stir-fried vegetables, fresh herbs, *goi* (meat and vegetable salads), and a *canh* (hot soup). The Vietnamese excel at savoury soups: popular varieties include fish, pork and papaya, and a broth featuring bitter melon stuffed with ground pork and mushrooms.

Dam gio, despite being an event to remember family members who have passed away, is generally a happy occasion, bringing the entire family together as well as friends and guests. It's an informal affair, and seating is on the floor, with a broad range of dishes set in the middle. These include beef and duck curries with baguettes, *goi* (a tangy salad of meats, herbs, chilli, garlic, onions and fruit) with large rice crackers, stir-fried noodles and pork, and boiled chicken. The food is served cold because it has already been sitting out for some time, presented as an offering to the deceased relative first.

At a wedding, it is considered good luck for the bride and groom to have foreign guests at their party, so any foreigner in the vicinity (at least in rural areas) is likely to be dragged in. If you received a printed invitation, bring it with you and enclose at least 200,000VND. This is deposited in a box at the reception table, in place of a wedding gift.

Bun cha, rice noodles with pork, is a popular northern dish

Fresh produce is available in abundance

Wedding parties held at home, under large outdoor tents full of dozens of round tables, always have better food than hotel banquet-hall weddings. Meals include five or more courses. The first is often crab and corn soup. It's followed by dishes such as fried beef in butter, *goi* with rice crackers, grilled prawn, and roast duck and sticky rice. The final main course is hotpot of some sort (typically beef, fish or seafood), and then a platter of fresh fruit or agar gelatine. In Vietnam, gelatine is usually flavoured with coffee, condensed milk, coconut and pandan (a grass-like plant that lends a nutty flavour and green colouring, especially to sweet coconut and rice dishes in Vietnamese cuisine), rather than fruit. Throughout the wedding, the bride and groom will go from table to table, making toasts with an unlimited supply of bottled beer.

Markets

Covered markets are the best place to pick up fresh fruit: durian, jackfruit, mango, dragon fruit, passion fruit, mangosteen… you can try a new fruit every day and probably never exhaust the selection. If you happen to be staying in a villa or bungalow with its own kitchen, you can of course buy ingredients and cook your own meals. Head to the back of the market for the best prices. The first few rows are the most expensive. Be wary of people approaching you and offering to help negotiate a price: they are usually in cahoots with the stall owners and you are almost certain to be cheated.

Every large market has a dine-in section. Usually, it's a selection of the most popular local dishes in town. Women sit at food stalls, surrounded by ingredients and a portable, charcoal-burning clay oven, where the food is prepared fresh for customers. Don't expect

Hoi An central market

any menus, or English to be spoken: market dining is strictly 'point-and-pray.'

Popular items include *hu tieu* (a rather firm rice-noodle soup that often includes diced internal organs), rice meals, *bun cha* (rice noodles and pork) and *bun thit nuong* (rice noodles and grilled meats). It's also a great place to pick up interesting – and often very pleasant – dessert items such as *che buoi* (pomelo pudding), *che dau xanh* (green-bean pudding), *sam bo luong* (a sweet iced 'soup' with dried longans, lotus root, fungus, seaweed, beans and lentils) and *banh bo* (sweet, coloured rice muffins).

Markets often serve the cheapest meals. The best selections are available early: usually between 6am and 8am. Hygiene varies from restaurant standard to very poor indeed – so if you notice anything that indicates the latter, avoid at all costs.

Cooking classes: taking the experience home

Cookery classes don't merely teach one how to cook the local food, they also teach the local culinary philosophy. Instructors discuss the local ingredients in the market, how they are grown and harvested, and their many uses in the kitchen. Such classes can be an interesting way to learn about Vietnamese culture.

In Hanoi, **Hidden Hanoi** (137 Nghi Tam, Tay Ho District; tel: 091-225 4045; www.hiddenhanoi.com.vn) runs hands-on cookery classes. There are five different menus (including a vegetarian option) to choose from and each has four courses. In Hoi An, **Red Bridge Cooking School** (Thon 4, Cam Thanh; tel: 090-545 2092; www.visithoian.com) is one of the most popular local cookery schools. The course begins with a trip to the

Items to avoid

The Vietnamese are adventurous eaters. They often say themselves that, whenever they see a new animal, the first question they ask is: 'Will it hurt me?' The second is: 'Can I eat it?'

Vietnam is famous for its dog-meat restaurants and, to a lesser extent, venues serving cat. Some will argue that there is nothing wrong with eating animals that would be considered pets by others. It's certainly not illegal. However, these animals are not part of the daily Vietnamese diet. They are novelty dishes. It should be understood that most of these animals are not raised for consumption. In fact, many are stolen house pets. Further, they are dispatched using what many would consider inhumane methods.

Visitors should avoid restaurants serving anything resembling a wild animal. It is illegal in Vietnam to buy, sell, eat or even advertise exotic game. Sadly, many guidebooks and travel shows continue to recommend these restaurants and they often appear on the itineraries of guided tours. Many restaurants will claim that the exotic animals on their menu were bred in captivity (citing a legal loophole). However, studies have shown that this is almost never true.

local market, followed by a lesson in the herb garden, and finally a very informative class teaching several Hoi An specialities, including creative garnishes. In Ho Chi Minh City, **Saigon Culinary Art Centre** (42/3 Nguyen Van Troi; tel: 08-3997 9569; www. vietnamsaigoncookingclass.com) is a small, dedicated cookery centre set in a traditional-style southern home. Standard classes involve the hands-on preparation of three dishes.

For more on Vietnamese food, see p.283–7.

Eating out in Vietnam

A cookery class in Ho Chi Minh City

Wild Vietnam

For such a small and densely populated country, Vietnam has a surprising amount of wilderness. Lofty mountain ranges are swathed in dense forests, with some cover surviving at lower altitudes, too. The extensive coastline is equally rich in coral reefs.

Vietnam's ecotourism industry is still in its infancy. This means that travellers who wish to pack their trips with multiple outdoor experiences may have to go it alone some of the time. Few destinations have qualified ecotourism companies (nearly all are based in Ho Chi Minh City, Dalat, Hanoi and Sa Pa) and few national parks (namely Cat Tien, Yuk Don and Cuc Phuong) have trained English-speaking guides. Therefore, some research before you set out is a good idea.

The surviving 'A-list' of Vietnam's once-abundant wild animals include small populations of Asian elephants (in Dak Lak province), leopards and clouded leopards, Indochinese tigers (very few), and lesser-known species such as the saola (the 'Asian unicorn', only discovered in 1992), gaur (Indian bison), sun bear, and various endangered primate species. A few black bears survive in the hills. The Javan rhinoceros, however, is thought to have recently become extinct in Vietnam.

Many travellers are disappointed when they spend hours hiking in the jungle but see very few, if any, animals. One of the dilemmas of jungle safaris is that the foliage tends to hide most animals from view. Likewise, hiking in tropical forests tends to be a noisy

Delacour's Langur, one of the endangered primate species at Cuc Phuong National Park

affair, and animals are alerted (and flee) from hikers long before they are in view. It's vital to move slowly and quietly, and for groups to stay together, if any wildlife is to be seen at all. Of course, many of the species are scarce, and many are nocturnal, which reduces the chances of wildlife sightings still further.

Common daytime animals throughout Vietnam include several

A forest giant, Cuc Phuong National Park

species of macaque, small carnivores such as civets and leopard cats, several species of deer, reptiles including the green vine snake and various skinks, geckos and other lizards, as well as saltwater crocodiles. Sadly, birdlife is scant in much of the country due to the local habit of hunting and caging wild birds. Nonetheless, over 800 bird species have been recorded, many of which can still be seen in the national parks, including such spectacular species as the green peafowl and hornbill. Vietnam is also estimated to have more than 1,000 species of butterfly.

Most jungle species tend to be nocturnal, so night safaris (especially popular in Cat Tien and Cuc Phuong national parks) are a great way to spot animals. Civets, deer, owls, fruit bats,

giant tokay geckos and tree frogs are all commonly sighted at night.

A range of habitats

Despite the inevitable deforestation and other pressures on the land, Vietnam's wild areas are still fairly extensive, and the range of habitats – from subalpine mountain peaks to tropical mangrove forests – means that tropical and temperate species are endemic.

The mountain chain that runs along the Lao border is still largely forested and, importantly, these forests are quite extensive, continuing a long way into Laos). There are numerous pockets of relatively untouched rainforest here and further south along the Cambodian border. The northern highlands around Dien Bien Phu and Sa Pa are

Wild Vietnam

Hazards

Mosquitoes are a concern when trekking, as both malaria and dengue fever are common in forested areas. Always use repellent, cover up and sleep under a mosquito net. Leeches are common, even in the dry season, but are not known to transmit any diseases. The bite wounds they cause remain open and bleeding for hours, however, and can be a source of infection.

Biting ants, red or black, are a constant problem when hiking. Be careful about leaning against trees, standing on top of ant trails, or brushing tree branches where ants like to build nests. Ants can swarm alarmingly in a matter of seconds and bite viciously.

The White Sand Dunes near Mui Ne

another relatively pristine area. At higher elevations, the rainforest gives way to a mix of deciduous and coniferous forest, which favour temperate species such as the Asiatic black bear.

By way of contrast, the Mekong Delta has a few mangrove forests and areas of swamp, while further up the coast in the vicinity of Mui Ne, is a drier area characterised by scrub vegetation and large sand dunes.

Vietnam has almost 130 natural protected areas, which includes approximately 30 national parks. Not all of these are well managed and some suffer extensive degradation. A few are truly remarkable, however: highlights are listed below.

Cuc Phuong National Park

The oldest and perhaps the most spectacular of Vietnam's national parks, **Cuc Phuong National Park** (*see p.123*) is located 120km (75 miles) southwest of Hanoi. The park has an almost prehistoric atmosphere to it. Limestone outcrops tower above the primeval forests, hiding dinosaur fossils and the relics of human cave-dwellers.

The park is a trekker's delight, with trails leading to Muong villages where visitors can spend the night in bamboo stilt-houses. There are hiking options to suit all fitness levels, and trips can last from a few hours up to three days. Proper attire and equipment (hiking boots, mosquito repellent, torch, etc) are essential due to the remoteness of the park and lack of facilities.

Because the wildlife in Cuc Phuong is so diverse (Indian flying squirrels, sambar deer, slow loris, pygmy loris, sun bears, and more than a dozen species of primate including the rare Delacour's langur), individual guided treks tend to focus on various wildlife themes (birdwatching, night-spotting, reptiles and amphibians, etc). There are also wildlife centres in the park, with captive animals in rehabilitation or breeding programmes for future release. Both the **Endangered Primate Rescue Center** and the **Turtle Conservation Centre** are open to the public as well.

Cat Tien National Park

About halfway between Dalat and Ho Chi Minh City, **Cat Tien National Park** (*see p.189*) is a nature lover's paradise, where seas of butterflies (there are over 400 species in the park) waft down the main path and regular wildlife sightings include golden-cheeked gibbons, sambar deer, sun bears, black bears, a few elephants and gaur.

The park currently has 14 official excursions and trails to explore. These include hikes through rainforest, grasslands, wetlands, lava fields, night-time safaris, and visits to a S'Tieng minority village. The crown jewel of the park is **Crocodile Lake**, one of the only locations in mainland Southeast Asia to see wild Siamese crocodiles, which were reintroduced in 2000.

Contrary to a wealth of misinformation circulated about the park, it is possible to hike most trails on your own, at no extra charge. Well-trained, English-speaking guides are available, and recommended so that your treks can be as fruitful as possible. Be sure to tell someone when and where you'll be hiking if you do go out alone. Visitors do get lost on the trails.

A Malaysian sun bear

A rescue centre at the park currently houses a dozen or so Asian black bears and sun bears. The bears were rescued from horrific 'farms', where many of them were de-clawed and their teeth pulled, kept in tiny cages that prevented them from moving, and their bile was extracted for traditional medicine. The rescue centre is open to park visitors.

Monkey World (www.go-east.org) has developed the **Dao Tien Endangered Primate Species Centre,** which rehabilitates primate species including golden-cheeked gibbon, black-shanked douc langur, and pygmy loris. The centre is located on an island in the Dong Nai River, inside the park. Tours of the rehabilitation centre are available, as well as guided hikes in the jungle to see wild gibbons.

Yok Don National Park
Yok Don National Park *(see p.190)* is a 115,545-hectare (285,520-acre) wildlife reserve in Dak Lak province (outside Buon Ma Thuot), near the Cambodian border. The park contains at least 63 species of mammal and 250 species of bird. More than 15 of these animals are listed as endangered. There are known to be around 50 Asian elephants, at least 10 Indochinese tigers, giant muntjac, golden jackals and a few leopards in the park. Most of these mammals live in a buffer zone along the Cambodian border, which means visitors are unlikely to see them without committing to an overnight, guided trek. For those who don't have time for the jungle hike, the main draws are elephant rides led by Ede trackers, and boat trips along the river

A mahout guides three young elephants at Yok Don National Park

Mount Fansipan, Hoang Lien Son National Park

Looming ominously over Sa Pa, **Mount Fansipan** entices the more adventurous to conquer its summit, conditions permitting. The mountain stands at 3,143m (10,311ft) in the middle of **Hoang Lien Son National Park**, 5km (3 miles) from Sa Pa. Vietnam's highest mountain offers stunning panoramic views.

The hike is more about taking in the mountain scenery than seeing any wildlife, and while it is not too technically demanding, it is still a challenging experience. It can take several days up steep, overgrown trails. The time required is very much dependent on weather conditions. Make sure that you arrange the trip with experienced operators that offer two- to four-

Beautiful countryside near Sa Pa

Wild Vietnam

Conservation in Vietnam

If you have already travelled in Vietnam, you might be asking, 'What conservation?'. Indeed, forests – including those in national parks – are being rapidly and openly harvested, illegally. Titanium mining is destabilising coastal dunes and destroying the fragile habitats. Dredging, dynamite fishing and fishing with poisons has destroyed many of Vietnam's coral reefs.

The country still has sizeable areas of wilderness, but as all manner of wild animal, from bears to monkeys and sea turtles, continue to be sold in markets and on restaurant menus, the wildlife within them steadily diminishes. Lacquered sea-turtle shells are sold openly in shops in Hanoi, Ho Chi Minh City and Nha Trang, while bear and tiger claws are sold in the Dalat market and the Ho Chi Minh Museum.

Unfortunately, the entertainment industry and foreign tourism hasn't helped the situation. A number of international travel shows have glorified the eating of wildlife in Vietnam. Traditional medicine is also a huge threat: tour groups out of Hanoi have made a big business out of taking busloads of Korean tourists to visit illegal bear-bile farms. Most major tourist attractions illegally sell bear claws and snake wine.

Vietnam has made the situation worse by legalising the farming of bears, tigers and even rhinos. As a result, many of these farms have become fronts for trafficking in wild tigers, and Vietnam is now the world leader of the illicit trade in African rhino horn.

For more on environmental issues, and how you can help, see p.264.

day packages with all the necessary porters, guides and equipment, such as tents and cooking facilities. **Topas Eco-lodge** (tel: 020-387 2404; www. topas-eco-lodge.com) is highly recommended for accommodation, and has 25 individual, eco-managed and solar-powered lodges set atop two remote hills, about a 1½hr drive from Sa Pa.

Diving and snorkelling

Vietnam's coral reefs are peppered all along the coast, but three sites have been developed as protected areas to preserve the reefs. These include dive sites in Nha Trang, the Con Dao Archipelago in the far south, and the Cham Islands off Hoi An. Nha Trang is by far the most visited.

Nha Trang

The star attraction of **Nha Trang** is its beautiful coral reefs, largely encompassed by the **Hon Mun Marine Protected Area**, and including several offshore islands. About 190 species of coral and 176 species of marine animal have been documented. Hawksbill turtles, morays and large rays are among the highlights.

Sadly, Nha Trang's reefs are rapidly in decline due to pollution, over-fishing and mismanagement by the government. Visibility, which once reached 30m (98ft), is often down to 10m (33ft). Of the 19 original dive sites, only five are now available. Boats provided to the government by NGOs to monitor the reef now sit idly by while fishermen in plain view drop nets, and even dynamite and cyanide on marked dive spots. Further south, at Ca Na Beach, two

Russian divers were killed in 2011 by fishermen using dynamite in a protected marine park.

Your support of ecotourism activities, like diving and snorkelling, promote further protection of the reef, but only if you support eco-friendly companies *(see p.264)*. Safety is also an important issue, as some companies have had certifications revoked, and have even accidentally abandoned divers in the bay.

Cu Lao Cham Marine Park

About 20km (12 miles), or 25 minutes by speedboat, from Hoi An, the **Cu Lao Cham Marine Park** surrounds the Cham Islands archipelago. The park is one of the finest diving areas in central Vietnam. The main island is known for the harvesting of swallow's

Bai Nhat beach, Con Dao

Scuba diving off Nha Trang

nests, a delicacy across Asia. Numerous boats take visitors to swim along the reefs each day, although few tourists venture on to the island itself.

Con Dao archipelago

The **Con Dao archipelago** is the centre of a national marine park covering 14 islands famous for dugongs and both green and hawksbill turtles. The World Wide Fund has been actively involved in programmes here to protect these beautiful creatures.

Since 1995, more than 300,000 baby turtles have been released and around 1,000 mature turtles have been tagged.

The waters here have escaped the destructive fishing practices that obliterated reefs in other places. There are over 1,000 hectares (2,470 acres) of pristine coral reefs and over 1,300 marine species identified thus far. Weather patterns alternate so that swimming, snorkelling and diving are excellent on at least one side of the islands all year long.

Dive centres

Rainbow Divers is arguably the top outfit in Vietnam, offering basic to advanced courses They have offices in Nha Trang (90A Hung Vuong; tel: 058-352 4351; www.divevietnam.com), Hoi An (39B Tran Hung Dao; tel: 0510-391 1914) and on Con Dao Island (tel: 090-516 2833).

Other options include the **Cham Island Diving Centre** (88 Nguyen Thai Hoc, Hoi An; tel: 0510-391 0782; www.

chamislanddiving.com), offering day trips to Cu Lao Cham Marine Park for beginners (diving or snorkelling) and certified divers.

The **Sailing Club Diving** (72–4 Tran Phu; tel: 058-352 2788; www.sailingclub diving.com) and **Octopus Diving** (24 Biet Thu; tel: 058-352 1629) are both run by the same reputable dive centre in Nha Trang. All of the above centres provide PADI certification classes.

Ancient cultures

For such a small country with a long history of Chinese domination, Vietnam has a remarkable foundation of unique, ancient civilisations, which all had profound cultural and political influence on the development of Southeast Asia. Although often overlooked and vastly underrated, Vietnam's ancient history is indeed fascinating.

Although Vietnam has been inhabited for more than four millennia, most of the communities and civilisations that colonised the region prior to the early 19th century have left little to remind us of their presence, apart from scattered burial grounds and buried relics. In fact, only the Champa – a matriarchal, Hindu culture thought to have arrived in Vietnam by sea – have left any substantial remains. Their ancient red-brick temples, still used by their descendants in the south of the country, are a highlight of any visit to Vietnam.

Way back in the mists of time, for a thousand years from around 1,000BC, the northern parts of the country were home to what is known as the Dong Son culture. Dominating the Red River Valley and northern mountains, this early civilisation owes its name to the first site, discovered by archaeologists on the edge of the Red River Delta. The Dong Son culture was apparently absorbed by the Vietnamese (as they moved southwards into the area from China), as well as by highland minority groups.

At roughly the same time, from 1,000BC to AD500, the Sa Huynh culture, believed to be ancestors of the Cham, dominated much of the length of Vietnam's coast. Further

Group B building, My Son

south, the Funan Kingdom ruled the Mekong Delta from approximately 400BC to AD600. Though Funan was absorbed by the Kingdom of Chen La and the subsequent Khmer Empire in Cambodia, Funanese religion and architecture is thought to have had a significant influence on the later Cham.

The Champa dominated all of central Vietnam for a full millennium, starting around AD600, with

a gradual decline thereafter, until
their autonomy was entirely dissolved
in the early 1800s by Vietnamese
emperor Minh Mang.

Sa Huynh

The **Sa Huynh** culture flourished
for nearly 1,500 years prior to the
Champa Empire. Their home range
stretched from north of Hue, south
to Saigon and into the Mekong
Delta. They are known from their
burial grounds in sand dunes and
river banks, and often buried their
dead with two styles of peculiar
earring, which travellers will frequently encounter in museums and
some shops. The first were circular
in shape with three arrow-points at
right angles, facing left, right and
downward. The second type had two
horned animal-heads facing in opposite directions at the ends of a cross-
bar, which dangled from the ear like a
set of scales. Both varieties were made
of obsidian, jade and other semi-
precious stones. They were traded,
and coveted, throughout Southeast
Asia and have been found in ancient

Ancient inscriptions telling the history
of the temple, Po Nagar Cham Tower

Ancient cultures

archaeological sites in Thailand,
Taiwan and the Philippines.

With no legacy in terms of ruins
or other sites, the only way to witness
Sa Huynh culture is by seeing their
artefacts on display in museums or
antique shops. Nearly every provincial
or city museum, from Ho Chi Minh
City to Hue, displays a few of their
artefacts. The best museums are the
Quang Ngai Provincial Museum (see
p.165), the **Hoi An Museum of Sa
Huynh Culture** (see p.151), and the
Vietnam History Museum in Hanoi
(see p.71). **Le Cong Kieu Street** (see
p.212) in District 1, Ho Chi Minh
City, is lined with antique shops
selling Sa Huynh earrings – most of
which are fake. A knowledgeable and
honest shop owner will sell a muse-
um-quality glass or stone reproduc-
tion for around US$10 each.

Dong Son

The **Dong Son** culture, though just as old as the Sa Huynh, is more visibly woven into the fabric of Vietnam's minority cultures. Masters of bronze casting, the Dong Son manufactured many different types of item in bronze, including swords, knives, axes, bracelets, necklaces and candle-holders – ornate and highly imaginative, they incorporate bizarre, otherworldly creatures.

They are best known, however, for their **bronze drums**, which were made with such expert craftsmanship that they were highly prized trade items as far away as China, Thailand and Java. Many examples still survive today in excellent condition. The drums can be seen in both museums and antique shops, though fakes are common.

The bird designs found on many drums, including jungle fowl, pheasants, spoonbills, peafowl and storks, are popular motifs also found in modern Vietnamese jewellery and art. They have also been incorporated into the traditional handicrafts of some minorities.

The **Khanh Hoa Provincial Museum** (see p.174) and **Vietnam Fine Arts Museum** in Hanoi (see p.76) have good sections on the Dong Son, and the better antique and handicraft shops are likely to have a few genuine antiques from the period: prices depend on the size and complexity of the piece. For genuine pieces, expect to pay anywhere from US$100 to $2,000.

Funan

The **Funan Empire** flourished in the waning years of Dong Son and Sa Huynh, when Champa was in its infancy. Thus it represents a crossroads in cultural development for the region. Most of what is known about Funan comes from artefacts recovered from the foundations of buried temples, the excavations at Oc Eo in the Mekong Delta, and limited references in ancient Chinese manuscripts. There is a great deal of confusion and misinformation over what constitutes vestiges of Funan and what might belong to other kingdoms, making it difficult to draw precise territorial boundaries.

Funanese statues of Hindu deities and Buddha images, made of stone and wood, are prized by museums and private collectors alike. The artistic legacy is most readily encountered at the

Bronze Dong Son tomb figure of a kneeling lamp bearer at the Fine Arts Museum, Hanoi

Vietnam History museums in Ho Chi Minh City and Hanoi, as well as the **An Giang Museum** on Ba The Mountain in An Giang province *(see p.240)*.

Oc Eo

The archaeological site of **Oc Eo** was excavated by French archaeologists in 1945. The site, near Long Xuyen in the Mekong Delta, can be visited but there is little to see. Oc Eo had a vast trade network extending to Rome and Egypt. Vietnamese scholars have ascribed nearly all archaeological finds in the Mekong to this 'Oc Eo culture.' However, there is no significant evidence to suggest that the culture or political identity of Oc Eo was distinct from the Funan Empire. In this book, archaeological sites outside of the port city itself have been categorised as Funan or Cham.

Champa

Unlike the aforementioned ancient civilisations, the culture of **Champa**, or rather the ethnic Cham people, still survives in modern form. Though the Kingdom of Champa once occupied all of central Vietnam, most ethnic Cham now reside in Binh Thuan and Ninh Thuan provinces, and the Mekong Delta.

For excellent tours (with knowledgeable, English-speaking guides) of ancient Cham temples, modern Cham communities and Cham culture in general, contact Inra Jaka (tel: 091-917 4987; email: inrajaka@yahoo.com) or Hung (tel: 090-443 4895; email: muinehung@gmail.com. There are no companies or government agencies that can be recommended.

Visitors at Po Ro Me Cham Tower

Temples

The most obvious way to experience ancient Cham culture is by visiting Champa's ancient temple sites, which are most accessible between Phan Thiet and Danang, along Vietnam's central coastline. **My Son** *(see p.154)*, near Hoi An, and the countryside around **Quy Nhon** *(see p.167)*, have the highest concentrations of temples. Other well-preserved temples worth visiting include **Po Sha Nu** in Mui Ne *(see p.177)*, **Po Ro Me** and **Po Klong Garai** in Phan Rang *(see p.173 and p.176)*, and the temples of **Chien Dan** and **Khuong My** near Tam Ky *(see p.155)*. The **Po Nagar Cham Towers** in Nha Trang *(see p.171)* are another noteworthy site, and because of their accessible location, they attract more tourists than the other sites.

In reality, there are far more undocumented temple ruins through

The Long Wall of Quang Ngai

It may not be particularly old (it has been dated to the early 19th century), but the recently discovered **Long Wall of Quang Ngai** *(see also p.166)* is still a remarkable sight. It was created to secure – from bandits and enemies in general – and regulate a centuries-old trade route developed by the Cham, and at the time used by the Vietnamese and H're (the minority group that is believed to have contributed to its construction) as well as Chinese merchants and other local minorities. The wall, which runs 127km (79 miles) from northern Quang Ngai Province south into Binh Dinh, is accessible by road in a few spots: head southwest from Quang Ngai City on Highway 624 and you will see signposts. There are, however, currently no hiking trails, maps or qualified guides to the wall, so visitors are on their own – for the time being at least. As camping is illegal, travellers will need to stay in Quang Ngai City and make daytrips out to the wall.

A protective corridor extending 500m (1,640ft) on either side of the wall has been established by the government. The landscape ranges from lush, forested mountains cut by waterfalls and rivers, to plains and farmland inhabited by Vietnamese, H're, Ca Dong and Cor villagers. In the rainy season, particularly September through December, the area can be hard to navigate.

Some of the most interesting archaeological sites around the wall are stone forts (some centuries older than the wall itself) and ruins of ancient Cham temples, dating back nearly 1,000 years.

Vietnam's countryside than are listed in tourist maps and guidebooks. Cham temple ruins can be found by following country roads along large river systems. Temples were often (but not always) built on hilltops or mounds in the vicinity of a village. Temple buildings were usually arranged in clusters of three or more, with the doorways facing east.

Most documented Cham temples have a government caretaker assigned to them who will charge a small, but variable, entry fee. None of the caretakers speak English, and signage is usually in Vietnamese, so visitors are on their own to explore.

It's difficult to get a sense of the scale of Cham temples through photos. Some are indeed small (only 3m/10ft tall), but others extend up

Cham man, Tuan Tu village, near Phan Rang

Monster makara, Cham Sculpture Museum, Danang

to 20m (66ft). Often called towers because of their tall, cylindrical shape, this is a misnomer. Temple buildings contain a single inner chamber with cathedral ceilings, no windows, and only one eastward-facing door. The damp, cavern-like interiors are home to bats, dung beetles and Tokay geckos.

Cham temple complexes usually consist of three or more buildings, all made of red baked bricks. In the centre of the main building sits a *linga* (phallus) or linga-yoni (male and female counterpart) or an image of the god-king to which the temple was devoted. Many of these religious objects have been taken away to museums or private collections.

Sculpture

Cham statuary – entirely religious in nature – can be found at nearly every provincial museum across the country, as well as the Vietnam History Museums in Hanoi and Ho Chi Minh City, although the **Museum of Cham Sculpture in Danang** *(see p.147)* has the best collection in the world.

Common subjects include Hindu gods, particularly Shiva, as well as Vishnu, Brahma, Ganesh, Nandin the bull, Garuda (a bird-like deity), *apsara* (magical dancing girls), *naga* (a serpent), *makara* (dragons, which unlike Vietnamese and Chinese dragons, were considered terrible creatures), *linga* and *yoni* (Hindu fertility symbols) fairies and demons, elephants, historical kings and consorts, and uniquely Cham deities such as the goddess Po Nagar.

Some of these characters still adorn well-preserved temples, particularly in Quang Nam province, where religious art reached its apex. Other temple-art motifs include lotus and other flowers, the female breast, scallop shells and monkeys.

Music and dance

Judging from the dance poses of apsara statues, ancient Cham dance was probably similar to traditional Khmer dance: slow and graceful movements by a single dancer or several, requiring a high degree of endurance, balance, flexibility and tolerance of pain due to the unusual body contortions typifying the dance style. Modern Cham dance has evolved into a simplified form, characterised by brief, wispy movements, performed by groups of dancers. Male and female dancers wear ethnic costumes, often holding props such as fans or jars.

Dancing is accompanied by a traditional Cham orchestra, which includes at least two large *ginang* drums (played by two men seated and facing each other), a *paranung* drum (a small, flat leather drum), a *xaranai* (reminiscent of an Indian snake-charmer's horn), and often hand bells (similar to sleigh bells) or gongs. The Cham do have other instruments but sadly there are very few musicians left who can play them, let alone make them.

Cham music and dancing is best observed in villages or temples during festivals such as Kate (Sept or Oct), Rija (Mar or Apr) and Ramuwan (usually Sept), or special occasions such as weddings and funerals. Po Nagar Temple in Nha Trang *(see p.171)* is the only temple with daily performances put on for tourists. A few resorts and restaurants in Binh Thuan and Ninh Thuan, such as **The Forest Restaurant** in Mui Ne *(see p.180)* present nightly performances.

Cham women dancing at Po Nagar

A 15-year-old Cham girl works at a loom in a Cham village near Chau Doc in the Mekong Delta

Ceramics

Cham ceramics have been prized since antiquity for their fine craftsmanship and durability. Many hilltribe minorities trade their goods for Cham jars in which to make *ruou can* rice wine *(see p.31)*. This pottery tradition can be traced all the way back to the Sa Huynh culture, and today's terracotta pottery is still made by hand, without the benefit of a conventional potters wheel. It is mesmerising to watch the potters (who are usually women) as they work, bent over their stands, crafting all manner of objects in various shapes and sizes. **Huu Duc Village** near Phan Rang *(see p.175)* is the best place to observe pottery being made as well as to purchase some. Good-quality examples are also sold in gift shops at the temples of Po Shanu in Phan Thiet and Po Nagar in Nha Trang *(see p.176 and p.171)*.

Textiles

The Cham have always been known for their brightly coloured textiles, which are still woven on looms in homes. Most temple statues were once adorned with these fabrics, in addition to lavish jewellery made of gold, silver and precious stones.

Traditionally, both men and women wore sarongs and turbans, but now, Balamon Cham (quasi-Hindu) men wear trousers and Bani Cham (quasi-Muslim) women wear hijab or veils. Cham holy men of both religious groups sport bright white robes with orange or red sashes and satchel, and a white turban with red tassels.

The village of **My Nghiep**, near Phan Rang, is most famous for its textile weaving. Visitors can observe the loom work and purchase the creations. Cham fabrics are also sold in gift shops throughout Vietnam.

PLACES

C H I N A

BIEN DONG

NORTHERN HIGHLANDS
Pages 96 – 115

HANOI AND ENVIRONS
Pages 64 – 95

NORTHEAST AND NORTH-CENTRAL
Pages 116 – 133

CENTRAL

VIETNAM

L A O S

Viangchan (Vientiane)

Vinh Bac Bo
(Gulf of Tonkin)

Cai Bau
Cam Pha
Vuon Quoc Gia Cat Ba (Cat Ba National Park)
Cat Ba
Ha Long
Halong Bay
Hai Phong (Haiphong)
Ninh Binh
Nam Dinh

Cao Bang
Ha Giang
Lang Son
Dong Dang
Bac Giang
Thai Nguyen
Viet Tri
Quang
Ha Noi (Hanoi)
Son Tay
Hoa Binh
Phu Ly
Phat Diep

Lao Cai
Phan Si Pan
Hoang Lien
Tuan Giao
Ky Trang
Son La
Phou Sam Soum
Moc Chau
Na Meo
Bim Son
Tam Diep
Thanh Hoa
Lam Son
Ky Son

Phan Thiet
Cao Vinh Quoc
Vuon Quoc Gia

Dien Bien Phu
Muong Nha (Nature Reserve)
Muong Lay
Pa

Hong

San Chau
Ha Tinh
Mui Ron
Cong Vien Quoc Gia Phong Nha-Ke Bang (Phong Nha-Ke Bang NP)
Dong Hoi
Dong Ha

Vinh

Getting
your bearings

A long, sinuous land on the eastern edge of Indo-China, Vietnam is essentially comprised of deltaic plains in the northeast and south separated by a long line of mountains that are flanked by narrow coastal plains. The major cities – from north to south, Hanoi, Hue, Nha Trang and Ho Chi Minh City – are linked by air, rail and long-distance bus routes.

For easy reference when using this guide, each region has a dedicated chapter and is colour-coded for quick navigation. Vietnam is divided into Hanoi and environs; the Northern Highlands, Northeast and North-Central Vietnam; Central Vietnam; the South-Central Coast; the Southern Highlands; Ho Chi Minh City and environs; and the Mekong Delta. Detailed regional maps are included within each chapter. As much of the country is mountainous, getting around isn't always easy. In the cities, traffic is often a problem. Therefore, to make the most of your time in Vietnam, planning your route in advance is advised.

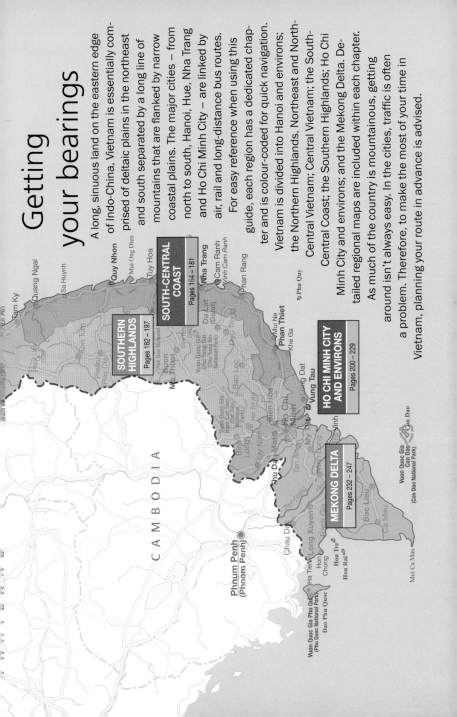

SOUTHERN HIGHLANDS
Pages 182 – 197

SOUTH-CENTRAL COAST
Pages 154 – 181

HO CHI MINH CITY AND ENVIRONS
Pages 200 – 229

MEKONG DELTA
Pages 232 – 247

Hanoi and environs

A complicated city torn between old and new, and an inimitable mix of ancient culture, colonial charm and modern-day luxury, Hanoi is in a constant state of flux and defies anyone who tries to box it in. It is, though, noticeably less frenzied than Ho Chi Minh City, and the picturesque old centre has retained its appeal. Beyond the city, a variety of day trips to pagodas and craft villages are possible.

Population: 6,452,000

Local dialling code: 04

Local tourist information centre: 7 Dinh Tien Hoang, Hoan Kiem District; tel: 04-3926 3366; www.ticvietnam.com

Main police station: Dial 113

Main post office: 75 Pho Dinh Tien Hoang; tel: 04-3825 7036

Main hospital: International SOS Clinic, 31 Hai Ba Trung, Hoan Kiem District; tel: 04-3934 0666

Local newspapers/listings magazines: *The Word* Hanoi

Today, **Hanoi ❶** is a rapidly developing city, but one that has kept its striking colonial embellishments. Indeed, it is ironic that this capital city of fiercely independent people, who have battled for generations against foreign invaders, possesses a decidedly European air. Hanoians may brag about their beautiful city while eating baguette sandwiches and sipping café au lait, but they are reluctant to admit that much of what makes it so is a legacy of the French. The colonial architecture, together with an abundance of trees and lakes, gives Hanoi an unmistakably romantic air, unusual for an Asian city.

Since the late 1990s, with the help of Korean and Taiwanese investors, the city has transformed itself from a rather sleepy backwater into a bustling metropolis. Luxurious shopping malls and apartment complexes have sprung up beside 200-year-old temples, and each day, new restaurants, cafés and shops open along the city's busy avenues. Despite, or because of, the rapid progress, Hanoians are passionate about protecting their ancient traditions and culture, and a number of preservation works have been announced to protect important historic sites.

Central Hanoi

At the heart of the town is **Hoan Kiem District**, which comprises the Old Quarter, just north of Hoan Kiem Lake, and the French Quarter, just east and south of the lake. Most of the action takes place in the Old Quarter, also known as the '36 Streets.'

Hoan Kiem Lake

A natural focus for any visitor to the city is picturesque **Hoan Kiem Lake** (Ho Hoan Kiem), the Lake of the Restored Sword. Also known to Hanoians as Ho Guom (Green Lake), early-rising visitors can catch locals seriously exercising before heading off to work. In the evening, especially during holidays, the lakeside has a carnival-like atmosphere, with vendors selling balloons and toys, teenagers racing around on motorbikes, and music blaring from loudspeakers. Around the perimeter are several pleasant outdoor cafés.

A legend that sounds like a Vietnamese version of the Excalibur one tells of how King Le Thai To, of the Le dynasty, received a magic sword from an ancient tortoise, which he

Nha Tho Street scene

used during his 10-year resistance against the Chinese in the early 1400s. After liberating the country, the king took a boat to the centre of the lake to return the magic sword given to him by the divine tortoise. The reptile is said to have snatched the sword from his hand and disappeared into the lake. Tortoises are still seen in the lake, though many believe that the tourism authority places them there as a publicity stunt.

Recalling the legend is a small 18th-century structure called **Tortoise Tower** Ⓐ (Thap Rua) in the middle of the lake. Perched on a tiny islet at the north end of the lake is **Ngoc Son Temple** Ⓑ, also known as the **Temple of the Jade Mound** (Den Ngoc Son; daily 8am–5pm; charge). The temple is reached from the shore via an arched bridge, painted bright red and known as **The Huc**, or the **Rising Sun Bridge**. Ngoc Son Temple is dedicated to, among others, the famous 13th-century general Tran Hung Dao and La To, the patron saint of doctors. Inside is a large stuffed tortoise, once caught in Hoan Kiem Lake.

A couple at Hoan Kiem Lake, with the Tortoise Tower in the background

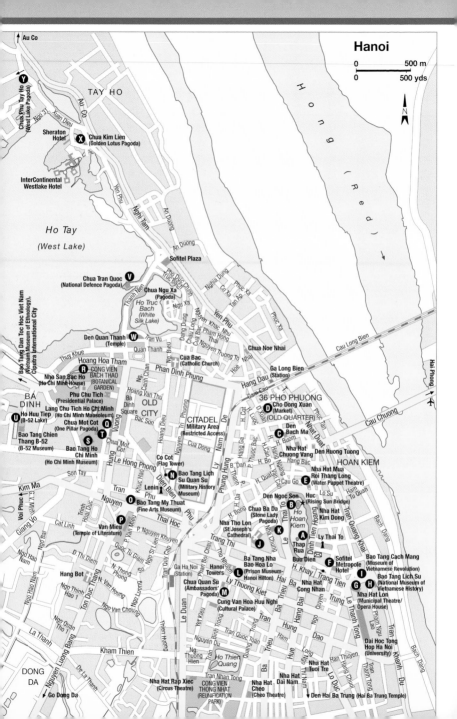

The Huc, or Rising Sun Bridge, leads to Ngoc Son Temple

The '36 Streets' of the Old Quarter

North of Hoan Kiem Lake is the area known as the **36 Streets**, or the **Old Quarter** (Pho Phuong). Today, it is the heart of the tourist district and a constantly bustling hive of backpacker hotels, cafés, shops and restaurants.

This part of town evolved in the 13th century, when artisan guilds were concentrated along each of the original 36 lanes. The guilds developed independently, separated from each other by

Hanoi transport

 Airport: Noi Bai International Airport is 35km (21 miles) north of downtown Hanoi. The best way to travel downtown is by airport taxi (fixed rate US$14). The trip takes 40–60 minutes. The airport minibus costs US$1.80 and only leaves when it is completely full. Public buses (daily 5am–10pm; VND5,000) are slow and crowded. The bus stop is on the right side of the terminal exit

 Taxis: Taxis charge by the meter, with a flag-fall rate that ranges from VND8,000–15,000 for the first 2km (1¼ miles), followed by about VND2,000 for every km thereafter. Stick to the major recommended taxi companies: Hanoi Taxi, tel: 04-3853 5353; CP Taxi, tel: 04-3826 2626; ABC Taxi, tel: 04-3719 1919; and Mai Linh Taxi, tel: 04-3822 2555. If you find yourself in a taxi that obviously has a rigged meter (the fare will rise very quickly), ask the driver to stop, tell him the meter is broken and get out of the cab

Motorbike Taxis (xe om): The most popular form of public transport, but they do require nerves of steel and a bit of good luck. *Xe om* can be found on almost every street corner and generally charge between US$1–2, depending on the destination. Settle the price beforehand and make sure the driver has a helmet you can use

 Cyclos: Hanoi's front-seater cyclos *(xich lo)* are three-wheeled rickshaws. Generally, an hour's tour around the Old Quarter or Truc Bach Lake should cost around US$7

 Trains: Hanoi's railway station is at 120 Le Duan Street; tel: 04-3942 3697 (western end of Tran Hung Dao St, 1km southwest of Hoan Kiem Lake). The ticket office is open daily from 7.30am–11.30am and 1.30–3.30pm. There are six trains daily to Ho Chi Minh City via Hue

 Buses: Hanoi's large city buses ply most major streets. The network is quite extensive and fares are a flat VND3,000 per person, but few foreigners are likely to use them

Hanoi and environs

Many Chinese merchants settled into the Old Quarter in the 17th century and it soon became Hanoi's most affluent area, as the Chinese monopolised local commerce. To some extent, they still do.

The Old Quarter retains many 'tube houses', so called because of their narrow facades and their length. These single-storey shops belie their depth, containing dwellings at the rear and tiny courtyards. Feudal laws taxed shops according to their width – explaining why many are less than 3m (10ft) wide – and decreed that buildings should be no higher than a passing royal palanquin, in deference to the emperor. Over the years, many buildings incorporated Western features, such as balconies and additional floors.

Originally, a tributary ran parallel to Hang Buom (Sails Street), enabling boats to sail up there to buy nautical supplies. When the French filled in the To Lich River, merchants switched to selling imported goods and dried foodstuff, still sold today.

walls and gates that were locked each night. Tinsmiths were found on **Hang Thiec** (Tin Street), bamboo-basket makers on **Hang Bo** (Bamboo Basket Street), and so on. The present-day commercial frenzy that the Old Quarter has become is all the more amazing considering that, with few exceptions, the Communists prohibited private trade until as recently as 1986.

The new tradespeople still tend to cluster along each street by speciality, but the trade doesn't necessarily match the street name any longer. Silver jewellery, as well as gravestones, can still be found on **Hang Bac** (Silver Street), but the future of this street clearly rests on travel agencies and tourist cafés. The street called **Hang Gai** (Hemp Street) specialises in silk,

Street stalls in the heart of the Old Quarter

and 19th centuries. In regular use, it remains in a good state of repair.

The area around **Dong Xuan Market**  (Cho Dong Xuan; daily 8am–5pm), in the northern part of the Old Quarter, rewards exploration. The original colonial-era market, destroyed by fire in 1994, has been replaced with an already grimy four-storey building; its escalator, perhaps the city's first, is permanently frozen. This is the wholesale source of many dry goods. It's a good place to shop for home wares or cheap souvenirs. On **Lang Ong Street**, traditional medicine shops sell all manner of cures and remedies.

Water Puppet Theatre

Most visitors to Hanoi will have heard about the city's famous water puppet theatre. You can book tickets in advance at the **Thang Long Water Puppet Theatre** (Nha Hat Mua Roi Thang Long, 57B Dinh Tien Hoang; www.thanglongwaterpuppet. org; Mon–Sat shows at 3.30pm, 5pm, 6.30pm, 8pm and 9.15pm, Sun 9.30am only; charge). The theatre is located on the northeast corner of Hoan Kiem Lake, along Dinh Tien Hoang Street. The nightly performance of traditional water puppetry is accompanied by live music and should not be missed if you want a dose (albeit a touristic one) of local culture.

East of Hoan Kiem Lake

To the east of Hoan Kiem lies an upscale, French-colonial quarter where some of the area's best hotels are located. On the east side of the lake, at 75 Dinh Tien Hoang Street, is

Mixing ingredients at a traditional medicine shop on Lang Ong Street

clothing and embroidered articles, while **Hang Dau** (Cooking Oil Street) is full of shoe shops. However, **Hang Chieu** (Mats Street) is still the place to find mats and **Hang Ma** (Paper Votive Street) has mainly stationery shops.

Bach Ma Temple (Den Bach Ma; daily 8am–5pm; charge), at 78 **Hang Buom Street** (Sail Street), is the Old Quarter's most revered temple and honours the white horse that appeared to King Ly Thai To in a dream and led him to build the walls of the old city. Aside from the giant wooden horse inside, there is a palanquin adorned with carvings of phoenixes, cranes and tortoises. Originally built in the 9th century, the temple was reconstructed in the 18th

Performers at the Thang Long Water Puppet Theatre

the city's **General Post Office** (Buu Dien), designed by French architects in 1942. One block north is a small patch of greenery called the **Ly Thai To Park** (formerly Indira Gandhi Park), where courting couples have late-night trysts and, during the day, young men gather to try out skateboard tricks, breakdance and play football. An emphatically large statue of King Ly Thai To, the founder of the Ly dynasty, dominates the park.

To the east of the park, on Ly Thai To Street, is the striking Art Deco-style former **Bank of Indochina**. Southwards, straddling Ly Thai To and Ngo Quyen streets, is the regal, whitewashed **Metropole Hotel** ⒻThis gem was the city's only international-standard hotel – then called the Grand Hotel Metropole Palace – in French-colonial days and was the venue for colonial society gatherings.

Famous guests from the glory days include writers such as Noël Coward and Somerset Maugham, and actors such as Charlie Chaplin. It was also here that Graham Greene wrote a few chapters of his visionary novel, *The Quiet American,* in the 1950s (most were written in Ho Chi Minh City – *see p.210*). During the Vietnam War years, the hotel was used as a base by diplomats and journalists. Thoroughly renovated by the new French management that took over and reopened in 1992, today its history, refined decor and excellent French restaurants make it a Hanoi institution.

From here it's only a short walk south, on Ly Thai To Street, to the grand columned **Municipal Theatre**, often referred to as the **Opera House** Ⓖ(Nha Hat Lon). This performing-arts centre was built in 1911 to keep the French entertained (and remind them of home). After years of renovation, it finally reopened in 1997 and hosts regular performances by foreign and local orchestras, as well as ballet, opera and pop concerts. Its basement boasts a gourmet restaurant called **Nineteen11**.

The Opera House is stunning, its interior embellished with a sweeping marble staircase, crystal chandelier, and red and gold-leaf decor. Unfortunately, there are no tours or any access unless you have a ticket for a show. Adjacent is the luxurious **Hilton Hanoi Opera**, with a pleasing facadious that replicates the style of the Opera House; the interior, however, is contemporary in style.

Heading back west and skirting the southern tip of the lake, **Trang Tien Street** – which ends in front of the Opera House – was once the main shopping street of the **French Quarter**. When the Communists closed private enterprises, Trang Tien Street was one of the few areas that retained any commerce; today it is home to up-market art galleries, bookshops, and – in the once-drab old government department

Nha Hat Lon, the city's Opera House

store – the **Hanoi Securities Trading Centre**. In the blocks to the south and west, on quiet tree-lined streets, the elegant former villas of the colonialists now house embassies, diplomatic residences and the headquarters of non-governmental organisations.

National Museum of Vietnamese History

Behind the Opera House, with a cupola resembling a pagoda, is the **National Museum of Vietnamese History** ⓗ (Bao Tang Lich Su Viet Nam, 01 Pham Ngu Lao and 01 Tran Tien; www.nmvnh.com.vn; Tue–Sun 8–11.30am, 1.30–4.30pm; charge). The museum occupies the old archaeological research institution of the French School of the Far East, which opened in 1910 and was substantially renovated in the 1920s. High on content and low on propaganda, this may be the best museum in town. The excellent archaeological collection includes relics from the Hung era and Neolithic graves, Bronze Age implements, Cham artefacts, stelae, statues, ceramics and an eerie sculpture of the goddess of mercy, Quan Am, with 1,000 eyes and arms.

Nearby, the **Museum of the Vietnamese Revolution** ⓘ (Bao Tang Cach Mang; Tue–Sun 8–11.45am, 1.30–4.15pm; charge), at 216 Tran Quang Khai Street, offers a carefully edited version of the struggles of the Vietnamese people, from ancient times up to 1975. Displays include long wooden stakes that crippled the Mongol fleet in Halong Bay during one of three invasion attempts

🚶 OLD HANOI WALK

The political and cultural capital of Vietnam, Hanoi is one of Asia's loveliest cities, with parks, lakes, tree-lined boulevards and history-drenched architecture. Take a stroll around the 1,000-year-old merchant's quarter and absorb the atmosphere and sights while snacking and shopping along the way.

Begin your tour at 8am; breakfast is taken en route. Walk north up **Ho Hoan Kiem Street** to get to Cau Go Street. Across the road is **Hang Be Market**, a good place to get street-food snacks, such as Hanoi's famous sweet black beans and yoghurt. Walk through the market, turn left and exit on **Dinh Liet**

The Old East Gate

Street – the start of Hanoi's most attractive neighbourhood, the Old Quarter, with its '36 streets' – the traditional trading places of local artisans.

Walk along Dinh Liet and turn right into Hang Bac, one of the oldest streets. Silversmiths settled here in the 13th century, casting silver bars and coins. and the shops still sell items, mainly jewellery, made from the precious metal. At the intersection with Dinh Liet and Ta Hien streets, the **Golden Bell Theatre** (Nha Hat Chuong Vang) – a traditional Vietnamese theatre – was once the Hanoi Imperial Guards' headquarters.

At the end of Hang Bac, gravestone workshops spill out on to the pavements. Head into **Ma May** (Rattan Street). Members of the notorious Chinese Black Flag Army – peasant mercenaries from Southern China – once lived here. In the 19th century, they helped with the Vietnamese struggle against the French.

The Old Quarter's most noteworthy antique house is at **No 87. Ma May Street**. This former Communal House (Gioi Thieu Nha Co So), beautifully restored to its late 19th-century condition, is open to the public. The restored building at No. 69, now transformed

Tips

- Distance: 1.3km (¾ mile)
- Time: Half a day
- Start at Hoan Kiem Lake at 8am and end at Cha Ca La Vong Restaurant for lunch
- Many attractions and services close at lunchtime and on Mondays

A colourful display on Hang Ma (Paper Votive Street)

into the **69 Bar-Restaurant**, once had a secret tunnel used by resistance fighters running through its walls. Don't miss **Huong Tuong Temple** (Den Huong Tuong) at No. 64, founded in 1450.

White Horse Temple (Den Bach Ma) at No.76 Hang Buom street, is the Old Quarter's most revered and ancient place of worship, its architecture influenced by the Chinese community. Founded in 1010 and restored many times, this stunning temple honours the white horse that appeared to Emperor Ly Thai To in a dream.

Turn right into **Hang Giay** (Paper Street) – with its dilapidated buildings crammed with goods – and into **Nguyen Sieu Street**. Hanoi's first inhabitants settled along the banks of the To Lich River, which flowed where this street now runs. **Co Luong Temple** (Den Co Luong) is at No. 28, its entrance flanked by two colourful guards.

Now pass along **Dao Duy Tu Street**, with its row of old houses, to reach **Old East Gate** (Cua O Quan Chong); the only city gate to remain from the original 16 that once marked the city's entry points. To your left is **Thanh Ha Street**, a fascinating alley lined with market and food stalls. Follow it until you reach **Hang Chieu** (Mat Street), which turns into **Hang Ma** (Paper Votive Street) – a mass of red, with lanterns and paper votive offerings used for Buddhist ceremonies. Turn south down Cha Ca Street, stopping at No. 14 for lunch at **Cha Ca La Vong**.

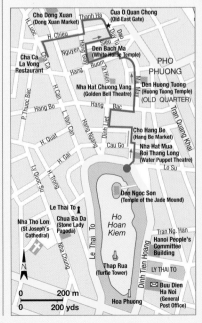

in the 13th century, and a bronze drum from 2,400BC.

West of Hoan Kiem Lake

Moving west from Hoan Kiem Lake, the Old Quarter is gradually replaced by more modern surroundings. Museums and religious architecture are among the highlights in these neighbourhoods.

Where Pho Nha Chung joins Ly Quoc Su Street is the oldest church in the city, **St Joseph's Cathedral** ❶ (Nha Tho Lon; the Vietnamese simply call it the 'big church'). Simplified Gothic in style – many visitors have commented that the Catholic cathedral resembles a smaller version of Paris's Notre-Dame – it was consecrated on Christmas night in 1886. The cathedral was built on the site of the Bao Thien Pagoda, razed to the ground by the French to make room for their edifice. Celebration of

Mass resumed here only in 1990, after more than 30 years of repression. On Sundays, the Masses are packed. Inside are beautiful stained-glass windows and an ornate altar decorated with gold leaf.

A narrow passageway at No. 5 Pho Nha Tho Street leads to **Ba Da Pagoda** ❿ (Chua Ba Da; daily 8am–5pm; free), tucked between the cathedral and Hoan Kiem Lake. This lovely pagoda was built in the 15th century after the discovery of a stone statue of a woman (hence its name, Stone Lady Pagoda) during the construction of the Thang Long citadel to the west. The statue, which was thought to have magical powers, disappeared and has since been replaced by a replica. The pagoda's modest exterior belies its exquisite interior. An impressive line-up of gilt Buddha statues forms the central altar. A sizeable number of resident monks and nuns live on site.

Statue of Ho Chi Minh in the Museum of the Vietnamese Revolution

Boys playing football outside St Joseph's Cathedral

About three blocks south of Hoan Kiem Lake is the site of the **Hoa Lo Prison Museum**  (Ba Tang Nha Bao Hoa Lo; Tue–Sun 8–11.30am, 1–4.30pm; charge). This is the infamous Hanoi Hilton, the moniker used by both American prisoners of war and present-day cyclo and taxi drivers. In 1994 it was almost entirely demolished to make way for an enormous steel and glass office and shopping complex called **Hanoi Towers**. The small section that remained was turned into the Ho Loa Prison Museum. Topped with barbed wire, Hoa Lo's yellow concrete main gate and a few cells have been preserved, along with exhibits of instruments of

Dining for a cause

Though Hanoi has made substantial economic progress over the last two decades, some people have been left behind. A few of Hanoi's top restaurants are trying to change this with training programmes for local youths.

Hoa Sua Training Restaurant (28a Ha Hoi Street; tel: 04-3942 4448) is part of the Hoa Sua Project for disadvantaged youth, housed in a beautiful restored villa. Service can be haphazard, but your patronage is for a good cause.

The cuisine – French influenced with some Vietnamese elements – can be surprisingly good and great value.

Koto (59 Van Mieu Street; tel: 04-3747 0337; www.koto.com.au) serves tasty multicultural food: the Mediterranean wraps and paninis, beer-battered fish and chips, lemon-grass chicken skewers, spring rolls and buffet breakfast are all recommended. Koto is a non-profit project providing hospitality training for Hanoi's disadvantaged young people.

torture and a guillotine. The vintage propaganda found here is amusing but increasingly out of sync with modern-day Vietnam.

One block southwest, the **Ambassadors' Pagoda** (Chua Quan Su; daily 8am–5pm; free), located at 73 Pho Quan Su Street, is perhaps the busiest pagoda in town. On the first and 15th days of each lunar month, crowds gather here to make offerings of incense, food and paper votives. In the 17th century, the site was a guesthouse for envoys from other Buddhist countries, hence its name. The long, low buildings surrounding the temples are schoolrooms for novice monks and contain a small library of parchment and texts in Vietnamese and Chinese.

Several blocks north, at 28A Dien Bien Phu Street, is the **Military History Museum** (Bao Tang Lich Su Quan Su; www.btlsqsvn.org.vn; Tue–Thur, Sat–Sun 8–11.30am, 1–4.30pm; charge), last renovated in the late 1990s. The museum exhibits chronicle Vietnam's battles for independence and unification against the French and American patrons of South Vietnam. The crumpled wreckage of a B-52 bomber sits in the outside courtyard. Inside are the uniforms of captured American pilots, photographs of Vietnamese war heroes and items belonging to the fallen leaders of what was then South Vietnam.

A short distance to the southwest is the **Vietnam Fine Arts Museum** (Bao Tang My Thuat; Tue–Sun 8.30am–5pm; charge) at 66 Nguyen Thai Hoc Street. Occupying a former boarding school for children of Indo-chinese officials, the exhibits at this highly regarded museum include displays on minority folk art and history, Dong Son bronze drums, Dong Noi stone carvings, Cham statues and carvings, communal house decorations from the 16th century, and 18th-century wooden Buddha statues in some surprisingly undignified poses. Particularly impressive are the displays tracing the development of Vietnamese paintings from the 20th century to the present.

To the south of the Fine Arts Museum, at Pho Quoc Tu Giam Street, is Hanoi's not-to-be-missed **Temple of Literature** (Van Mieu; Tue–Sun 8.30–11.30am, 1.30–4.30pm; charge). Built in 1070 under the reign

Lighting incense at Chua Quan Su

The Temple of Literature

of King Ly Thanh Tong, the temple is dedicated to Confucius. When it was first built, the Quoc Tu Giam, or School of the Elite of the Nation – Vietnam's first university – adjoined the temple's grounds. Under the Tran dynasty, the school was renamed the Quoc Hoc Vien, or the National College, in 1235.

After passing exams at the local levels, scholars aspiring to become senior mandarins came here to study for rigorous triennial examinations. The subjects included literature, philosophy and ancient Chinese and Vietnamese history, which Confucians believed provided the ideal training for government administrators. It became known as the Temple of Literature when the capital was transferred to Hue at the beginning of the 19th century.

The large temple enclosure is divided into five walled courtyards. After passing through the main **Van Mieu Gate** (Van Mieu Mon) and the first two courtyards past this gate, one arrives at the **Pleiade Constellation Pavilion** (Gac Khue Van), where the men of letters recited their poems. Through the **Great Wall Gate** (Dai Thanh Mon), an open courtyard surrounds a large central pool known as the Well of Heavenly Clarity (Thien Quang Tinh). Now regrouped and sheltered under a roof, the **82 stelae**, survivors of an original 117, rest on the backs of stone tortoises.

Ho Chi Minh Mausoleum and West Lake

Hanoi's **West Lake** (Ho Tay) is one of the most up-and-coming areas of the city. Property is extremely expensive and some of Vietnam's most exclusive restaurants, hotels and boutiques are located on the lake shore. Ho Chi Minh's Mausoleum and the surrounding area are, by contrast, a masterclass in stark Communist sobriety.

Ho Chi Minh's Mausoleum illuminated at night

Ho Chi Minh Mausoleum and Museum

The massive marble- and granite-clad **Ho Chi Minh Mausoleum ⓠ** (Lang Chu Tich Ho Chi Minh; Tue–Thur, Sat–Sun 8–11am; charge) is built on the spot in **Ba Dinh Square** where Ho Chi Minh delivered Vietnam's declaration of independence in 1945. The embalmed corpse of Uncle Ho lies in a glass casket within this monumental tomb, contrary to his alleged wish to be cremated and have his ashes scattered in the north, centre and south of the country. In late autumn/early winter, it is advisable to check beforehand whether his body is in residence – rumour has it that he is packed off to Russia for embalming for three months each year. Dressed in his trademark khaki suit, the heavily guarded body lies displayed on an elevated platform in a dark and chilly room. Upon entering the mausoleum, visitors should adopt a respectful demeanour. Foreigners may find the process of paying homage to a cold, lifeless body strange, but to the average Vietnamese, paying respect to 'Uncle Ho' is a sacred duty.

When you leave the mausoleum you will find yourself in the wooded grounds of the grand **Presidential Palace** (Phu Chu Tich). Built in 1906, the palace was formerly the residence of the French governor-general. Today, it has been turned into a government guesthouse for foreign dignitaries (no entry to visitors). Ho lived in two unassuming houses on the same grounds: the first was his abode from 1954 to 1958, before he moved to a specially constructed but still austere house on stilts. The **Ho Chi Minh House ⓡ** (Nha San Bac Ho; daily except Mon and Fri, 7.30–11.30am; charge), with its immaculately varnished wooden exterior, overlooks a carp pond in a quiet and leafy section of the park. The modest living quarters consist of two small rooms with an open-air

The political career of Uncle Ho

While wandering the world, a young Vietnamese revolutionary, Nguyen Ai Quoc, better known as Ho Chi Minh, developed a strong sense of political consciousness. Leaving his homeland aged 21, in 1911, to begin 30 years of self-imposed exile, he was educated in Paris and founded the Indochinese Communist Party in 1930. Returning to Vietnam in 1941, he co-founded the League for the Independence of Vietnam (Viet Minh). His goal was not only independence from French colonial rule and Japanese occupation, but also 'the union of diverse nationalist groups under Communist direction'.

Ho formed the National Liberation Committee and called for an uprising, the August Revolution, after which Vietnam came under the control of his political party, the Viet Minh. On 2 September 1945, Ho established the Democratic Republic of Vietnam with his Declaration of Independence Speech in Ba Dinh Square. This date became Vietnam's National Day and was also that of Ho's death, at home in Hanoi, in 1969.

meeting room below. Ho lived here from May 1958 to August 1969.

Behind the park with the pagoda rises a massive, angular Soviet-style structure, the **Ho Chi Minh Museum** ❺ (Bao Tang Ho Chi Minh; Tue–Thur and Sat 8–11.30am, 2–6pm; charge). Arranged into three sections and opened on 19 May 1990 (the 100th anniversary of Ho's birth), the museum celebrates the great man's revolutionary life and the pivotal role he played in Vietnam's history and international Communist development. It contains photos, documents and numerous personal effects, such as Ho's rubber sandals, walking stick and the disguise he used to flee to Hong Kong in 1933. However, all this is often overshadowed by the museum's modern, abstract and often bizarre displays,

Hanoi and environs

The Presidential Palace

including a gigantic lopsided table scene, a car crashing through a wall, and a cave-like hide-out re-imagined as the inside of Ho's brain.

Just north of the museum is the **One Pillar Pagoda** ❼ (Chua Mot Cot) and the Ho Chi Minh complex. Originally built in 1049 by King Ly Thai Thong, this unique wooden pagoda rests on a single concrete pillar rising out of a murky green pool – it is supposed to symbolise the sacred lotus sprouting from the waters of suffering. The pillar that you see is a late 1950s replacement, erected after French soldiers blew up the original in 1954. Prime Minister Nehru of India planted the banyan tree behind the pagoda in 1958 during an official visit to the then fledgling Vietnamese republic.

Just a kilometre from the Ho Chi Minh Mausoleum, on Hoang Hoa Tham Street, tucked down a winding alley, is **B-52 Lake** ❿ (Ho Huu Tiep). Sticking out of this small, brackish pond is the engine and landing gear of the **Rose 1**, an American B-52 bomber that was shot down on 19 December 1972. Of its crew of six, four survived the attack and were taken prisoner.

West Lake and surroundings

North of the main city centre lies the vast **West Lake** (Ho Tay), formerly known as the Lake of Mists, an area popular with wealthy expats and an emerging shopping and dining district. This lake, the largest in Hanoi, lies on an ancient bed of the Red River (Song Hong). The palaces of emperors and generals once graced its banks, all of which have been destroyed in feudal battles. Since the 1990s, the desirable area surrounding the lake has seen considerable building activity.

The unique One Pillar Pagoda

A residential street near West Lake

During an uprising against the occupying Chinese, AD545, the national hero Ly Bon built the National Foundation Pagoda (Chua Khai Quoc) beside the Red River. In the 17th century, the pagoda was transferred to its present site on a tiny peninsula off West Lake and renamed the **Tran Quoc Pagoda** ⍰, or the **National Defence Pagoda** (Chua Tran Quoc; daily 8am–5pm; free).

Separated from the lake by Thanh Nien Road is **White Silk Lake** (Ho Truc Bach). This was the ancient site of Lord Trinh's summer palace, which later became a harem where he detained his wayward concubines.

The lake derives its name from the beautiful white silk that these concubines were forced to weave for the princesses. The lakeside area is home to various hotels and restaurants.

Nearby, the rather ornate **Quan Thanh Temple** ⍰ (Den Quan Thanh; daily 8am–5pm; free) beside the lake was originally built during the Ly dynasty (1010–1225). This temple has a huge bronze bell and an enormous, 4-tonne bronze statue of Tran Vu, guardian deity of the north, to whom the temple is dedicated.

Further up the northern bank of West Lake, in a small neighbourhood beside the plush InterContinental Hotel, are **Kim Lien Pagoda** ⍰, also

Restaurants along White Silk Lake (Ho Truc Bach)

known as **Golden Lotus Pagoda**
(Chua Kim Lien; daily 8am–5pm;
free) and the **Kim Lien Flower Village.** In the three lanes that wind
their way towards the lake from the
pagoda, courtyards spill over with an
abundant array of tropical flowers,
most notable amongst them being the
varieties of orchid.

Further north still, at the tip of
a small peninsula at the end of
Dang Thai Mai Street, is **West Lake
Pagoda**  (Chua Phu Tay Ho; daily
8am–5pm; free), a popular destina-
tion for pilgrims and unmarried
Vietnamese, particularly on the 15th
day of each lunar month – a holy
day in the Buddhist calendar and an
auspicious time to visit any temple.
The lane just before the pagoda is
lined with lakeside restaurants specialising in *banh tom* (shrimp cakes).
Inside the pagoda, the hall on the
right is especially garish, its altars

crammed with statuettes of strange
beasts, grottoes and miniature sailing ships.

Around Hanoi
The area surrounding Hanoi is rich
in history and natural beauty and
can be explored on an easy day trip.
The land is extremely fertile, the
bright-green paddy fields being nur-
tured by the Red River (Song Hong),
which spreads its alluvial deposits
over much of northern Vietnam. The
most interesting sights are the craft
villages just outside the city that produce fine silks, pottery and wood-
carvings. Further out, several ancient
pagodas are just a few hours' drive
away, as are a number of highland
escapes and national parks. Most day
trips can be booked with tour agencies in Hanoi, while others require
the use of slow and uncomfortable
local buses or hired cars.

On the far western side of Hanoi is the **Vietnam Museum of Ethnology** (Bao Tang Dan Toc Hoc Viet Nam, Nguyen Van Huyen Road; www.vme.org.vn; Tue–Sun 8.30am–5.30pm; charge), which is perhaps Vietnam's most progressive museum. It serves to promote a greater understanding of Vietnam's 54 ethnic-minority groups and has gathered nearly 15,000 ethnic artefacts from across the country, including musical instruments, masks, baskets and garments, as well as maps, wall charts and photographs. Check the boards outside the main entrance for information on daily water puppet shows.

You will also find a permanent display of authentic, life-size minority dwellings, as well as a Jarai-minority grave house (a covered tomb surrounded by wooden totems) behind the museum building.

After exploring the museum, grab a light lunch at **Baguette & Chocolat** (tel: 04-2243 1116; www.hoasuaschool. com), the pleasant café situated behind the main building. This excellent bakery has seating both indoors and outside on the patio. The restaurant is run by Hoa Sua, a highly respected culinary school for disadvantaged youths. Try the citron tarts and pastries.

Craft villages

Just 10km (6 miles) southeast of downtown Hanoi, potters continue a 500-year-old tradition in the village of **Bat Trang ❷**. Rather incongruously, large showrooms with wide glass windows dominate the main street, while the oldest part of town, near the river, is threaded with walled alleyways. What look like cowpats stuck on the brick walls are really blobs of coal drying out for use as fuel. A ceramics market has been built for tour groups, but the most interesting areas are hidden in the alleys behind the modern shop

Ceramics for sale at Bat Trang craft village

Travelling by boat to the Perfume Pagoda

fronts. Inside these tiny workspaces are brick kilns and great vats of white liquid clay fed by a network of troughs. Bat Trang artisans used to make bricks, but now they concentrate solely on glazed ceramics, which include teapots, dinnerware and 3m (12ft) -tall blue-and-white urns destined for temples and pagodas.

Another village worth visiting is Chuong (also known as Phuong Trung), known for the manufacture of traditional hats, roughly 13km (8 miles) along Highway 21B from Hanoi. The conical hat *(non la)* is the typical headgear worn by Vietnamese women, especially in the countryside, protecting them from rain and sun. There are many types of conical hat, solid and thick for farm work and everyday use, or thinner and more elegant for decorative purposes. Chuong village specialises in the former.

Another variety, with a stencilled poem inserted between the hat's layers, is mainly produced in Hue.

South to the Perfume Pagoda

When it comes to visiting the **Perfume Pagoda ❸** (Chua Huong; daily 7.30am–6pm; entrance fee included in boat trip), the journey is just as important as the destination. Around 60km (38 miles) southwest of Hanoi, this sacred pilgrimage site, with dozens of Buddhist pagodas and shrines, is best approached by rowing boat on the dramatic and swiftly flowing **Yen River** (Song Yen). Looming over the quiet countryside is the jagged karst of the **Hoang Son Mountains**.

After a winding 4km (2½-mile) river journey that takes about 90 minutes (*see p.25*), the boat will pull up to a cluster of pavilions and market stalls – most tour groups will have lunch at the food stalls here. To reach the temple complex from there involves either a 2hr hike up the lower flanks of the Huong Tich Mountains or, alternatively, a cable-car ride.

The collection of pagodas and Buddhist shrines at the top of the moutain are built into the limestone cliffs and caves. Among the sites are the **Pagoda to Heaven** (Chua Thien Chu), the **Pagoda of Purgatory** (Giai Oan Chu) and, the main attraction itself, the **Pagoda of the Perfumed Vestige** (Huong Tich Chu).

The last is located inside the **Huong Tich Grotto**, an enormous Buddhist cave-temple which lies just below the summit of the mountain. Some 120 stone steps bedecked with Buddhist flags lead down to the 'dragon's mouth' entrance, where worshippers jostle to rub banknotes on a large, wet stalactite

said to bestow wealth. Chinese characters etched on the outside of the cave in 1770 declare that you are entering 'the most beautiful grotto under the southern sky.' In the darkness of the 50m (160ft) -high cave, surrounded by stalactites and stalagmites, are numerous gilded Buddhist statues with altar offerings of fruit and incense. Visiting during the pagoda's annual seven-week festival, from March to April, is not advised as the grounds are thronged with thousands of worshippers and, although picturesque, it can be a struggle to get around.

West and north of Hanoi

One of Vietnam's oldest pagodas, **Thay Pagoda** ❹ (Chua Thay; daily 8am–5pm; free), also known as the **Pagoda of the Master**, is nestled against the hillside in **Sai Son**

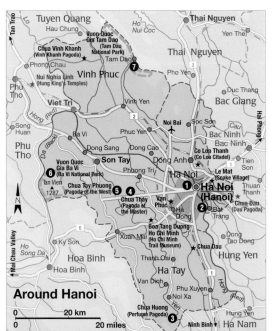

The Perfume Pagoda

Village, 37km (23 miles) west of Hanoi. It shares its compound with the smaller **Ca Pagoda** (Chua Ca).

Founded in 1132 by King Ly Thai To, Thay Pagoda has been renovated a number of times. It is dedicated to three individuals: Ly Than Tong, king of the Ly dynasty from 1127 to 1138; Sakyamuni, the historical Buddha and his 18 disciples (Arhats); and the venerable monk Dao Hanh. All are represented by elaborate lacquer statues, some dating back to the 12th and 13th centuries. The pagoda complex itself is divided into three sections: the outer section is used for ceremonies, the middle section is a Buddhist shrine, while the inner temple is dedicated to Dao Hanh.

On the fifth, sixth and seventh days of the third lunar month, the districts' premiere puppet troupes stage elaborate shows on the pond in front of the pagoda. Folk plays, chess tournaments, a recital of Dao Hanh's feats and a procession of tablets are other features of the festival, which draws participants from nearby villages. The two arched, covered bridges – **Moon Bridge** and **Sun Bridge** – date from 1602.

About 6km (4 miles) from the Thay Pagoda complex – and usually visited in conjunction with it on day trips from Hanoi – is **Tay Phuong Pagoda** ❺, or the Pagoda of the West (Chua Tay Phuong; daily 8am–5pm; free), in the picturesque village of **Thac Xa**. It is perched atop the 50m (164ft) Tay Phuong hill, which is said to resemble a buffalo. The pagoda dates from the 8th century, though the present structure was rebuilt in 1794. It is particularly famous for its **74 statues of Arhats** (Buddhist saints) carved from jackfruit wood, which are said to illustrate stories from the Buddhist scriptures and all aspects of the human condition.

Built of ironwood with bare brick walls, the pagoda comprises the **Prostration Hall** (Bai Duong), the **Central Hall** (Chinh Dien) and the **Back Hall** (Hau Cung). Together they form the **Three Gems** (Tam Bao).

Ba Vi National Park

Some 48km (30 miles) west of Hanoi is the scenic **Ba Vi Mountain** (Nui Ba Vi) and **Ba Vi National Park** ❻ (Vuon Quoc Gia Ba Vi; daily, daylight hours; charge). The park's protected forest boasts a number of rare and endangered plants and animals, including several varieties of flying

The entrance to the Temple of the Jungle God in Ba Vi National Park

Tam Dao, Hanoi's local hill station

squirrel. However, the wildlife is elusive and it is rare actually to spot anything. Regardless, the park's large orchid garden and many hiking paths make it a favourite destination for many city-weary Hanoians looking to commune with nature. At the summit of the 1,276m (4,186ft) Ba Vi Mountain is an interesting temple dedicated to Ho Chi Minh. From here there are astounding views of the surrounding countryside and even Hanoi on clear days. At the base of the mountain is Vietnam's oldest golf course, the public **Kings' Island Golf Club** (www.kingsislandgolf.com).

Tam Dao hill station

To escape the capital's summer heat and humidity, wealthy Hanoians head to the cooler climes of **Tam Dao ❼**, established as a hill station by the French in the early 1900s. Located at an altitude of 880m (2,886ft), Tam Dao sits on a large plateau 70km (43 miles) north of Hanoi in the Tam Dao mountain range. Tam Dao means 'three islands', the name deriving from three mountains – **Thien Thi**, **Thach Ban** and **Phu Nghia** – that rise to around 1,400m (4,600ft) and dominate the landscape, appearing like three islands jutting above a sea of clouds.

The hill station lies within **Tam Dao National Park** (Vuon Quoc Gia Tam Dao; daily, daylight hours; charge). A dense cover of trees and plants grows on the mountain slopes, while the forests shelter various rare mammals (including civets, muntjac, wild boar, pangolins and porcupines), although you are most likely to see only the colourful butterflies and birds.

As far as hiking options go, a 20-minute walk from Tam Dao leads to the popular 45-metre (148ft) **Silver Waterfall** (Thawc Ba). To reach the more remote forest is a full day's walk.

ACCOMMODATION

Hanoi has a wide variety of hotels to satisfy all budgets. The central Hoan Kiem District (which includes the Old Quarter) has the largest choice of hotels. Most budget hotels and guesthouses are concentrated in the side streets of the Old Quarter. The West Lake area has some excellent luxury hotels, though little else in terms of moderate or budget lodgings.

Accommodation price categories

Prices are for a standard double room in peak season:

$ = under US$20
$$ = $20–50
$$$ = $50–100
$$$$ = $100–150
$$$$$ = over $150

Central Hanoi (Hoan Kiem District)

Church Hotel
9 Nha Tho
Tel: 04-3928 8118
www.churchhotel.com.vn
This gem of a boutique hotel, in a prime location just a few steps away from St Joseph's Cathedral, was built in 2004 and features stylishly appointed rooms overlooking trendy Nha Tho Street and the Ba Da Pagoda. Features free Wi-fi and made-to-order breakfast. **$$$**

De Syloia Hotel
17A Tran Hung Dao
Tel: 04-3824 5346
www.desyloia.com
A small, pleasant boutique hotel situated just to the south of the Old Quarter, the De Syloia has an excellent restaurant and compact, but good, gym facilities. Windows are soundproofed so rooms remain blissfully quiet. **$$$$$**

Hilton Hanoi Opera hotel

Hanoi Elegance Emerald Hotel (formerly Hanoi Elegance II)
85 Ma May
Tel: 04-3926 3451
www.hanoielegancehotel.com
A stylish, modern hotel built in 2006 right in the heart of the Old Quarter. Large, airy well-furnished rooms and helpful English-speaking staff. **$$**

Hanoi Paradise Hotel
53 Hang Chieu
Tel: 04-3929 0026
www.hanoiparadisehotel.com
One of few Old Quarter hotels to boast a pool. Opened in 2006, all rooms have an internet-connected computer. The complimentary bottle of red wine, fruit and flowers on arrival is a nice touch. **$$**

Hilton Hanoi Opera
1 Le Thanh Tong
Tel: 04-3933 0500
www.hanoi.hilton.com
An architecturally impressive hotel built to complement the neighbouring Opera House. Rooms are large, airy and modern. The wide, spacious lobby features live music and free Wi-fi. Great pool, gym facilities and beauty salon/spa. **$$$$$**

Hoa Binh Hotel
27 Ly Thuong Kiet
Tel: 04-3825 3692
www.hoabinhhotel.com
A small and elegant hotel with a sweeping wooden staircase and lovely French colonial touches. Rooms facing the street can be

noisy in the morning. There are French and Vietnamese restaurants on site. **$$$**

Melia Hanoi
44B Ly Thuong Kiet
Tel: 04-3934 3343
www.meliahanoi.com
Located in Hanoi's business and diplomatic district. On site are five excellent restaurants, bars, a deli and a pool. Also features a helipad on its rooftop and the largest pillarless ballroom in Vietnam. **$$$$$**

Sofitel Legend Metropole Hanoi
15 Ngo Quyen
Tel: 04-3826 6919
www.sofitel-legend.com/hanoi/en/
Built in 1901 and renovated by the French Sofitel company in 2005, this grande dame has maintained its colonial-era atmosphere while improving on its comfort levels. Former guests include kings, princes, presidents and an assortment of celebrities. **$$$$$**

Hotel Nikko Hanoi
84 Tran Nhan Tong
Tel: 04-3822 3535
www.hotelnikkohanoi.com.vn
A high-rise hotel with airy, modern rooms and excellent, attentive service. Overlooking Thong Nhat Park, with a good-sized pool and fitness centre. Three excellent restaurants (Chinese, Japanese and French), bar and bakery. Disabled-friendly. **$$$$**

Zenith Hotel Hanoi
96–98 Bui Thi Xuan
Tel: 04-3822 9797
www.zenithhotel.com.vn
A distinguished hotel with all the expected amenities. The lobby is a little shabby, but the rooms are quiet, comfortable and well maintained. Also has a good restaurant, bar and fitness centre. **$$$$**

Ho Chi Minh Mausoleum and West Lake

Flower Hotel
55 Nguyen Truong To
Tel: 04-3716 3888

The Sofitel Metropole

www.flowerhotel.com.vn
A bright and cheery hotel just north of the Old Quarter. Pleasant, quiet rooms with wooden floors and large windows. The best rooms are on the upper floor. **$$$**

Hanoi Daewoo Hotel
360 Kim Ma
Tel: 04-3831 5555
www.hanoi-daewoohotel.com
This immense complex in western Hanoi has every conceivable facility. Rooms are large, quiet and comfy. Rooms on the uppermost floors have amazing views over Hanoi. Features one of the city's best Chinese restaurants. **$$$$**

InterContinental Westlake Hanoi
1 Nghi Tam
Tel: 04-6270 8888
www.intercontinental.com
A luxurious new hotel built over the West Lake and overlooking an 800-year-old pagoda. The rooms are large, comfortable and elegantly outfitted. Features three restaurants and two bars, plus a pool and gym. Watching the sunset at the Sunset Bar is a must. **$$$$$**

Sofitel Plaza Hanoi
1 Thanh Nien
Tel: 04-3823 8888
www.sofitelplazahanoi.com
The 20-storey Sofitel Plaza dominates the

Listings

Sheraton Hanoi Hotel

skyline at the edge of West Lake and is home to the best indoor/outdoor swimming pool in the city. Two restaurants, three bars and a spa. Overlooks Truc Bach Lake. **$$$$$**

Sheraton Hanoi Hotel
11 Xuan Dieu
Tel: 04-3719 9000
www.sheraton.com
The lakeside swimming pool, floodlit tennis courts, conference facilities and staff are all excellent. The more expensive rooms have lake views. Features three restaurants and a rather raucous late-night bar. **$$$$$**

RESTAURANTS

Just 10 years ago, most of the places to eat in Hanoi were basic rice and noodle stalls where people gobbled food down while sitting on plastic chairs on the dusty sidewalk. Today, there are dozens of excellent restaurants in the capital, serving a variety of cuisines. The largest concentration is in the central Hoan Kiem District.

Restaurant price categories
Prices are for a full meal per person, with one drink

$ = under US$5
$$ = $5–10
$$$ = $10–15
$$$$ = over $15

Central Hanoi (Hoan Kiem District)
Alfresco's
23L Hai Ba Trung
Tel: 04-3826 7782
98 Xuan Dieu
Tel: 04-3719-5322
This family-orientated restaurant is popular with expats for its jumbo ribs, imported Australian steaks and burgers, fish and chips, plus decent Mexican dishes, all with generous portions. There are two locations. **$$$**

Chim Sao
65 Ngo Hue
Tel: 04-3976 0633
www.chimsao.com
Great local food at reasonable prices set in comfortable but low-key surroundings. Its art gallery always has an interesting exhibition going on. Try the sausages. **$**

Bun Cha
20 Ta Hien
Bun cha is seasoned and grilled pork pieces served with fresh rice noodles and drenched with a piquant sweet-and-sour sauce. This small streetside restaurant in the Old Quarter serves some of the best in town. **$**

Cha Ca La Vong
14 Cha Ca
Tel: 04-3825 3929
One of Hanoi's most famous dishes, *cha ca* is the only thing served here – fish grilled on a clay brazier at your table, with rice noodles, peanuts and herbs. **$$$**

Green Tangerine
48 Hang Be
Tel: 04-3825 1286
Located in a gorgeous restored French villa in the heart of the Old Quarter. Lounge in the

atmospheric interior, or dine in the garden courtyard. The French chef creates mouth-watering international fusion and traditional dishes from his homeland. **$$$$**

Hapro Café
38-40 Le Thai To
Tel: 04-3828 7043
A small alfresco café in a prime location on the banks of Hoan Kiem Lake under leafy boughs. The light menu offers coffee, juices, ice creams, plus sandwiches and breakfast. **$$**

Highway 4 Bar & Restaurant
3 Hang Tre
Tel: 04-3926 0639
www.highway4.com
Specialises in rice-wine liquors and North Vietnamese cuisine, especially hotpot, fish, spring rolls (try the catfish spring rolls with wasabi-based dip) and caramelised clay-pot dishes. There are three other Hanoi branches at 25 Bat Su, 54 Mai Hoc De and 575 Kim Ma. **$$$**

La
25 Ly Quoc Su
Tel: 04-3928 8933
Tall, wooden double doors open to a casual bistro run by friendly and knowledgeable staff. The menu is a mix of Western tastes and Asian fusion. The pork tenderloin is tasty, and the ample side dishes are a delight. **$$$$**

Highway 4 Bar & Restaurant

Le Tonkin
14 Ngo Van So
Tel: 04-3943 3457
Set in a century-old restored French villa, filled with regional antiquities and ambi-ence. The Vietnamese cuisine is modified to suit Westerners. Evening traditional-music performances on Mondays and Fridays. **$$$**

Nineteen11
1 Trang Tien
Tel: 04-3933 4801
www.nineteen11.com.vn
Named after the year the Hanoi Opera House was completed, it features a walk-in wine cellar and serves gourmet Continental and refined Vietnamese dishes. Both the service and the food are exquisite. **$$$$**

Quan An Ngon
18 Phan Boi Chau
Tel: 04-3942 8162
Sit at simple tables set in a pretty alfresco villa courtyard and enjoy traditional Viet-namese dishes served from the surrounding mock street-food stalls. The restaurant can get very busy, so book ahead. **$$$**

Ho Chi Minh Mausoleum and West Lake
Au Lac Do Brazil
6A Cao Ba Quat
Tel: 04-3845 5224
www.aulacdobrazil.com
This all-you-can-eat Brazilian barbecue is a little unusual for Vietnam, though there are now three outlets in Hanoi and Ho Chi Minh City. Twelve types of meat are served for about $25 per person. **$$$$**

Classico Café & Restaurant
68 Quan Su
Tel: 04-3941 2327
www.classico.com.vn
Heavy, cheesy pizza loaded with toppings: you'll think you've died and gone to America. The private museum of ancient Dong Son relics inside the restaurant is delightful. **$$**

Around Hanoi
Bamboo Restaurant
Mela Hotel, Thi Tran, Tam Dao Town,
Van Phuc Province
Tel: 021-182 4321
A good spot to find relatively decent Western meals while in Tam Dao. Also serves a selection of Vietnamese dishes, which perhaps come closer to hitting the mark. **$$**

Tan Da Restaurant
Tan Da Spa Resort, Tan Linh Mountain,
Ba Vi District, Ha Tay Province
Tel: 034-388 1047
This resort in Ba Vi National Park features two restaurants: Vietnamese dishes (outside) and Western favourites (indoors). Ask for a table in the adjoining traditional Muong stilt house. **$$**

NIGHTLIFE

Hanoi is still way behind Ho Chi Minh City in the nightlife stakes. There are few glitzy clubs or bars as the city's 'morality police' are notorious for shutting down any venue that becomes too popular or stays open too late at night. However, a few tried-and-tested venues do their best to serve the late-night crowd.

Dance clubs
Dragonfly
15 Hang Buom, Hoan Kiem District
Tel: 04-3926 2177
www.dragonfly.vn
A newly relocated favourite, with a dance floor and an upstairs *shisha* (water pipe) lounge.

Funky Buddha
2A Ta Hien, Hoan Kiem District
Mobile tel: 091-488 6689
A slick and shiny dance club/lounge on the bar street of Ta Hien.

Stones 1
769 Bach Dang, Hai Ba Trung District
Mobile tel: 098-276 6527

Open-air bar and nightclub with food, *shisha* lounge, a large dance floor and late hours.

Bars and pubs
Daluva
33 To Ngoc Van, Tay Ho District
Tel: 04-3243 4009
www.daluva.com
This wine bar/restaurant serves great tapas and excellent wine and cocktails.

Le Pub
25 Hang Be, Hoan Kiem District
Tel: 04-3926 2104
www.lepub.org
One of those places where travellers, expats and locals mix easily.

Funky Buddha, one of the city's most popular clubs

ENTERTAINMENT

As both the modern political and ancient cultural capital of Vietnam, Hanoi has a thriving arts scene. Whether it is water puppetry, modern drama, traditional Vietnamese opera or Western classical music, there is usually something worth seeking out.

Performing arts venues

Opera House
1 Trang Tien, Hoan Kiem District
Tel: 04-3993 0113
www.ticketvn.com
Built in the early 1900s by the French, Hanoi's Opera House holds regular performances of classical and traditional music, as well as dance.

Youth Theatre
11 Ngo Thi Nham, Hai Ba Trung District
Tel: 04-3943 0820
Focuses on three art forms: drama, music and dance. Particularly worthwhile are the stagings of contemporary Vietnamese dramas.

Traditional Vietnamese theatre

Cheo Hanoi Theatre
15 Nguyen Dinh Chieu, Hai Ba Trung District
Tel: 04-3943 7361
Cheo theatre is a uniquely northern-Vietnamese music and drama folk-art that originated in the Red River Delta.

Vietnam National Tuong Theatre
51 Duong Thanh, Hoan Kiem District

Water puppets at Thang Long

Tel: 04-3828 7268
www.vietnamtuongtheatre.com
This beautifully restored national theatre has regular performances of excerpts from traditional *tuong* (Vietnamese classical opera).

Water puppetry

Thang Long Water Puppet Theatre
See p.69

SPORTS AND ACTIVITIES

There's not much in the way of sports and outdoor activities on offer in the city centre. Instead, the focus is on tranquil pastimes such as an afternoon of spa treatments or a day of cooking classes. There are golf courses further out.

Golf

Kings' Island Golf Course
Dong Mo, Son Tay Town, Ha Tay Province
Tel: 034-368 6555
www.kingsislandgolf.com

With two 18-hole courses, Kings' Island is the first 36-hole facility in northern Vietnam.

Tam Dao Golf & Resort
Hop Chau Commune, Tam Dao District,

Tam Dao Golf course

Vinh Phuc Province
Tel: 021-189 6554
www.tamdaogolf.com
This golf club is about two hours from Hanoi, nestled at the foot of the mountains near Tam Dao.

Spas
Spa La Madera
18 Tong Duy Tan, Hoan Kiem District

Tel: 04-3938 0549
A self-styled wellbeing centre that uses natural, local products in reflexology and traditional Vietnamese body massages.

Zen Spa West Lake
100 Xuan Dieu, Tay Ho District
Tel: 04-3719 9889
www.zenspa.vn
A wide range of massages and spa treatments are offered inside traditional wooden houses close to Hanoi's picturesque West Lake.

Cooking classes
Highway 4 Restaurant
575 Kim Ma, Ba Dinh District
Tel: 04-3771 6372
www.highway4.com
The class starts with a market visit in the Old Quarter followed by a hands-on cooking class during which students whip up three dishes.

TOURS

In the Old Quarter, just about every second shop front seems to be that of a small travel agency or guesthouse, and all seem to offer the same tour excursions – most often to Halong Bay or Sa Pa – at similar prices. The main advantage of booking through an established, well-known travel agency is that it is more likely to be concerned about its reputation and will ensure that tour groups are small and all costs are clearly spelt out.

Buffalo Tours
94 Ma May, Hoan Kiem District
Tel: 04-3828 0702
www.buffalotours.com
A pioneer in responsible travel in Vietnam, Buffalo Tours offers some interesting off-the-beaten-track adventures, as well as more typical tour outings.

Exotissimo Travel
26 Tran Nhat Duat, Hoan Kiem District
Tel: 04-3828 2150
www.exotissimo.com
This travel agency specialises in tailor-made vacations for those with bigger budgets.

Handspan Tours
78 Ma May, Hoan Kiem District
Tel: 04-3926 2828
www.handspan.com
This long-established travel agency offers reliable and reasonably priced tours of Vietnam's major destinations.

Offroad Vietnam
36 Nguyen Huu Huan, Hoan Kiem District
Tel: 04-3926 3433
www.offroadvietnam.com
The best option for those wanting to explore northern Vietnam on a motorbike. Most tours use 4-stroke Honda 160cc motorcycles that

have been tried and tested in the field; some larger machines are also available for hire.

Topas Adventure Travel
52 To Ngoc Van, Tay Ho District
Tel: 04-3715 1005
www.topasvietnam.com
A high-end tour and travel company that specialises in package trips to Sa Pa, as well as tours of Vietnam, Laos and Cambodia.

Walking tour
Hidden Hanoi
137 Nghi Tam, Tay Ho District
Mobile tel: 091-225 4045
www.hiddenhanoi.com.vn
This small, locally run company offers the best walking tours of the Old Quarter, the French Quarter, street food and temples. The guides are young, energetic and excellent English-speakers.

FESTIVALS AND EVENTS

Reflecting its long history, Hanoi's festivals are much older than most others celebrated around the country, and are thus more distinctly Kinh (ethnic Vietnamese) – lacking Khmer or Cham influences. Some are religious, others tied to eccentricities of village life, and others designated to celebrate ancient military victories.

January–February
Hai Ba Trung Festival
This festival takes place in Hanoi, at the Hai Ba Trung Temple. It honours the heroic resistance of the Trung sisters against the Chinese.

March–April
Perfume Pagoda Festival
Thousands of Buddhist pilgrims flock to one of Vietnam's most revered pilgrimage sites, southwest of Hanoi *(see p.84–5)*, to pray for good luck in the coming year. The festival actually starts on the 6th day of the 1st lunar month and lasts until the

middle of the third lunar month, but the 15th day of the second lunar month is the principal day.

Thay Pagoda Festival
In celebration of the pagoda's revered Buddhist monk and puppeteer, the festivities include traditional water puppetry and rowing contests.

Le Mat Festival
The 'Snake Village' of Le Mat celebrates a local legend, with snake dishes, snake dances and a rather gruesome snake-beheading act.

Pilgrims during the Perfume Pagoda Festival

Northern Highlands

A striking blend of jagged mountain ranges, lush valleys and jungle, the northern provinces of Vietnam are culturally diverse and largely inhabited by ethnic minorities. The region was important in the revolution against the French and suffered during more recent conflict with China. It remains a rural backwater and largely isolated from the country's recent economic achievements.

Northern Highlands transport

 The Northern Highlands are one of the most difficult regions of Vietnam in which to travel. There are no major airports and most destinations are serviced by a motley collection of small buses, vans, taxis and private cars, which can be booked at town bus stations, travel agents or hotels.

Motorbike hire is possible from Hanoi, but be aware that it is inadvisable to pick up hitchhikers in this region – drug traffickers take advantage. If someone is caught in your company with drugs, then you could also be held responsible

 Trains: The only rail line in the region runs from Hanoi to Lao Cai on the Chinese border (onward travel to Kunming is by sleeper bus), taking 8 hours. Minibuses at Lao Cai station wait for travellers to Sa Pa

 Buses: Public buses and privately run minibuses ply the main routes. Hanoi to Dien Bien Phu takes around 12 hours. Dien Bien Phu to Sa Pa is around 9 hours. Most people travelling to Sa Pa take the Hanoi-Lao Cai train (see above); from Lao Cai, minibuses operate every half hour for the 1¼-hour journey

Vietnam's untamed northwest does not yield itself up easily. Those who dare to brave the winding roads and rough terrain are treated to wonderful mountain scenery, primordial forests and remote ethnic-minority villages. To the west and northwest of Hanoi, the flat rice-growing delta of the Red River (Song Hong) quickly gives way to deep green valleys, hilly orchards and craggy mountain ranges inhabited by a number of ethnic-minority groups. These days, the people farm in the shadow of modern hydroelectric dams supplying power to much of

the rest of the country. Bounded on the north by lengthy borders with Laos and China, this is a stunningly wild and picturesque region, but there is the usual caveat: travellers on the 'northwest loop' can expect poor roads, treacherous passes and few modern tourist amenities. Nonetheless, they will be rewarded for their efforts with some of the most spectacular mountain vistas anywhere in Southeast Asia.

Largely bypassed by the modernisation coursing through other parts of Vietnam, the people living in the northern hills have retained their long-established culture, the rites and rituals of religion, and a shared history of struggle.

There is a great deal to see across the region, although the vast majority of visitors head for the beautiful hill retreat of Sa Pa, in Lao Cai province. The town has become reknowned as a high-altitude getaway, with treks into minority villages and homestays in stilt houses.

Sa Pa rice terraces

Hanoi to Dien Bien Phu

The stretch northwest from Hanoi to the Laos border includes Mai Chau, Moc Chau, Son La and Dien Bien Phu. The last is significant to many Vietnamese as the point of decisive victory in the struggle for national independence from the French. At

A farmer in the Mai Chau Valley

times of political tension between the Vietnamese and local minority groups, portions of this area may be closed to outsiders.

Around 135km (85 miles), or 3½ hours' driving time, from Hanoi on Highway 6 is the serene **Mai Chau Valley ❶**. If you've made a stop at Hoa Binh City, Mai Chau is only 60km (40 miles) further along the road. The valley makes for an excellent weekend outing from Hanoi and is an ideal base for treks to nearby highland villages. Known for its *ruou can* (a unique rice wine drunk through long bamboo straws), Mai Chau is a collection of small villages, farms and individual stilt houses spread out over a vast and verdant valley. Peaceful and charming, it is also the closest place to Hanoi where one can trek in the countryside from and stay overnight in an authentic ethnic-minority village.

While most tour agencies drop off their charges at **Lac Village** (Ban Lac), a very commercial White Thai village popular with Vietnamese tourist groups, it's better not to linger here.

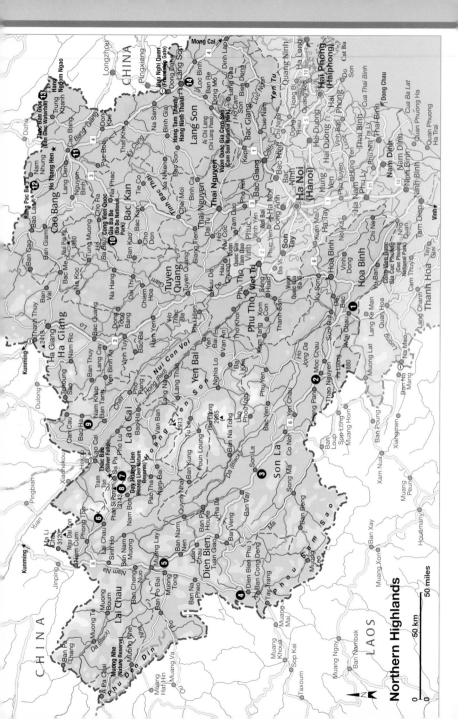

Northern Highlands

'Penitencier' is engraved above the original main gate to Son La's old French prison

Stop for a meal after the drive from Hanoi and then set off with a guide to one of the farther-flung and more authentic White Thai villages located deeper in the valley.

Son La province

Continuing northwest, **Moc Chau** ❷, in neighbouring Son La province, is a stunningly beautiful highland valley surrounded by low mountains. Sprinkled with prosperous villages of Muong and White Thai and Black Thai people, it is laced with a vast irrigation network that feeds the fields of wet rice and manioc, as well as the stilt-house villages. Traditionally fishermen, each Thai household will have its own fishpond and prominently displayed nets.

You will know you are approaching the sprawling market town of Moc Chau by the presence of black-and-white dairy cows, originally imported from Holland, wandering across the road. Much of the area is devoted to dairy farming, so be sure to try out some of the famously rich yoghurt, ice cream or Moc Chau-branded chocolate bars. Be aware that during the coldest months, January and February, night-time temperatures can fall to –3°C (27°F). With central heating nearly impossible to find, visitors are advised to pack appropriate clothing.

Highway 6 from Moc Chau climbs to the west past hills cultivated with tea, coffee, cotton and fruit trees, including mulberry, the leaves which are fed to silkworms. The road winds

through the mountainous landscapes of Son La, close to the border with Laos. The region is home to many ethnic minorities, including the Hmong, Mnong, Muong, Mun, Kho Mu, Dao, Tay, White Thai and Black Thai, Xinh Mun and Hoa peoples.

The capital of Son La province, **Son La City** ❸, is some 100km (60 miles) northwest of Moc Chau. The minuscule 'city' runs for just over a kilometre on the southwestern bank of the **Nam La River** (Song Nam La). Despite increased development and a scattering of shiny new government buildings, it is still the familiar, rather anonymous Vietnamese provincial town of dusty roads and tall, narrow houses. In the early mornings, many traditionally garbed Hmong, Muong, Xinh Mun, and Black and White Thai people gather to trade in the market.

99

Northern Highlands

Soldiers cross the Muong Thanh Bridge, Dien Bien Phu

Above To Hieu Street, on a wooded promontory, the brick ruins of a former French prison have been converted into the **Son La Provincial Museum** (Bao Tang Tinh Son La; daily 7.30–11am, 1.30–5.30pm; charge). Built in 1908, the prison was once the residence of many a political prisoner. Visitors can take a look at the prison's original cells, with their food slots and leg shackles. Partially rebuilt for tourists, most of the compound was blasted away during the war with the French. After the drabness of the city, Son La's environs are refreshingly verdant and lush, with rice fields, orchards and attractive ethnic-minority villages.

Dien Bien Phu

Continuing west for about 90km (56 miles) from Son La brings you to the small town of Tuan Giao. The intersecting road to the west is Highway 279, the route to **Dien Bien Phu** ❹, which is a further 80km (50 miles) and at least 3½ hours' driving time away. The capital of Dien Bien province, it lies on the east bank of the **Nam Rom River** (Song Nam Rom) at the northern end of the Muong

Tension with China

It's no secret that the Vietnamese have no love for China. Some of these feelings derive from centuries of Chinese domination and the ensuing territorial disputes. Others are due to more recent military aggressions from China. Official relations have improved, but resentment lingers over the People's Liberation Army's destruction of the city of Lao Cai in 1979 as part of China's 'lesson' to Vietnam for invading Cambodia and overthrowing the murderous Khmer Rouge regime.

Thanh valley. This was the site of a 57-day siege – the famous Battle of Dien Bien Phu – which brought an ignominious end to French colonialism in Asia. It is encircled by steep green hills from which tens of thousands of Viet Minh troops launched their assault on the French garrisons in 1954.

Visitors can visit a reconstruction of **General de Castries's main command bunker**, set amid a litter of rusty tanks and artillery. Not far away, **A1 Hill**, known as 'Eliane 2' to the French, was the scene of fierce fighting and is now a war memorial dedicated to the Viet Minh who died here. There's also a bunker and entrance to a tunnel dug by coal miners. The miners stuffed the tunnel with 1,000kg (2,205lbs) of explosives and detonated it on 6

May to signal the final assault on the French bases.

On the edge of the downtown area, the **Museum of the Dien Bien Phu Victory** (Nha Trung Bay Thang Lich Su Dien Bien Phu; daily 7–11am, 1.30–4pm; charge) has black-and-white battle photos, an illuminated electronic model of the valley and battle positions, and a collection of Chinese, American and French weapons. Across the street is a **Viet Minh Cemetery,** where some of the Viet Minh soldiers killed in the battle are buried.

Towering over town from its vantage position at **D1 Hill** is the **Dien Bien Phu Victory Monument**. Unveiled in 2004, this huge bronze statue measures 12.6m (41ft) and weighs 220 tonnes. It depicts three soldiers standing atop the French garrison, one holding a flag, another holding a gun, and the third carrying a child with flowers. On the flag is written: *Quyet chien, quyet thang* (Determined to fight, determined to win).

The far north (Northern Lai Chau and Lao Cai provinces)

Stunning mountainous scenery and exotic hill-tribe villages are the main attractions in the far-northern provinces of Lai Chau and Lao Cai, with the old colonial hill station of Sa Pa as the base of operations. Hike along terraced rice paddies in hanging valleys to Hmong and Dao villages, or trek up Vietnam's highest peak, Mount Fansipan.

Children at the entrance to the tunnels at A1 Hill, Dien Bien Phu

Lai Chau province

Wedged in between China to the north and Laos to the west, Lai Chau province was once known for its wildlife, including tigers, but sadly this is now hugely diminished (with no tiger sighting for several years) due to rampant deforestation, slash-and-burn farming and the lucrative trade in illegal animal products.

Running due north of Dien Bien Phu, Highway 12 connects with the historic town of **Muong Lay** ❺ (formerly known as Lai Chau – confusingly, there is now a new Lai Chau, see below), some 104km (65 miles) away. The surroundings are striking: jagged, unforgiving peaks set against dense tiers of thick forest. The road into town is in good condition but, during heavy rains between May and August, landslides can cause serious delays.

The new capital of Lai Chau province is 150km (93 miles) to the northeast: **Lai Chau** ❻ town, formerly known as Tam Duong, bustles with new shops and hotels. Besides visiting the market – frequented

> ### Being followed
>
> The Hmong and Dao women of Sa Pa are friendly and polite, but extremely persistent. Unlike in other parts of Vietnam, the hill-tribe vendors here will follow you all morning – everywhere you go – until you've made a purchase. They will grab you the moment you walk out of your hotel and follow you into restaurants, shops, the market, the church, and all the way to the bus. They are actually good company, great conversationalists and can answer a lot of common questions. Don't bother to appease them right away, though; they will just be replaced by other equally persistent sellers. The best strategy is simply to smile, be patient, make the most of the extra company... and eventually buy some souvenirs.

by White Hmong and Flower Hmong, White Thai and Black Thai, Dao Khau and Giay hill tribes – travellers can visit a a number of ethnic-minority villages that are only accessible by motorbike. The immediate surroundings here are

View of Sa Pa, its market and the Catholic church

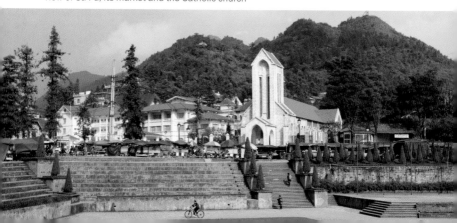

Black Hmong in the Sa Pa countryside

unattractive and dusty, as the nearby hills have been dug out to create more flat land for construction.

Sa Pa and Lao Cai province

The 90km (56-mile) stretch of road from Lai Chau to the hill-town retreat of Sa Pa – Highway 4D – runs southeast along the dramatic Hoang Lien mountain range. Here, the mountains become higher and craggier and are more thickly forested. The road winds through **Tram Ton Pass**, the highest mountain pass in the country. Travellers will know they are approaching **Sa Pa ❼**, the northwest's tourism capital, upon nearing the village of **Binh Lu**. The ethnic-minority people in this region are neither shy nor indifferent to tourists or their cameras. On the contrary, they usually take off their metal jewellery and headpieces and proffer them for sale.

Originally a Black Hmong settlement, Sa Pa was used by the French as a hill-station retreat during the summer months. The temperate climate, at an elevation of 1,650m (5,413ft), was a welcome respite from the stifling humidity at the lower levels, and reminded the French of home. Sa Pa's current incarnation as a bustling tourist town only took off in the mid-1990s with the arrival of large numbers of backpackers.

Dramatically perched on the edge of a high plateau, it is surrounded on all sides by theatrical dark-blue peaks enveloped by shifting mist and cloud. All along the lower hillsides of the valleys are terraced rice fields interspersed with hill-tribe villages. It is all unbelievably scenic and, best of all, it doesn't take more than 10 minutes to stroll beyond the town and into the breathtaking countryside.

All manner of hill-tribe clothing, jewellery and handicrafts, some quite old, are on sale – after fierce

★ SHOPPING IN VIETNAM

Shopping can be a memorable highlight of any visit to Vietnam. The settings are as diverse as the goods on offer, whether paddling through Mekong floating markets, buying hill-tribe textiles right from the loom, souvenir shopping in Hanoi's swanky boutiques, assembling a picnic lunch in open-air markets, or procuring brand names at Saigon's high-rise shopping malls. Bring plenty of dong or crisp new dollars, as many shops still don't take plastic.

Apart from Hanoi and Ho Chi Minh City, the main shopping destinations for tourists in Vietnam are likely to be Hoi An (selling every conceivable souvenir, in addition to numerous tailor shops) and the ethnic-minority markets of the far north. Interesting souvenirs – for example, buffalo-horn servers, marble boxes, ceramic tea sets, lacquerware bowls, silk lanterns and acrylic paintings – are sold at countless outlets across the country, however. In many cases it is the hill-tribe handicrafts that are the most interesting – and difficult – to procure. Common items include hand-woven fabrics, silver jewellery, baskets, ethnic costumes, wood-carvings, musical instruments made from gourds and bamboo, and pottery. For many visitors, the Hmong and Dao markets in and around Sa Pa provide the best opportunities to purchase these items.

Prices are usually negotiable. When haggling, it is important to smile and remain polite. If a price seems high, counter-offer 50 percent and then

Making traditional pottery at Bat Trang craft village near Hanoi

negotiate to a happy medium. It's simply not worth fretting too much over a few thousand dong. The difference is minimal to most foreigners, but helps locals to feed their families. The most important principal in haggling is arriving at a price both parties are happy with, but not necessarily reaching the cheapest price possible.

Outdoor markets open very early, often at sunrise. The best time to go is before 10am. Shops and boutiques open around 8am and close around 8 or 9pm. Some shops close for lunch, usually from 11.30am to 1.30 or 2pm.

The biggest recent changes in the shopping scene have been the creation of new, home-grown designer brands, as well as a trend towards high-rise shopping malls. Stricter laws on copyright have also meant a reduction, but not elimination, of counterfeiting.

Vietnam has very strict regulations on the sale and export of genuine antiques, thus most 'antique' pieces sold to tourists are fakes or copies. If someone claims to be selling an original piece, ask to see a certificate of authenticity and ownership.

Strict laws prohibit the sale of products made from endangered species and other wild animals, but there are still too many loopholes (and people also break the law outright). To be safe, don't buy insect or butterfly collections, snake wine, coral pieces, sea-turtle shells, bear-teeth or tiger-claw necklaces. Unfortunately, all are readily available and usually come from wild animals rather than those raised in captivity.

Ipa-Nima, a boutique in Hanoi

A vegetable seller at Tan An Market, Can Tho

Mount Fansipan viewed from Sa Pa

bargaining – in the main **Sa Pa Market**. The ethnic-minority attire has been cleverly altered for foreign body shapes. Vendors gather at the market every day, but the best time to visit is early on Saturday and Sunday mornings. Throughout the week, Black Hmong and Red Dao women wander about town, aggressively touting their clothing and jewellery.

Replaced in the last decade with all manner of mini-hotels and karaoke bars, only a few original buildings, replete with balconies and cupolas, linger from Sa Pa's days as a French hill station. One of the most noteworthy is **Sa Pa Catholic Church**. Built in 1930, it was shelled in 1952 by the French and again, in 1979, by the Chinese. Repaired in 1994, a priest comes in from Lao Cai twice a week to preach to a packed congregation able to recite Mass from memory.

Just 3km (2 miles) outside of Sa Pa is the well-trodden Black Hmong village of **Cat Cat**. The Black Hmong children here squat bare-bottomed in the dirt and pose for tourists' cameras (in return for money, of course). Dozens of visitors tramp through this small stilt-house village daily on their way to the nearby **Silver Falls** (Thac Bac), about 12km (7 miles) out of town. Also near the falls is a long wooden suspension bridge called **Cloud Bridge** (Cau May). Several outlying villages, such as **Ta Van**, **Sin Chai** and **Ta Phin**, make for pleasant and relatively easy treks. Hotels and travel agencies in Sa Pa will have more details.

For the truly adventurous (or foolhardy), there is **Mount Fansipan** ❽ (Nui Phan Si Pan), Vietnam's highest peak at 3,143m (10,310ft) to conquer. A guide is mandatory (by law) for the trek to the summit, which takes a minimum of three days to complete. Directly west of Sa Pa and located in **Hoang Lien Son National Park**, the scenery is utterly magnificent, notable for its rhododendron-rich forests and exceptional birdlife (see p.49).

While there is some rather threadbare camping equipment available for rent in Sa Pa, most climbers choose to outfit themselves for the trek in Hanoi, where it's easy to find good fleece jackets and sturdy shoes. While not technically demanding, it's a long way up the mountain and the trek is not to be underestimated, particularly in rain or misty conditions. Closer to the summit, the ascent involves negotiating a number of steep, rocky patches and can be treacherous if the ground is wet. March is perhaps the best time to visit as this is the peak of the dry season. If you decide to make the trip, be sure to book with an experienced local operator.

About 80km (50 miles) east of Sa Pa, little **Bac Ha** ❾ is best known for its colourful and lively **Sunday market**. The town itself is smaller,

usually warmer on account of its lower altitude, and has more of a frontier feel than Sa Pa. The market's appeal stems from the sheer variety of hill-tribe minorities represented. Most people in this area belong to one of the Hmong groups, including the colourfully dressed Flower Hmong people, but there are also Dao, Giay, Laichi, Lolo, Nhang, Nung, Phulao, Tai, Thulao and Hoa, as well as Vietnamese. Each Sunday, the women gather to socialise and trade, while their husbands drink themselves under the table on rice wine.

Around 2km (1¼ miles) from Bac Ha, through cornfields, is a Flower Hmong village called **Ban Pho**, known for its maize alcohol. Further afield, the **Can Cau Market**, in a village 18km (11 miles) north of Bac Ha, runs on Saturday. It is a diverse market that does sell some souvenirs.

Flower Hmong women selling clothes at Bac Ha market

Ba Be Lake, within the eponymous national park

Bac Kan, Cao Bang and Lang Son provinces

Moving to the far northeast of Vietnam, Bac Kan, Cao Bang and Lang Son provinces border China's karst-filled Guangxi province. The picturesque limestone mountains spill over into Vietnam, creating dramatic, rugged landscapes cut by rivers and waterfalls. Ba Be National Park, Ban Gioc Waterfall and numerous caves are among the many natural wonders. Peaceful and serene now, the area was a battleground between the Chinese and Vietnamese in the not too distant past, and still bears many scars.

The most significant attraction in Bac Kan province is **Ba Be National Park ❿** (Cong Vien Quoc Gia Ba Be; daily, daylight hours; charge). The protected area covers an area of more than 7,000 hectares (17,300 acres) and is characterised by high mountains and deep valleys, as well as waterfalls, lakes and caves.

In the southwest of the national park, **Ba Be Lake** (Ho Ba Be), or Three Seas Lake, is the largest natural body of water in the country. Comprising three linked lakes stretching 9km (6 miles) in length and over 1km (½ mile) in width, Ba Be reaches a depth of over 30m (98ft) and is surrounded by limestone cliffs and forests. The lake's major attractions are boat trips to nearby caves, waterfalls and minority villages, where visitors can stay overnight. In July and August, the height of the tourist season for the Vietnamese, the normally peaceful lake is crowded with tour boats for hire.

Highlights in the area include **Dau Dang Waterfall** (Thac Dau Dang), which can only be reached by boat, and **Puong Cave** (Hang Puong), which runs deep into a mountain and is traversed by a river, which allows exploration by boat.

Minority women in northern Vietnam often carry large woven baskets, called *gui*, on their backs. These handmade backpacks are an ingenious and beautiful art form themselves, though rarely for sale to tourists. Inside the baskets, however, are a wealth of hand-crafted souvenirs that the women are all too eager to hawk. Silver jewellery is very popular, from necklaces to rings and bracelets. Before you invest too much money, be aware that much of the silver is impure. Fabrics are also highly prized, often made from hemp and dyed or embroidered. Local tribes are especially known for their indigo batik (a process of applying beeswax to fabric before dyeing to create patterns). The hands and fingers of Hmong women tend to be black and blue as the dye readily stains skin.

For visitors wishing to spend the night, there are two options. The Tay minority, who live in the park and surrounding areas, have cottages and rooms for rent inside the park boundaries. Outside the park, slightly more expensive lodgings in the form of guesthouses and air-conditioned villas are available.

Wildly beautiful Cao Bang province sits in the far northeast of the country. **National Highway 4** runs down to the coast through ravines and mountain passes parallel to the Chinese border. This highway was the site of numerous clashes in the late 1940s between French colonial troops and the Viet Minh guerrillas. Protected by a thin string of French forts that were constantly under attack, French-speaking soldiers dubbed the then-Highway 4 'the Street without Joy.'

The provincial capital is also called **Cao Bang ⓫**. Shelled by the Chinese in 1979, the town itself has limited tourist appeal, its main function being that of a launch point for visits to the nearby mountains and the Chinese border. In the past five years, the town has undergone significant development, with new government buildings, hotels and shops popping up all over. The hill leading up to the war memorial offers spectacular views from its summit.

Cao Bang province shares a long border with China. Much of the land

Cycling through the Chi Lang Gorge, near Lang Son

Ban Gioc Waterfall

is still forested and the climate is quite cool, with chilly winters. Throngs of hill tribes, including the Tay, Hmong, Nung, Dao and Lolo, gather at the morning markets in the villages around the provincial capital. Enquire at your hotel about these markets, and be prepared to make an early start.

A good 90-minute drive north of Cao Bang City is **Pac Bo Cave** ⑫ (Hang Pac Bo), a stop for people on the Ho Chi Minh trail. Just a kilometre from the Chinese border, this is the spot where, in 1941, the man then known as Nguyen Ai Quoc crossed into his homeland for the first time in 30 years. Later, after taking the name Ho Chi Minh, he lived in a cave near the Nung village of Pac Bo – the proximity of the Chinese border providing a quick escape route if French soldiers discovered his hiding place. In Pac Bo there is a small **museum** (daily 7.30–11.30am, 1.30–4.30pm; charge)

with information on the surrounding area, as well as artefacts that belonged to Ho, his jungle hut, a replica of his simple bed and, of course, tourist trinkets. In true Communist style, Ho named the stream flowing in front of the cave **Lenin Creek** and a nearby mountain **Karl Marx Peak**.

Also close to the Chinese border, about 80km (50 miles) northeast from Cao Bang, is **Ban Gioc Waterfall** ⑬ (Thac Ban Gioc), sometimes written Ban Doc. This is the country's largest (but not highest) waterfall, and is very popular with both Vietnamese and Chinese tourists. The 300m (984ft) width of the falls stretches from Vietnam and across the border into China, and the waterfall is at its most spectacular during the rainy season, from May to September, although it is worth seeing at any time of the year. Ask your hotel to arrange a visit, as the border area around Ban Gioc is a military area and access can be restricted. Boat trips can be arranged to within fairly close range of the falls.

Some 2km (1¼ miles) away from the waterfall is **Nguom Ngao Cave** (daily, daylight hours; charge), a 3km (2-mile) subterranean network. There are two sections; the smaller cave is beautifully lit, but to explore the second, larger cave you need a torch and a guide. The latter apparently has a secret entrance near Ban Gioc Waterfall.

Limestone mountains and forests surround another of the province's beauty spots, **Thang Hen Lake**. This is one of seven scenic lakes in the area, but access to it can be difficult and any tourism infrastructure is scant. Wild orchids grow in profusion throughout the region.

Lang Son province lies to the east of Cao Bang and shares a border with China's Guangxi province. High mountains and thick forests cover around 75 percent of the land area and shelter wildlife including leopards, monitor lizards and muntjacs. Tay, Nung, Hmong, Dao, Nghia and Hoa are among the ethnic minorities living in this part of Vietnam. The **Ky Cung River** that flows through the province is unique in that it flows northwards to China; the other rivers in the region all flow south.

The Vietnamese have fought numerous battles against Chinese invaders in the narrow gorge at **Chi Lang**. There are a series of passes connected by tortuous tracks that thread their way between high mountains here – good for defensive positions.

To the west of **Lang Son city** ⓮ is an area riddled with caves and grottoes, many of which are used for the worship of spirits. The two main examples, **Tam Thanh Cave** and **Ninh Thanh Cave** (both daily, daylight hours; charge), are illuminated and contain Buddhist altars. Also in the region is a highland valley called **Bac Son** and a market town inhabited by Tay (Tho) and Nung people. An unmarked white building perched on stilts, the **Museum of Bac Son** (Bao Tang Bac Son; open on request; donation) contains a small collection of artefacts from the Bac Son culture (5,000–3,000BC), as well as exhibits and displays related to the Bac Son Uprising of 1940.

Nguom Ngao Cave

ACCOMMODATION

From December to February, Sa Pa is often cold and sometimes wet. Few hotels have heating; instead, most prefer to offer fireplaces, though these rarely warm the rooms. Many visitors opt for a homestay in an ethnic-minority village in the valley. Most hotels in Dien Bien Phu are

government-run, which generally means poor service, low standards and a less-than-enthusiastic staff. In the rest of the region, most accommodation is of the small generic hotel and family-run guesthouse variety.

Hanoi to Dien Bien Phu

Brewery Guesthouse (Khach San Cong Ty Bia)
Tran Can, Dien Bien Phu
Tel: 0230-382 4635
This brewery-operated guesthouse has clean and comfy rooms, with the best featuring hot water and TV. For the full experience, spend the evening at one of the local bars nearby. **$**

Huyen Tran Guesthouse
Lai Chau
Tel: 0231-387 5829
This quaint little guesthouse along the main road is popular with Vietnamese business-men, and offers pleasant rooms with air conditioning, TV and a balcony that looks out over the rice paddies. **$**

Mai Chau Lodge
Mai Chai Town
Tel: 0218-386 8959
www.maichaulodge.com
This gorgeous resort/lodge has large, comfortable rooms decorated in natural woods and local handicrafts. A full-service resort with English-speaking staff, guests are treated to a free bottle of rice wine on arrival. **$$$**

People's Committee (Uy Ban Nhan Dan) Guesthouse
Off Highway 6, Son La City
Tel: 022-385 2080
An interesting government-run guesthouse

that has been expanded and renovated and offers clean, comfortable rooms with all the standard amenities. Has great views over the nearby hills. **$**

The far north

Cat Cat View Hotel
46 Fan xi Pang Road, Sa Pa Town
Tel: 020-387 1946
www.catcathotel.com
Don't confuse this long-established favou-rite with the numerous copycats; this is the authentic Cat Cat Hotel. Located on the Cat Cat-village side of town, its comfortable rooms are located up a hillside, making for breathtaking views at the top. **$$**

Cha Pa Garden Boutique Hotel and Spa
23B Cau May, Sa Pa Town
Tel: 020-387 2907
www.chapagarden.com
Once Sa Pa's best-kept secret, this lovely little boutique hotel features clean and well-appointed rooms in a renovated French villa. The friendly owners, Tommy and Chai, go out of their way to make their guests happy. **$$$**

Topas Eco Lodge
24 Muong Hoa
Tel: 020-387 2404
www.topasecolodge.com
Located south of Sa Pa, this environmen-tally friendly lodge generally enjoys warmer weather and clearer views than hotels in the main town due to its location. The 25 rooms

The Victoria Sapa Resort

are located within bungalows, each powered by solar panels. **$$$$**

Victoria Sapa Resort
Sa Pa Town
Tel: 020-387 1522

www.victoriahotels-asia.com
This charming chalet-style resort is located just above the town and offers stunning views of the valley and Mount Fansipan. Rooms are warm and luxurious, with attractive Vietnamese embellishments. **$$$$**

RESTAURANTS

In the wild northwest, travellers eat where they can and food is a fuel to push onwards into the mountains. At pit stops along the way, restaurants mainly serve ethnic-minority delicacies heavy with grilled pork, beef and vegetables.

Restaurant price categories

Prices are for a full meal per person, with one drink

$ = under US$5
$$ = $5–10
$$$ = $10–15
$$$$ = over $15

Hanoi to Dien Bien Phu

Lien Tuoi Restaurant
64 Muong Thanh, Dien Bien Phu
Tel: 0230-382 4919
Long popular for its high-quality Vietnamese and Chinese dishes. The translated English and French menu might bring a smile to your face but there are no mistakes in the food, which is reliably good. **$**

Mai Chau Lodge
Mai Chau Town
Tel: 0218-386 8959

www.maichaulodge.com
This upscale resort has a lovely open-air restaurant overlooking the valley and surrounding hills. On the pricey side for this neck of the woods, but the quality is high. **$$$**

Muong Thanh Hotel & Restaurant
25 Him Lam, Dien Bien Phu
Tel: 0230-381 0038
This hotel restaurant serves a variety of typical Vietnamese meat and rice dishes, as well as passable pasta ones. It's not terribly exciting, but good value for the money. **$$**

Street food in Song La

Baguette & Chocolat
Thac Bac Street, Sa Pa
Tel: 020-387 1766
www.hoasuaschool.com
The ground floor of this guesthouse is a quaint restaurant and café, with a bakery attached. Great cakes and pastries and you can order a packed picnic lunch if you're heading out on a trek. **$$**

Camellia
22 Tue Tinh, Sa Pa
Tel: 020-387 1455
A warm, friendly place with delicious and reasonably priced Vietnamese comfort food. The spring rolls and salads are fantastic, as is the mountain-apple rice wine. **$$**

The far north
Auberge
7 Rue Muong Hoa, Sa Pa
Tel: 020-387 1243
www.sapanowadays.vnn.vn
This guesthouse has a restaurant on a terrace overlooking the owner's delightful garden. Delicious snacks and mains (both Vietnamese and Western), with a nice selection of vegetarian options. **$$**

Delta Restaurant
33 Cau May, Sa Pa
Tel: 020-387 1799
www.deltasapa.com
This Italian restaurant features delicious pizzas, pastas, soups and steaks. Warm and cosy, upstairs is a romantic wine bar with private booths. Credit cards accepted. **$$**

SPORTS, ACTIVITIES AND TOURS

Most activities in the far north involve trekking and mountain climbing, or some form of do-it-yourself adventure sport. Most activities are best arranged in Sa Pa or pre-arranged in Hanoi. *For more on local activities, see the Hill tribes Unique experience, p.30.*

Mountain climbing

For hardy travellers hoping to scale Vietnam's highest peak, Mount Fansipan, the three-day trip (including guides) can be organised by any of the hotels listed in the Sa Pa section on Accommodation *(see p.112)*. The climb can also be booked in Hanoi with travel agents such as Buffalo Tours *(see p.94)*. Another possibility is the well-regarded Active Travel Vietnam (3/F, 303 Nguyen Du, Hoan Kiem District, tel: 04-3944 6230; www.activetravelvietnam.com).

Trekking

To book treks to the villages surrounding Sa Pa, it's best to hire a guide from a local hotel. All of the hotels listed under Accommodation *(see p.112)* have enthusiastic and (mostly) knowledgeable English-speaking guides, usually young Hmong women, who are experienced in leading groups of foreigners through the picturesque valleys. Non-English-speakers can request French-, German- or Chinese- (Mandarin) speaking guides.

French veterans at Dien Bien Phu

Tours

Kangaroo Café Tours
18 Bao Khanh, Hoan Kiem District,
Hanoi
Tel: 04-3828 9931
www.kangaroocafe.com
Organises cheap but reliable (and fun) tours
of Sa Pa, as well as shorter day trips. Offers
excellent travel advice.

The Dien Bien Phu battleground sites are
toured independently, but for those with an
interest in the history, it might be a good
idea to hire a guide who can explain the
stories behind the most important sites.
Guides are best booked at the Muong Thanh
Hotel (25 Him Lam, tel: 023-381 0038),
where staff can also arrange transportation,
or by asking around on the street. Many of
the city's *xe om* drivers double as guides,
though finding one who speaks good English
can present a challenge.

FESTIVALS AND EVENTS

In the Northwest, the vast majority of festivals relate to hill-tribe religious
practices and are particularly influenced by China. Nearly all occur around the
Lunar New Year. Sa Pa is the best base to experience these festivals, though
many villages will have their own distinct celebrations.

January–February

Red Dao Dance Festival
Sa Pa
On the first and second days of the Lunar
New Year (Tet), the Red Dao of Sa Pa gather
in homes to dance in the new year.

Gao Tao – Hmong Festival
Sa Pa
On the second and fifth days of the Lunar New
Year (Tet), the Hmong of Sa Pa invite shamans
to pray for good health, fertility and longevity.

Thuong Temple Festival
Lao Cai
A Buddhist pilgrimage festival celebrated
on the 14th and 15th days of the first lunar
month (the close of Tet).

Ta Van Giay Dragon Festival
Ta Phoi
(Cam Duong)
Celebrated on the day of the Dragon, during
the first lunar month, this is a time of feast-
ing and parties.

Northeast and north-central Vietnam

The northeastern corner of Vietnam – easily accessed from Hanoi – is made up of rugged mountain ranges, broad agricultural plains and an extensive, curving coastline. Here, ancient history and wild, natural beauty come together to create one of the most diverse regions in the country.

Northeast and north-central Vietnam transport

 Getting around the northeast of Vietnam is easier than the northwest. Buses or trains north to China can all be readily booked in Hanoi. Buses south can also be booked at any tour agent or hotel reception desk in Hanoi. Almost all travel overnight

 Taxis: Haiphong taxis: the best are Haiphong Taxi, tel: 031-383 8383, and Hoa Phuong Taxi, tel: 031-364 1641. Halong City taxis: Mai Linh Taxi, tel: 033-362 8628, is the most reliable company here. Motorbike taxis (xe om) are probably the best way to get around in Bai Chay and Hon Gai

 Trains: The region is well connected by railways. Services run from Hanoi to Lang Son and the China border (around 5½ hours), and on to Beijing. There are several daily trains between Hanoi and Ninh Binh (2½ hours) and other points on the main north-south line. Vinh is around 6 hours from Hanoi. Two daily trains run between Hanoi and Haiphong (2 hours)

 Buses: Often the only means of transport between provincial towns. There are numerous daily buses (and private minibuses) between Hanoi, Haiphong (2½ hours) and Halong City (4 hours)

Between the Red River Delta and the sea, northeast Vietnam is an area rich in agriculture and history, as well as a regional engine of growth for industry and tourism. At Mong Cai, the easternmost border gate with China, people and goods pass in and out between the two countries, and beach resorts and colourful markets abound. Scenic Halong Bay and Cat Ba Island draw endless crowds who sail peacefully through a dreamy seascape of rocky limestone outcrops, while the hustle and bustle of Haiphong makes it clear that this area is a vital artery for the country's industry and trade.

Further south along the Tonkin Coast, which sees far fewer tourists, the landscape is enlivened by dramatic limestone peaks, towering waterfalls and lush national parks. Ethnic hill-tribe minority villages, tucked away at the foot of mountains, offer cross-cultural opportunities, while seaside and lakeside retreats are an escape from the stifling summer heat. At the southern reaches, poverty and the scars of war become more apparent as one nears the former border between North and South Vietnam.

Halong Bay and the Northeast Coast

Vietnam's northeast corner is the country's gateway from China, or alternately the exit route to Beijing. Further south is the Unesco World Heritage site of Halong Bay, one of Vietnam's top tourist attractions. Limestone cliffs tower above a peaceful bay where junks ferry visitors to hidden caves, lagoons and floating fishing villages.

Mong Cai

Mong Cai ❶ is one of three land-border gates to China open to foreigners, though visas must be issued in either Hanoi or Beijing beforehand.

Sowing rice seedlings near Ninh Binh

A few kilometres to the east, on an island separated from the mainland by a narrow channel, is Tra Co Beach. It may be the north's longest beach, at 17km (11 miles), which makes it relatively easy to find a quiet spot, but the sand is coarse and uninviting. At the southern end of the beach, you can catch a hydrofoil to **Van Don Island** (Dao Cai Bau), which is part of Halong Bay (*see p.119*).

Haiphong

Haiphong ❷, Vietnam's third-most populous city and the north's most important port, is located in the northeast of the **Bac Bo Delta**. A small port town at the time of the French conquest in 1873, it quickly grew as the Europeans set about draining the surrounding swamps and constructing monumental buildings. Inside the boundaries of the Old City, wide shady streets, well-tended stands of greenery and a surprising number of colonial-era buildings are still in excellent condition.

The Haiphong Museum

Northeast and north-central Vietnam

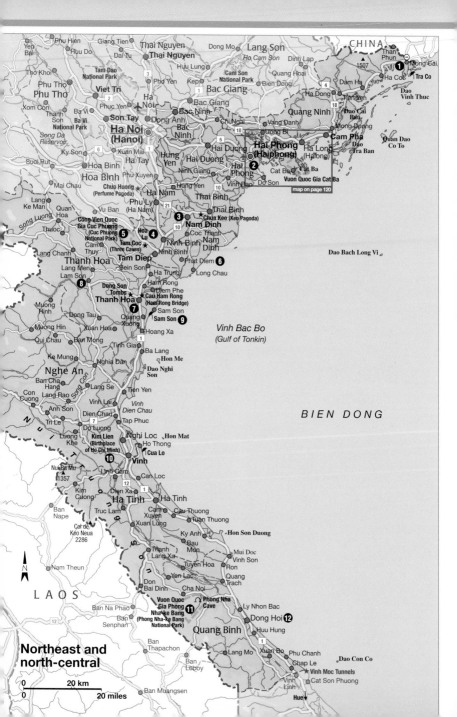

warrior who aided the Trung sisters in the uprising against the Chinese, AD39. The long, low wooden building, with its magnificent carvings and its swooping roof, is reached by passing through a triple-tiered bell tower and an open courtyard. Behind the carved offering table is a baby Buddha protected by nine dragons. The pagoda is situated on Pho Chua Hang, a lively and attractive street.

Halong Bay

No trip to northern Vietnam would be complete without visiting **Halong Bay** Ⓐ (Vinh Ha Long), one of the natural wonders of the world and truly one of the most stunning places in Southeast Asia. The bay's tranquil beauty encompasses some 1,500 sq km (579 sq miles) of indigo sea and is dotted with over 3,000 limestone

The city centre curves around the **Tam Bac River** (Song Tam Bac). In this area there are several impressive colonial-era hotels, administrative buildings and the **Haiphong Museum** (Bao Tang Haiphong; Tue and Thur 8am–10.30pm, Wed and Sun 7.30am–9.30pm; charge). At 56 Dinh Tien Hoang there is a square overlooked by the yellow, neo-colonial **Grand Theatre**, which dates back to 1912. The government has spent over US$6 million renovating the lavish interior.

The **Du Hang Pagoda** (Chua Du Hang; daily 8am–5pm; charge), in the south of the city, was built in 1672 by a wealthy mandarin-turned-monk. It is dedicated to Le Chan, a female

Northeast and north-central Vietnam

Getting to Halong Bay

The best way to get to Halong Bay or Cat Ba Island is by booking a tour through an agency in Hanoi, as it will arrange the rather complicated transport links. For those doing it on their own, travel from Haiphong or Halong City (Bai Chay) to Cat Ba Island via hydrofoil or ferry; the hydrofoil will take an hour and the ferry at least double that. The ferry and hydrofoil schedules change according to the season, but at least one hydrofoil departs from both Haiphong and Halong City to Cat Ba daily, and there are at least two ferries. Confirm hydrofoil and ferry schedules at your hotel or the pier. For more on Halong Bay tours, see p.23.

Have a safe cruise

The best time to visit Halong is in warmer weather, from April to October, as you can swim off the boat and relax on sundecks. During the peak typhoon season in September, boats may cancel due to bad weather. Between January and March, the weather can be cool and drizzly, but even then, Halong Bay is a worthwhile excursion. It is important to note the weather before setting out as rough seas have led to serious accidents. Indeed, in 2011, two accidents, the first killing 12 tourists (the other, fortunately, had no fatalities), led to much new government oversight but little real development of safety standards. When it comes to Halong Bay tours, you get what you pay for. More expensive tours tend to have newer boats and higher safety standards.

islands and rocky outcrops, almost all of them uninhabited. Oddly shaped rock sculptures jut dramatically from the sea, and numerous grottoes create an enchanted, timeless and almost mystical world. *For more on Halong Bay, see p.22–24.*

Halong City (Ha Long) – about 3½ hours from Hanoi – is the main departure point for boat trips. It comprises two smaller towns, **Bai Chay** and **Hon Gai**: Bai Chay is the departure points for boat trips around the bay and is where the majority of hotels, tour agencies and restaurants are located. Shops here specialise in kitsch souvenirs fashioned from pearl, coral and limestone.

Cat Ba Island and National Park

The **Cat Ba Archipelago** consists of 366 islets and islands peppered with

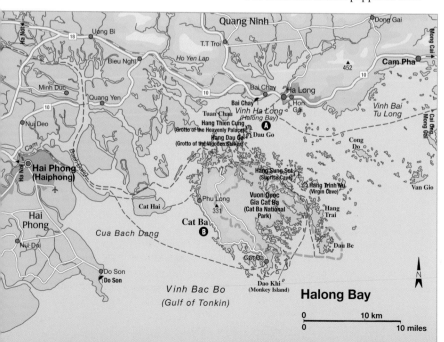

Halong Bay

beautiful beaches and grottoes. Just 20km (12 miles) from Haiphong, with the Gulf of Tonkin to the west and Halong Bay bordering to the east, the main **Cat Ba Island**  covers about 354 sq km (137 sq miles), with a stunning landscape of forested hills, coastal mangroves and freshwater swamps, as well as lakes, waterfalls and reefs.

   Cat Ba, overlooking the Gulf of Tonkin, is the island's main settlement and port. Scattered along the coast are a number of floating fishing villages, best visited by boat. Half of the island and 52 sq km (20 sq miles) of the surrounding inland waters are part of the **Cat Ba National Park** (Vuon Quoc Gia Cat Ba; park office: daily 7–11.30am, noon–5.30pm; charge). The thickly forested island has a rich diversity of flora and fauna, including 69 bird species, numerous reptiles and 32 species of mammal, including the Cat Ba langur, leopard cat and serow.

The Tonkin Coast

Heading south out of Hanoi, **National Highway 1A** passes through varied landscapes as it enters the area known as the Tonkin Coast. Comprising several provinces that contain just about every terrain imaginable, the vistas include mountains, limestone hills, low-lying plains, inland waterways, rice paddies and long stretches of sand along the **Gulf of Tonkin** (Vinh Bac Bo). Rich in culture and revolutionary history, the area is home to several ancient citadels and temples and was the birthplace of Ho Chi Minh. One of the poorest parts of the country, the people here are among the friendliest anywhere in Vietnam.

Nam Dinh to Ninh Binh

The city of **Nam Dinh** ❸, on Highway 21, about 90km (56 miles) south of Hanoi, is the capital of Nam Dinh province and a large industrial city famous for its textiles. In 1899, the French built the **Nam Dinh Textile Mill**, which still operates today. The most interesting part of the city is by the old riverside, where artisans and merchants are still concentrated in an area similar to Hanoi's Old Quarter.

To the east, small Thai Binh province has one of the highest population densities in the country. Salt flats cover extensive areas on the coastal shores. On the road to Haiphong is the site of the 11th-century **Keo Pagoda** (Chua Keo; daily 8am–5pm; free), considered one of the finer examples of traditional Vietnamese architecture. It is dedicated to Buddha, his disciples, and an 11th-century monk named Minh Khong, who is said to have cured King Ly Thanh Ton of leprosy.

At the intersection of National Highway 1A and Highway 10, about 30km (20 miles) south of Nam Dinh, the dusty city of **Ninh Binh** in the eponymous province has few redeeming features. However, it makes a good base for exploration of the eminently redeeming ancient capital of Hoa Lu, the scenic beauty of Tam Coc and Cuc Phuong National Park, and Phat Diem Cathedral.

Hoa Lu and Tam Coc

Hoa Lu ❹, the site of the 10th-century capital of the Vietnamese kingdom known as Dai Co Viet, is just 13km (8 miles) from Ninh Binh. Though much of the site has long

since been destroyed, there remain vestiges of the earthen citadels, palaces, shrines and temples, albeit in a state only archaeologists could appreciate. What has survived are two 17th-century temples modelled on 11th-century originals, which were built after the capital was transferred from Hoa Lu to Thang Long (now Hanoi) in 1010. The **Dinh Tien Hoang Temple** (daily 8am–5pm; free), reconstructed in 1696, features the **Dragon Bed**, an ancient stone altar in the centre of the courtyard in front of the main building. This area was once used for sacrifices. Nearby, **Nhat Tru Pagoda** (Chua Nhat Tru; daily 8am–5pm; free) is a lively and active place of worship. In front of the entrance stands a stone column engraved with Buddhist sutras dating from 988.

Adjacent is the steep **Ma Yen Hill** (Nui Ma Yen). Those who are willing to climb the 260-plus stone steps (and ignore aggressive hawkers flogging souvenirs) will be rewarded with a panoramic view of the ancient

The hilltop temple at Ninh Binh

Boats passing through the caves at Tam Coc

Northeast and north-central Vietnam

kingdom, as well as the site of **Dinh Tien Hoang's tomb**.

The enchanting scenery of **Tam Coc** (Three Caves) is known as 'Halong Bay on Rice Paddies' on account of the jagged limestone out-crops that jut out dramatically from the flooded rice paddies. Usually com-bined with a visit to Hoa Lu on day trips from Hanoi, Tam Coc can also be accessed from the Van Lam Wharf, 9km (6 miles) southwest of Ninh Binh City. If not travelling with a tour group, this is where travellers can hire a small, flat-bottomed boat manned by two people (a rower and poler, both usually women) for the stunning journey along the atmospheric **Ngo Dong River** – as featured in the 1992 film *Indochine*. See also p.26.

Cuc Phuong National Park

Continuing west 24km (15 miles) along the same road that runs past the Kenh Ga pier, you will arrive at the entrance to the 25,000-hectare (61,000-acre) **Cuc Phuong National Park ❺** (Cong Vien Quoc Gia Cuc Phuong; www.cucphuongtourism. com; daily, daylight hours; charge). If visitors can only visit one national park in northern Vietnam, this should be the one. Declared open by Ho Chi Minh in 1962, the biodi-versity here is compelling: mammal species include Delacour's langur, the black giant squirrel, Indian flying squirrel, sambar deer, slow loris, clouded leopard, Owston's civet and Asian black bear. Some of the 307 species of rare bird identified here include the silver pheasant, brown hornbill, red-collared woodpecker and bar-bellied pita. Some of the trees (*Parashorea stellata* and *Terminalia myriocarpa*) reach over 50m (165ft) in height and are estimated to be over 1,000 years old. Cuc Phuong's

⭐ VIETNAMESE TRAINS

Train rides are a great way to cover distance in Vietnam, whether it's a short scenic ride or a long overnight trip designed to save airfare and hotel expenses. Vietnam's train lines run from Ho Chi Minh City all the way to Hanoi, stopping at major cities along the way. Two of the prettiest stretches are between Hue and Danang and the stretch in Phu Yen Province to the north of Nha Trang.

Hotels and tour companies don't tend to sell train tickets. This is because the original price is marked on tickets, leading to arguments with budget travellers when agencies try to charge a commission rate on top of the base fee. To purchase a ticket, therefore, you'll have to go directly to the train station, which is often outside tourist areas (and sometimes in the next town). Fortunately, the women selling tickets usually speak enough English to ensure that you purchase the correct one. Do verify that the price on the ticket matches the price you are quoted.

There are several classes of train, depending on the rail line and times. The choices are hard seat (wooden benches), soft seat (similar to bus seats), hard sleeper (a cabin with six bunks with very thin padding) and soft sleeper (like a hard sleeper but with

A hard-seat carriage on the Lang Co to Danang train

The attractive restaurant car on the Victoria Resorts line

thicker mattresses and, usually, four bunks instead of six). Air conditioning is available in all sleeper cabins but may not be in all sitting cars. The trains between Lao Cai and Hanoi and the direct service between Ho Chi Minh City and Phan Thiet offer better facilities.

Meal, snack and beverage carts generally pass by every few minutes. There is also a kitchen car where meals can be purchased, and passengers are permitted to hop off the train at stops to buy snacks. Do not linger, however, or you will be left behind. The food available is strictly Vietnamese (often rice, boiled cabbage and pork) and not very good.

Facilities are cramped, especially in sleeper cars. The cabins are often full, which may mean that you are sleeping with five strangers. The Vietnamese have a habit of sneaking children on board without tickets, which makes things all the more cramped. Large people may have trouble sitting up straight in the bunks or having enough room to lie flat.

From Hanoi, routes branch off to Lao Cai (from where buses travel to Kunming in China), Lang Son (leading to Beijing) and Haiphong. Other routes under construction may link Dalat to Phan Rang, and Ho Chi Minh City to the Cambodian border – if they are ever completed.

Unfortunately, windows are usually locked and usually dirty, making picture-taking difficult. Your best bet is to stand in the lavatory, generally the only place where windows may be opened.

The Hanoi to Ho Chi Minh City train begins its 1,700km (1,050-mile) journey

Sunday morning Mass at Phat Diem Cathedral

many caves and grottoes are also easily accessible within two mountain ranges that enclose a valley with a microclimate quite different from that of the surrounding region. As the park is only 45km (30 miles) from Ninh Binh (and 140km/87 miles from Hanoi), it can be easily visited on a day trip. *For more on Cuc Phuong, see p.46–7.*

Phat Diem

The towering stone edifice of **Phat Diem Cathedral** (Mass celebrated Mon–Sat 5am and 5pm, Sun 5am, 9.30am and 5pm) is an architectural wonder that is little known outside of Vietnam. It is located in the town of **Phat Diem ⑥** (also known as Kim Son), close to the coast to the southeast of Ninh Binh. Built in 1891, the Sino-Vietnamese-style cathedral, with elements of European Gothic, has sturdy stone walls and is fringed with boxy cupolas with upturned tiled

roofs. Climbing the internal staircase of the magnificent bell tower, visitors will eventually reach the enormous bronze bell protected by a Vietnamese-style tiled roof. The complex

Catholic country

Travelling south from Ninh Binh for 30km (19 miles), you pass through 'Catholic country', with numerous churches and distant spires scattered across rice fields. Catholic graveyards line the road, their white, coffin-shaped tombs sinking into the marshy ground. Sixty-five parishes belong to Phat Diem, with a church in almost every village. Before 1954, around 90 percent of the area's population were Catholic. From 1954 to 1980, however, Catholicism was forbidden in the region and 60,000 locals – including more than 100 priests – fled south to Ho Chi Minh City. Today, only a third of the area's population are Catholic.

around the catehdral consists of five separate chapels, three grottoes and a bell tower set before a small lake.

Thanh Hoa province to the DMZ

Beautiful but impoverished Thanh Hoa province marks the northern boundary of Annam, the traditional central region of Vietnam. This is the first of a succession of seven coastal provinces hemmed between the the East Sea (Bien Dong) – and the Truong Son mountain range.

From Thanh Hoa down to the former Demilitarised Zone (DMZ) – that is, through Thanh Hoa, Nghe An, Ha Tinh and Quang Binh provinces – National Highway 1A is crowded with trucks, cars, motorbikes, bicycles, buffalo carts and pedestrians. Given the sporadic road construction along the way, the train is an attractive option.

There is little to see in Thanh Hoa's provincial capital, **Thanh Hoa City ❼**, although just 3km (2 miles) to the northeast of the city limits, the historic 160m (525ft) span of **Ham Rong Bridge** (Cau Han Rong) crosses the Ma River (Song Ma) to link the central and northern sections of Vietnam. A crucial transport link for the Vietcong during the Vietnam War, the bridge was continuously targeted by the US Air Force from 1965.

At the beginning of the 20th century, archaeologists discovered many relics of the **Dong Son civilisation** (which lasted for approximately the entire millennium from 1000BC) dispersed along the length of the **Ma River** (Song Ma) **Valley**: bronze drums, musical instruments, statues, jewellery, various tools and domestic objects. Some of these are now displayed at the Fine Arts Museum in Hanoi (*see p.76*).

The Ham Rong Bridge marks the traditional divide between northern and central Vietnam

Thanh Hoa's highlands surrounding the area are beautiful and relatively untouched, supporting an array of wildlife and various hill tribes. The Muong village of **Lam Son** , in the Thanh Hoa highlands about 50km (30 miles) west of Thanh Hoa City, was the birthplace of Vietnam's national hero, Le Loi, who became King Le Thai To. It was from here that Le Loi launched a successful decade-long uprising against the Chinese occupiers in the 15th century. In the village is the **Le Loi Temple** (Den Le Loi; daily 8am–5pm; free), dedicated to Le Loi. It contains a bronze bust of him cast in 1532. Nguyen Trai, Le Loi's adviser, penned the epitaph on the large stone stelae, dedicated to the king's life and works.

Some 16km (10 miles) southeast from the city of Thanh Hoa, the white sands of **Sam Son Beach** ❾ stretch for 3km (2 miles) along the coast. There are actually two beaches here, separated by rocks. Both are busy, but more businesses are located on the northern beach. Superb scenery surrounds Sam Son, named after the coastal mountains.

South of Thanh Hoa is Nghe An province. With a long history of peasant uprisings, this is the birthplace of several revolutionaries, including Phan Boi Chau and Nguyen Ai Quoc (more famously known as Ho Chi Minh), as well as the national poet Nguyen Du (1765–1820), author of the *Tale of Kieu*, Vietnam's epic poem.

The city of **Vinh** is the capital of Nghe An province, and immediately known to most Vietnamese as the birthplace of Ho Chi Minh. Uncle Ho was actually born just 15km (9 miles) out of the city, in the humble hamlet of **Kim Lien** ❿. The city itself isn't

Sam Son Beach, a popular resort

The shrine to Ho Chi Minh at his birthplace in Kim Lien

terribly exciting. A modern industrial base, it was bombed to smithereens by the US Air Force and then completely rebuilt in drab Soviet Communist style. The beach at **Cu Lo** is nice enough, though dominated by massage parlours and prostitutes. Most travellers will come to Vinh as a rest stop, or use the city as a transit point en route to the Lao border.

In Nghe An province and its neighbour to the south, Ha Tinh, the mountains give way to wide plains along a 230km (143-mile) coastline, and forests cover around half of the land. There are more than 100 rivers and streams, the longest of which is the **Lam Dong River** (Song Lam Dong), which feeds the two provinces.

Quang Binh province was one of the earliest battlegrounds between the Viets and the Champa, in their struggle to control Vietnam. Although a quiet backwater now, it is the home of several well-known historical figures in Vietnam, including the poet Han Mac Tu, former president Ngo Dinh Diem, and one of the most respected Communist war veterans in the country, Vo Nguyen Giap.

The Unesco World Heritage **Phong Nha-Ke Bang National Park ⓫** was created to protect some of the world's most extensive karst landscapes. The park has a unique forest ecosystem but is most known for its caves, including Phong Nga, which is home to the world's longest underground river, and what the Vietnamese claim to be the largest cave in the world, Son Doong, which was discovered by British explorers in 2009.

Phong Nga Cave is open to the public but Son Doong is not (yet). 'Discovered' by a Frenchman in the 19th century, it was actually used by the ancient Cham in the northern reaches of their kingdom. This is evidenced by Cham inscriptions still visible inside the cave. A tour of the cave by boat is the highlight of any visit to this region.

About 55km (34 miles) from Phong Nga, **Dong Hoi ⓬** is a quaint base to explore the DMZ and make day trips to see the caves. There was once an ancient citadel here but little remains other than moats and vestiges. The local beach, **Nha Le,** is a lovely and very quiet place to get away – there's little there in the way of service and accommodation, apart from **Sun Spa Resort.**

ACCOMMODATION

Most visitors to Halong Bay book their tours in Hanoi, and many opt to stay overnight on board one of the bay's many cruise boats or on Cat Ba Island, where there are dozens of mini-hotels and guesthouses, and many more still being built. For those who prefer to base themselves in Halong City, there is a huge variety of hotels and guesthouses from which to choose, so feel free to bargain hard for the best rates.

Accommodation price categories
Prices are for a standard double room in peak season:
$ = under US$20
$$ = $20–50
$$$ = $50–100
$$$$ = $100–150
$$$$$ = over $150

Halong Bay and the northeast coast

Halong 1
Halong Street, Bai Chay, Halong City
Tel: 033-38 6320
Catherine Deneuve stayed in this beautiful French colonial villa during the filming of the movie *Indochine*; room 208 to be exact. Features charming rooms with huge bathrooms and amazing views. **$$**

Catba Island Resort and Spa
Cat Co 1 Beach, Cat Ba Island
Tel: 031-368 8686
www.catbaislandresort-spa.com
Set on a hill and surrounded by forest, this plush resort features tastefully outfitted rooms with gorgeous views of the bay and Cat Co Beach. Great free-form pool with waterslides and private beach to laze on. **$$$$$**

Harbour View Hotel
4 Tran Phu, Haiphong
Tel: 031-382 7827
www.harbourviewvietnam.com
This lovely, old colonial hotel has huge, well-appointed rooms with views over the bay and friendly staff. Located on the edge of downtown Haiphong, it has a nice pool, the Mandara Spa and an excellent fitness centre. **$$$$$**

Saigon Halong
168 Halong Street, Bai Chay, Halong City
Tel: 033-384 5845
www.saigonhalonghotel.com
This large, imposing hotel has seen better days, but still offers spotlessly clean rooms with amazing views of the bay. There are heavily discounted room rates on offer during the low season. **$$$**

The Tonkin Coast

Cuc Phuong National Park
Nho Quan District, Ninh Binh Province
Tel: 030-384 8006
www.cucphuongtourism.com
There are lodgings in three different areas of the park. At the headquarters visitors can choose a hotel room (basic with air conditioning, hot water and TV), a stilt house (hot water, fan) or a detached bungalow (en suite bathroom, hot water, TV, air conditioning). At Mac Lake, there are detached bungalows; large groups can rent a stilt-house dormitory (no hot water, separate bathroom). Furthest into the park, the Bong substation offers detached bungalows and stilt houses, though the electricity is only turned on during the day. Two restaurants on site. **$$**

Ben Ngu Guesthouse
5 Ben Ngu, Thanh Hoa City
Tel: 037-385 4704
A motel-style guesthouse featuring clean, comfortable rooms with basic amenities, overlooking a leafy courtyard. The friendly staff can arrange tours, though English is not their forte. **$**

Huu Nghi Hotel
74 Le Loi, Vinh
Tel: 038-384 2520

Cat Ba Island

www.huunghina.com.vn
Comes with all the basics such as cable TV,
air conditioning and hot water. Rooms on
the uppermost floors are quiet and have
good views. **$$**

Ngoc Anh Hotel
30 Luong Van Tuy, Ninh Binh City
Tel: 030-388 3768
A small hotel with large, clean rooms, a
fairly good restaurant and friendly, helpful
owners. **$**

Saigon Kim Lien Hotel
25 Quang Trung, Vinh
Tel: 038-383 8899
This quality business hotel with friendly
staff features all the basic amenities (TV, air

conditioning, mini bar, hot water and safe)
at reasonable prices. Often offers room dis-
counts. **$$**

Van Xuan Hotel
National Road 12, Hoa Lu
(just off Highway 1)
Tel: 030-362 2615
This well-run hotel is located in a lush garden
at the bottom of Thien Ton Mountain. **$**

Vi Hoang Hotel
153 Nguyen Du, Nam Dinh City
Tel: 0350-384 9290
Located in the centre of Nam Dinh City next
door to the city's cultural house. Features
large rooms, a swimming pool, massage
facilities and a restaurant. **$$**

RESTAURANTS

If there's one thing that coastal
northeastern Vietnam has in spades, it
is excellent seafood. In Haiphong and
Halong, check out the street stalls and
get cracking on some freshly caught
crabs and prawns. South of Hanoi
and down towards the central coast,
restaurants cater to busloads of domestic tourists hell-bent on reaching the beach.

Restaurant price categories

Prices are for a full meal per person,
with one drink

$ = under US$5
$$ = $5–10
$$$ = $10–15
$$$$ = over $15

Halong Bay and the northeast coast
Au Lac Vegetarian Restaurant
276 Cat Dai, Haiphong
Tel: 031-383 3781
Most popular on the first and 15th days of

each lunar month when tradition dictates
that Buddhists eat vegetarian meals. **$**

Bamboo Forest (Truc Lam) Restaurant
Group 19, Zone 4, Cat Ba Town, Cat Ba Island
Serves a good variety of the area's justifiably

famous seafood, as well as many vegetarian options. The owner, Mr Dau, is very friendly and has a wealth of information on the area. **$**

Bien Mo Floating Restaurant
35 Ben Tau, Bay Chay, Halong Bay
Tel: 03-382 8951
Climb aboard this floating restaurant and dig into some of Halong Bay's best seafood dishes. Specialities here include succulent oysters, crab, lobster and prawns – all cooked local-style. **$$**

Green Mango
Group 19, Block 4, 1-4 St, Cat Ba Town, Cat Ba Island
Tel: 03-188 7151
A hip restaurant and bar overlooking Cat Ba harbour. Serves an electic mix of Vietnamese, Asian and Western cuisines, along with some creative fusion dishes. Relax in comfortable yet classy surroundings and chill. **$$**

Hoai Len Restaurant
14 Van Don St, Mong Cai City
In the evening the streets near the market transform into open-air restaurants, and

Prawn and noodles

this is the best of them. Ask for help and the genial owner will usher you down the alley to help you to choose your ingredients. **$**

Tonkin Coast
Cuc Phuong National Park Restaurant
Tel: 030-384 8006
Two simple, but efficient, restaurants serving local fare are found at the entrance, just inside the Cuc Phuong National Park. Both local Vietnamese and passable foreign favourites are on offer. **$**

Hoa Hong Hotel & Restaurant
102 Trieu Quoc Dat, Thanh Hoa City
Tel: 037-385 5195
www.hoathanh.com
A nondescript hotel restaurant offering generously sized meals. Mostly Vietnamese standards, with a few pasta dishes thrown in for good measure. **$**

Lounge Bar & Lighthouse Café
Thuy Anh Hotel, 55A Truong Han Sieu, Ninh Binh City
Tel: 030-387 1602
www.thuyanhhotel.com
This well-managed hotel is home to one of Ninh Binh's best restaurants. There's a dining room on the ground floor, but head to the rooftop terrace to eat. Serves simple but well-prepared local dishes and some Western standards. **$$**

Vanchai Resort
Quang Cu, Sam Son Beach
Tel: 037-379 3333
www.vanchai-vn.com
Tucked away on the edge of a private beach, this hotel restaurant is a nice place to lunch on fresh crab and other seafood. The set dinners are good value. **$$**

Van Xuan Hotel & Restaurant
Thien Ton Street, Hoa Lu
This hotel has a clean restaurant and makes for a good lunchtime stop when travelling to or from the Hoa Lu complex. There is a selection of Vietnamese and Western dishes on offer. **$**

SPORTS, ACTIVITIES AND TOURS

Most activities in the region are of the outdoor-adventure variety. The main centres of activity are Halong Bay, Cat Ba Island and the national parks. Make arrangements in advance for Halong Bay, usually via tour companies in Hanoi. Cat Ba activities can be arranged on the island by your hotel. Any activities in the national parks can be arranged at respective park headquarters.

Biking

Biking is a great way to see Cat Ba island or the national parks. The majority of hotels and guesthouses rent out cheap Chinese-made bicycles. For those hoping to do more serious trips, good-quality mountain bikes can be rented on Cat Ba Island at the Flightless Bird Café (south end of Nui Ngoc Street; tel: 031-388 8517). In the national parks, it's possible to rent them from the reception building.

Boat tours

Tours of Halong Bay and Cat Ba Island, including kayaking trips, are usually organised by Hanoi-based tour operators. *See the On the water Unique Experience, p.23.*

Kayaking

Kayaking is perenially popular in Halong Bay and Cat Ba. A number of hotels and guesthouses along Nui Ngoc Street rent kayaks for visitors wanting to tour the calm waters of the bay. Expect to pay about US$2–5 an hour.

Trekking

Trekking around Cat Ba and Cuc Phuong is one of the main draws of the parks, and there are numerous trails for the intrepid hiker to explore. The scenery is magnificent but don't expect to see much in the way of wildlife. Bring sturdy shoes, breathable clothing and lots of water – it can get extremely hot and humid between April and October.

FESTIVALS AND EVENTS

In the northeast of Vietnam, the ancestral homeland of the ethnic Kinh, festivals are quintessentially Vietnamese, with little influence from minority groups. Many commemorate ancient military victories and most occur around Halong Bay.

January–April
Cua Ong Festival
Cua Ong Temple, Cua Ong Ward
This three-month long temple-pilgrimage festival celebrates one of the sons of general Tran Hung Dao, and his many victories against the Chinese.

April
Long Tien Pagoda Festival
Long Tien Pagoda, Bai Tho Mountain, Ha Long City
A Buddhist pilgrimage festival for prayer, lighting incense and making offerings at the popular temple.

May–June
Bach Dang Festival
Yen Giang Commune, Yen Hung District
The four-day festival celebrates the Vietnamese heroes Ngo Quyen, Le Hoan, Tran Hung Dao and others, and their victories over Chinese invaders and occupiers.

June–July
Quan Lan Festival
Quan Lan Commune, Van Don District
This 10-day festival commemorates the 1288 victory against Mongol invaders and the exploits of the renowned general, Tran Khanh Du.

Central Vietnam

Vietnam's central zone is the geographical and cultural heart of the country, and with its heady blend of historic sights, fine beaches and beautiful old towns, is a priority on most travellers' itineraries. The region's most important city, Hue, was the seat of the last royal dynasty, and just to the south, My Son was the ancient holy city of the Champa Kingdom, with nearby Hoi An an associated port.

The central region of Vietnam is a showpiece of the country's rich history and a must-see for visitors, with a fascinating array of sights all in close proximity to each other. At its heart is the historic city of Hue, the imperial capital of the Nguyen kings. Nearby Danang is the central commercial hub of the country and boasts all the modern conveniences of Ho Chi Minh City and Hanoi, in addition to the fine Museum of Cham Sculpture. The expansive sands and big surf of China Beach lie just to the east.

South of Danang, the charming old town of Hoi An makes for an exquisitely relaxing break. The 15th-century town was once the biggest sea port and most important centre of trade in the country. Its beautifully preserved assembly halls, merchant shops and family homes reflect the influence of the Chinese, Japanese and Westerners who settled in the region. In the jungled hills inland from Hoi An are the atmospheric Cham ruins of My Son.

The DMZ (Quang Tri province)

Contrary to its name, the Demilitarised Zone (DMZ), was the location of some of the bloodiest fighting of the American War. The DMZ stretched for 8km (5 miles) on either side of the Ben Hai River, 100km (60 miles) north of Hue. This was the line of demarcation between North Vietnam and South Vietnam, established at the Geneva Conference in 1954 after the end of the war against the French. Following the 17th parallel, the border was intended as a temporary measure, to be removed after elections took place in 1956. The elections, however, never happened and Vietnam remained divided along this line until the two countries were officially reunified in 1976, following the collapse of South Vietnam.

Today, there are still desolate stretches of scorched earth. Just south of the Ben Hai, Highway 9 passes sites of famous Vietnam War battles and old US military bases such as **Con Thien** and **Khe Sanh**.

North of the DMZ, in **Vinh Moc** ❶ (daily 7am–5pm; charge), are a series of tunnels where an entire village camped out for several years to escape the bombings. Most of the people evacuated to other parts of the country after the bombings began,

Group B towers, My Son

but some stayed put. For five years, from 1966 to 1971, around 300 people lived in the 2,000m (6,500ft) -long network of tunnels.

Another important DMZ site is the **Truong Son National Cemetery** ❷ (Nghia Trang Liet Si Truong Son). Located 17km (11 miles) off Highway 1A and 13km (8 miles) north of Dong Ha, this large memorial is dedicated to the North Vietnamese soldiers who died along the Ho Chi Minh Trail during the war.

Hue and environs

Once the capital of Vietnam and the seat of the Nguyen dynasty (1802–1945), **Hue** ❸ is located roughly midway between Hanoi and Ho Chi Minh City and a few kilometers inland from the coast. Today, the city is one of Vietnam's most noteworthy attractions thanks to its eventful history and its cultural and intellectual connections, made all the more inviting by a scenic location along the banks of **Song Huong** – the Perfume River. This is an attractive city, crisscrossed by dozens of bridges, lakes, moats and canals.

Ngo Mon Gate, Hue

Central Vietnam transport

 Airports: Da Nang International Airport (tel: 0511-382 3377) is just 2km (1¼ miles) from the city centre. Vietnam Airlines (35 Tran Phu, tel: 0511-382 1130) is the preferred carrier. Airport taxis (tel: 0511-327 2727) and *xe om* are readily available. Phu Bai Airport is 15km (9 miles) southeast of downtown Hue. Vietnam Airlines (24 Nguyen Van Cu, tel: 054-824 709) has several flights per day to Ho Chi Minh City and Hanoi. Taxis between the city and the airport cost over $10. Buses also run from the airport to most hotels for $2 per person

 Taxis: Taxis, *xe om* and cyclos are widely available in Hue and Danang. Mai Linh (Hue: tel: 054-389 8989; Danang: tel: 0511-352 5252) is one of the best companies

 Trains: Danang's station is just a few kilometres west of the town centre. The 2½hr trip between Danang and Hue, one of the most pleasant in the country, costs less than $5 and runs 9 times per day, both directions. Hue Train Station (2 Phan Chu Trinh, tel: 054-382 2175) is located less than 2km (1¼ miles) west of town. For a complete list of schedules and prices, visit **www.vr.com.vn**

 Buses: Most tour companies sell bus tickets between Hue and Hoi An, with a stop in Danang. However, Sinh Café (Danang: 154 Bach Dang, tel: 0511-384 3258; Hue: 7 Nguyen Tri Phuong, tel: 054-382 3309) is the only company that reliably stops in Danang as promised, for $4 per person. Most buses skip Lang Co, despite claims to the contrary by most open tour companies. Hue–Danang takes around 3 hours; Danang–Hoi An, 1 hour

Palace detail, Hue

Central

0 50 km
0 50 miles

Citadel Gate, Hue

Hue's prominence in Vietnamese history goes back to 1601, when Nguyen Hoang, of the powerful Nguyen Lords faction, arrived. He found a particularly good location to build a capital and erected the citadel of Phu Xuan. It became the centre of a new kingdom under the reign of Vu Vuong in the mid-1700s, independent of the north. In 1802, after quelling the Tay Son uprising, the 10th Nguyen Lord proclaimed himself Emperor Gia Long and founded the Nguyen dynasty, which would last for 143 years, until 1945. Yet, just 33 years into the dynasty's reign, the French invaded Hue. They retained the Nguyen as something of a puppet regime, with nominal governance over central Vietnam (Annam) and northern Vietnam (renamed Tonkin).

Anti-French demonstrations and strikes were followed by the Japanese occupation in World War II, before Hue became part of South Vietnam following the country's division. During the Tet Offensive of 1968, Hue's imperial city suffered extensive damage when the Viet Cong held out in the fortified ancient citadel against American attack for nearly two months.

The Imperial City

On the northern side of the Perfume River, Hue's **Citadel** (Kinh Thanh) is enclosed by a wall made of stone, brick and earth, and measuring 8m (26ft) high and 20m (65ft) wide. The wall – all 10km (6 miles) of it – is punctuated by 10 large fortified gates, each topped with watchtowers, and surrounded by a moat.

A second defensive wall – 6 metres (20ft) high – within the Citadel guards a far smaller area, the **Yellow Enclosure** (Imperial Enclosure – Hoang Thanh; daily 7am–5.30pm;

★ THE LEGACY OF WAR

War tourism is a significant part of many visits to Vietnam. Whether one visits the Cu Chi Tunnels, the DMZ, the War Remnants Museum in Ho Chi Minh City, or the mausoleum of the man himself in Hanoi, memories of war are ever present. When embarking on war tourism, it is important not only to remember the suffering of those who endured the war but also the hardships that came after it.

The years immediately following the American war, as the conflict is called in Vietnam, were brutal. Anyone who worked with the US regime was sent for re-education, which meant prison, labour camps or some other form of punishment. Many, weakened by overwork and a poor diet, died from disease or starvation. When the government seized private property, families lost their homes and often their life savings. Food and common wares were all rationed. In the north, several million people starved to death from a disastrous, mismanaged Mao-style collectivisation of farming.

On the surface, it may seem that this legacy has passed away with the social and economic liberalisation following the *doi moi* policies of the 1990s. However, many aspects continue behind the scenes. Not only are people who worked with the South kept from holding high-level jobs or penalised in other ways, but their children and grandchildren suffer discrimination, too.

Memorials of the war remain scattered around the country. Most

The remains of an American tank at Cu Chi

Display at the Son My Massacre Memorial

common are venerated cemeteries for the Viet Cong (Communist soldiers), although the fallen soldiers of the southern regime receive no such honour. A number of prisons have been turned into museums open to tourists, such as the 'Hanoi Hilton' (see p.75) or the prison camp on Con Dao Island. Likewise, the War Remnants Museum (see p.208) is an ideal place for Vietnam to show visitors the horrors endured by its citizens during the war. One of the most popular war tourist 'attractions' is the Cu Chi Tunnels (see p.219), northwest of Ho Chi Minh City, which demonstrate an important 'weapon' in the war against America. DMZ tours in Central Vietnam, while relatively popular, are more about showing what used to be there, but was destroyed in the war. More than 35 years after the end of the war, bomb craters and the effects of napalm can still be seen in many places.

In schools, history education normally starts at the birth of Ho Chi Minh, with an emphasis on his life, Communism and the push for national independence. Youths are still taught to revere Uncle Ho with religious fervour. Although Vietnam spent a great deal of time at war with France and China, as well as Cambodia and Japan, the emphasis in formal education is on the war with America. Children are not taught a message of reconciliation, but thanks to American movies, television, music, food and the influx of foreign tourists and expats, most lessons go in one ear and out the other.

A gruesome reconstruction of the cells at Tiger Cages Prison, Con Dao

The rush to preserve

For a country with a long and rich history, Vietnam boasts relatively few ancient architectural landmarks. Those that have survived the centuries of war, typhoons and harsh climate have suffered from neglect. Vietnam has actively begun to show interest in saving its historical sites. In part, this movement to preserve is part of the government's emphasis on nationalism. Restoring architectural ruins is one way to develop national pride.

More importantly, however, restoration is commercially viable. Watching tourists flock to Cambodia's Angkor Wat convinced local authorities that there is money in a pile of old rocks. If the rocks are well maintained, that is.

However, when restoration decisions are based on the lowest bidder, the end result isn't always as authentic as one might hope. Restored buildings quickly begin to sag and crumble only a few years after they are repaired. Conservationists have their work cut out for them.

charge), with its palaces, temples and flower gardens. Most of what visitors come to see today is found within this inner zone, which was fashioned after Beijing's Imperial City and built during the reign of Emperor Gia Long. Four richly decorated gates provided access: **Hoa Binh** (northern gate), **Hien Nhon** (eastern gate), **Chuong Duc** (western gate) and the **Ngo Mon** Ⓐ (southern gate, or noon gate), first built of granite in 1834 during the reign of Emperor Minh Mang. The gate, the main entrance point into the Imperial Enclosure, is topped by the **Five Phoenix Watchtower** (Lau Ngu Phung), with its roofs brightly tiled in yellow over the middle section and green on either side.

Outside of the gate – between it and the outer wall (and the **Flag Tower**) – are the **Nine Deities' Cannons** Ⓑ (Sung Than Cong). The

Cyclos riding past Ngo Mon Gate

five cannons on the western side represent the five elements – metal, water, wood, fire and earth – while the four to the east represent the four seasons. Each cannon weighs about 10 tonnes.

Pass through Ngo Mon Gate and walk across the **Golden Water Bridge** (Trung Dao), which at one time was reserved for the emperor. It leads to **Thai Hoa Palace**  (Dien Thai Hoa), or Palace of Supreme Harmony, the most important administrative structure in the Imperial City. Here the emperor would hold bimonthly audiences with the court, including male members of the royal family. Civil mandarins were seated on the left and military mandarins on the right. Built in 1805 during Gia Long's reign, the palace was renovated first by Minh Mang in 1833 and later by Khai Dinh in 1923. Today, it stands in excellent condition, its ceilings and 80 beams decorated with red lacquer and gold inlay.

Beyond Thai Hoa lies the third and final enclosure, the **Forbidden Purple City** (Tu Cam Thanh). This city within a city was reserved solely for the emperor and the royal family, who resided here behind a 4m (13ft) -thick brick wall. It was almost completely destroyed during the Tet Offensive of 1968, when the Viet Cong used it as a bunker. Today, the structures within are undergoing reconstruction work.

To the left and right are the **Halls of the Mandarins**, which are annexes to the demolished Can Chanh Palace. In the **Left Hall** (Ta Vu), visitors can be photographed in period costumes, while the **Right Hall** (Huu Vu) houses an extension of the **Royal**

Tourists pose for the camera in the Halls of the Mandarins

Antiquities Museum, with small but representative exhibits of silver, bronze and wood belonging to the Nguyen royalty.

The **Royal Theatre**  (Duyet Thi Duong; charge), behind and to the right (east), stages 30-minute shows (daily 9.30am, 10.30am, 2.30pm and 3.30pm) that feature dancers in elaborate costumes backed by a traditional orchestra. The more expensive entrance tickets include a cup of tea and snacks.

The emperor's **Reading Pavilion** (Thai Binh Lau) sits behind the theatre, ornately decorated with ceramic tiles. This is one of the few structures to have survived the Tet Offensive, although it is in a poor state of repair and looks as if it could collapse at any time.

Beyond, a number of covered **walking corridors** (*truong lan*) have been reconstructed, imitating (albeit poorly) the Nguyen-dynasty style. In the empty expanse behind to the left

and right is a pair of octagonal **Music Pavilions** (Nhac Lau).

To the west, between the walls of the Forbidden City and the Imperial Enclosure, is **Dien Tho Palace** (Cung Dien Tho) **E**, the residence of the various queen mothers, which dates back to 1804. There are some 20 structures in the complex, most notably the **Phuoc Tho Pagoda**, the **Residence of Emperor Bao Dai** and the lovely **Truong Du Pavilion**, which is nestled over a small lotus pond. The beauty of this complex rivals that of Thai Hoa Palace.

Just behind Dien Tho Palace is **Truong Sanh Residence**, which served as a sort of social area for the queen mothers. Constructed during

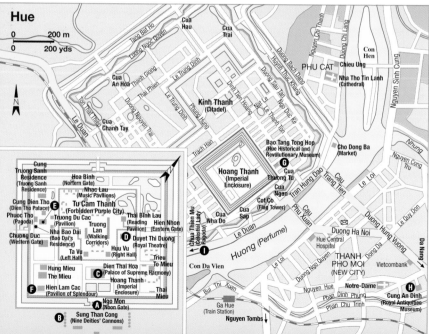

Hue

0 — 200 m
0 — 200 yds

the time of Emperor Minh Manh, the building is in a severe state of disrepair and not easily accessible.

The temples within the Imperial Enclosure are dedicated to various lords and royal family members: in the southeast corner, the temple of **Trieu To Mieu** (now used as a plant nursery) was built to honour Nguyen Kim, while the adjacent **Thai Mieu** was dedicated to Nguyen Hoang and his successors.

The **To Mieu** complex in the southwest corner houses numerous shrines of significance as well. The **Hung Mieu** is devoted to Nguyen Phuc Luan, Gia Long's father. To its left is the well-preserved **The Mieu**, dedicated to the sovereigns of the Nguyen dynasty. This structure houses the shrines of seven Nguyen emperors, as well as monuments to the revolutionary emperors Ham Nghi, Thanh Thai and Duy Tan, which were added in 1959.

In front of The Mieu temple, and completely restored, is the magnificent **Pavilion of Splendour** ❻ (Hien Lam Cac), with the **Nine Dynastic Urns** (Cuu Dinh) lined up before it. The urns, cast between 1835 and 1837 during Minh Mang's reign, are decorated with motifs of the sun, moon, clouds, birds, animals, dragons, mountains, rivers, historic events and scenes from everyday life. Each urn represents an emperor of the Nguyen dynasty and weighs up to 2,500kg (5,600lbs).

Elsewhere in Hue

Another world lies beyond the walls of the Imperial City, which is flanked to the south and east by Hue's commercial centre. The modern downtown area is south of the river between **Trang Tien Bridge** and **Phu Xuan Bridge**. Trang Tien Bridge is the most recognisable modern structure in the city and is lit up every evening in a multicoloured light show. The hotel, shopping and restaurant district is concentrated within a triangle formed by Ben Nghe and Ha Noi streets. There are attractive parks on both sides of the river, abuzz with stalls and cafés in the evening.

Near the east gate of the Imperial City, the **Hue Historical and Revolutionary Museum** ❼ (Bao Tang

143

Central Vietnam

Hue tips
• The Imperial City and most Nguyen tombs have entrance fees of 55,000VND each. Add another 5,000VND for parking if you take a motorbike. English-speaking guides are also available for hire at the Ngo Mon Gate.
• You may exit the Imperial City and re-enter later in the day to attend a performance at the Royal Theatre. Just check with the ticket takers at the front gate when you exit.
• For the best cityscape and waterway photo opportunities, head to the bar on the top floor of the Imperial Hotel. It also has the best Wi-fi connections in town.
• Beware of friendly people who pull up beside you on motorbikes, offering to show you the way to tombs and temples outside the royal city because it's 'on the way home to their village'. Several scams start this way.

Night view over Hue, with Trang Tien Bridge to the right

Tong Hop; Tue–Sun 7.30–11am, 1.30–5pm; free) is easily recognised by the tanks and artillery sitting out front. The central building, built in the style of a traditional *dinh* (communal house), contains a humble collection of archaeological discoveries (mainly pottery and Cham relics) from the surrounding area.

Southeast of Trang Tien Bridge is the **Royal Antiquities Museum** ⓗ (Cung An Dinh; daily 7am–5pm; charge) at 150 Nguyen Hue Street, which occupies the former private residence of Emperor Khai Dinh and his adopted son, Bao Dai. The elaborately ornamented facade of the house and gazebo, the murals and gaudy finishes reflect Khai Dinh's flamboyant personality. The exhibits in the museum include porcelain, silver objects and items from the royal wardrobe.

Some 3km (2 miles) west of the citadel, situated on a hill overlooking the Perfume River, is **Chua Thien Mu** ❶ (Celestial Lady Pagoda; daily, daylight hours; free). The seven tiers of the temple's octagonal tower each represent a different reincarnation of Buddha. Many generations have heard the tolling of the pagoda's enormous 2,000kg (4,400lbs), 2m (6ft) -high bell since it was cast in 1701. In the right conditions it can be heard from fully 16km (10 miles) away.

In 1963, Thich Quang Duc, a monk from Thien Mu, travelled to Saigon and burnt himself to death in protest against President Diem's regime in South Vietnam. The Austin car that he drove to Saigon, as well as the notorious photo that shocked the world, are on display behind the pagoda.

Outside Hue: the Nguyen Tombs

The tombs of the Nguyen emperors are well spread out and could easily take up two full days if you visited all of them. Each tomb has a large brick-paved courtyard, called *bia dinh*, which contains several stone figures. In front of this stands the stelae pavilion, containing the tall marble or stone stelae engraved with the biography of the deceased king. Beyond this is the temple, or *tam dien*, where the deceased king and queen are worshipped by their families and their royal belongings are displayed. Behind and on either side of the temple are the houses built for the king's concubines, servants and the soldiers who guarded the royal tomb. The emperor's body would be laid in a concealed place, or *bao thanh*, enclosed by high walls behind securely locked metal doors.

To reach the tombs from Hue, head south on Dien Bien Phu Street, first passing **Nam Giao Dan** (Terrace of Heavenly Sacrifice; daily 8am–5pm; free) on your left, an esplanade surrounded by a park of pine trees

The tomb of Minh Mang

around 2km (1¼ miles) from Hue's commercial centre. Built by Gia Long in 1802, in its day it was considered a most sacred and solemn place. Alternatively, **boat tours** (see p.27) on the Perfume River depart from Hue and stop at the tombs along the way, bypassing Nam Giao Dan.

The **tomb of Tu Duc** (daily 8am–5pm; charge) is less than 3km (2 miles) west of Nam Giao Dan, and is surrounded by a clutch of incense and souvenir shops. The mausoleum resembles a royal palace in miniature and harmonises beautifully with the natural surroundings. It is perhaps the loveliest of all the Nguyen tombs.

The **tomb of Dong Khanh**, the nephew and adopted son of Tu Duc, who ruled for just four years from 1885, lies just outside the complex. The smallest of the Nguyen tombs, it has been under restoration for several years and is expected to continue in this state for a few more.

The **tomb of Thieu Tri** (daily 8am–5pm; charge) is located a few kilometres to the south. Thieu Tri, Minh Mang's son, was the third Nguyen emperor and reigned from 1841 to 1847. His tomb was built between 1847 and 1848, in the same elegant architectural style as his father's but on a much smaller scale.

The **tomb of Minh Mang** (daily 8am–5pm; charge) is located about 5km (3 miles) south, where the Ta Trach and Huu Trach tributaries of the Perfume River meet. Minh Mang was Gia Long's fourth son and the Nguyen dynasty's second king. He was responsible for the building of the Imperial City and was highly respected for his Confucian outlook and opposition to the French. He was not so well loved by the Cham however, whose autonomy he finally dissolved. The setting is at its best in mid-March, when Trung Minh Lake and Tan Nguyet Lake bloom with a riot of lotus flowers.

About 4km (2½ miles) south of Nam Giao Dan, on Minh Mang Street, the **tomb of Khai Dinh** (daily 8am–5pm; charge) somewhat resembles a European castle, its architecture a blend of the oriental and the occidental. Made of reinforced concrete, it took 11 years to complete and was only finished in 1931. A grandiose dragon staircase leads up to the first courtyard, from where further stairs lead to a courtyard lined with stone statues of elephants, horses, and civil and military mandarins.

Gia Long's tomb (daily 8am–5pm; charge) is best reached by boat. Gia Long was the founder of the Nguyen dynasty, and his tomb, dating from 1820, perhaps served as a model for the later tombs. It has become rather neglected, but the wild beauty of the site itself, with its mountainous backdrop, makes the effort to get there worthwhile.

Danang and environs

The region around Danang, the business and commercial centre of central Vietnam, is an often-overlooked treasure trove of natural beauty and local culture. Nearby – and very much on the tourist trail – is the once-important port of Hoi An, preserved today as a Unesco World Heritage site. It still retains its appealing old-town atmosphere and architecture, but also has the dubious honour of being central Vietnam's top shopping destination – there are more bespoke tailors per square foot here

The tomb of Khai Dinh

The Lang Co peninsula

than anywhere else in the country.

The 110km (68-mile) route from Hue to Danang via the 1,200m (4,000ft) **Hai Van Pass ❹** is one of the most spectacular in Vietnam. The 3½-hour drive over Highway 1A follows a vertiginous route up, down and around mountains that hug the coast.

Along the way is the palm-shaded peninsula of **Lang Co ❺**, which rates as one of the most superb beaches in the country. To one side lies a stunning blue-green lagoon and on the other, miles of white sandy beach.

Danang

Danang ❻ lies at the midpoint of the country, about 800km (500 miles) from both Hanoi and Ho Chi Minh City, and is Vietnam's fourth-

147

Central Vietnam

Bread of Life project

Bread of Life (Dong Da Street at Bach Dang Street Roundabout; tel: 0511-356 5185; www.breadoflifedanang.com; Mon–Sat 7am–9.30pm) is more than an outstanding bakery, Wi-fi café and restaurant that happens to be run by deaf staff. They have brought heart and hope to the deaf community of Danang and the surrounding area. The deaf are viewed as a burden in Vietnam, incapable of learning basic life skills. Most have never been taught to read or write, nor are they necessarily aware that sign language even exists. Bread of Life teaches young people Vietnamese Sign Language (a cousin of ASL), trains in vocational skills, provides housing and enables deaf young people to build a firm, independent future for themselves. Enjoy home-cooked meals crafted by the American management in a cosy environment, between visiting the Marbled Mountains and Cham Museum, and support a great cause!

Marble Mountains

The mountains were once a valuable source of red, white and blue-green marble – most marble used in Vietnam is shipped in from elsewhere these days. Nonetheless, at the foot of Thuy Son and the other mountains, skilful marble carvers still chisel out a great variety of objects ranging from small souvenirs to giant statuary. Some will proudly tell you that they worked on the construction of Ho Chi Minh's mausoleum, but most will just nag you incessantly until you visit their shop. If the ticket office is closed, they'll also offer to watch your motorbike and lend you a flashlight (the cave is never closed – only the lights are turned off), hoping you'll buy something when you come back outside.

largest city, straddling the east and west banks of the Han River. While it's nowhere near as hectic as Hanoi or Ho Chi Minh City, this is central Vietnam's economic centre, host to the country's third-busiest port. It is as good a place as any to gauge the flavour of modern Vietnam, and has prospered in the economic boom of recent years.

Danang's **Cao Dai Temple** (63 Haiphong Street) dates back to 1956, and locals claim that it is the second-largest temple for the Cao Dai religion outside its base in Tay Ninh *(see p.220)*. Visitors are not allowed into the temple, but are welcome to observe from the periphery.

For an insight into Vietnam's ancient Cham civilisation *(see p.55)*, visit the excellent **Museum of Cham Sculpture** (Bao Tang Dieu Khac Champa; daily 8am–5pm; charge) at the corner of Trung Nu Vuong and Bach Dang streets in the southern part of the town. Danang's most note-worthy attraction, it was established in 1915 and contains the largest display of Cham artefacts in the world.

Outside Danang

Son Tra Peninsula, also known as Monkey Mountain to US servicemen during the Vietnam War, is a beautiful nature reserve just northwest of Danang. The mountain is best explored by motorbike or bicycle, taking the new road winding around steep cliffs and dense rainforest. Macaques and civet cats are among the wildlife sometimes spotted.

China Beach is the name given by American servicemen during the Vietnam War to the 30km (19-mile) stretch of white-sand beach extending

Shiva carving at Danang's Cham Museum

Sun, sand and surf on China Beach

from Son Tra Peninsula, past Danang, all the way east to Cua Dai Beach, near Hoi An. The section of China Beach closest to Danang, called My Khe, was the R&R hangout of American soldiers seeking reprieve from the rigours of the Vietnam War. The local government is sensitive about the name 'China Beach' and has officially banned the term, though it will probably never stamp it out (the official name is Non Nuoc Beach).

About 11km (7 miles) south of Danang, not far from China Beach, stand five large hills known as the **Marble Mountains** (Ngu Hanh Son). Each hill is named after one of the five Taoist elements: **Kim Son** (metal), **Thuy Son** (water), **Moc Son** (wood), **Hoa Son** (fire) and **Tho Son** (earth). These mountains were once a group of five offshore islets, but due to silting over the years, they eventually became part of the mainland. The caves within were once used by Cham people and now shelter altars dedicated to the Buddha, and various bodhisattvas and local deities worshipped by the area's inhabitants. The most famous peak, which is riddled with caves, temples and paths, is **Thuy Son** (daily 7am–5pm; charge). Nearly all tour buses stop at the large cave at the base.

Just west of Danang, at an elevation of 1,136m (3,727ft), is the **Ba Na Hill Station** ❼ (daily, daylight hours; charge), built by the French on **Chua Mountain** (Pagoda Mountain) in the 1920s to escape the summer heat. The hill station, where temperatures are typically around 10°C (18°F) lower than on the coast, was later abandoned and reclaimed by the jungle and the ravages of war. In recent years, the government and private enterprise have built extensive new resort properties and have constructed a gondola up the mountain. A great variety of flora and fauna can be seen along walking trails at **Ba Na-Nui Chua Nature Reserve**, including various monkeys and birdlife, colourful butterflies and delicate orchids.

Towering 1,450m (4,757ft) northwest of Danang is **Bach Ma Mountain**, which, like Ba Na, served as a hill-station resort for the French in the 1930s. Even before the French discovered it, the area had caught the attention of conservationists seeking to protect the resident population of rare Edward's pheasants.

Today, **Bach Ma National Park** ❽ (Vuon Quoc Gia Bach Ma; www.bachma.vnn.vn; daily, daylight hours; charge) is a 22,031-hectare (54,440-acre) treasure trove of flora and fauna. Nine species of primate have been recorded in Bach Ma, including macaques, langurs, slow loris and gibbons. A few leopards still prowl the remote areas of the park.

Hoi An and environs

Located some 25km (15 miles) southeast of Danang is the ancient town of

Linh Ung Pagoda in the Marble Mountains

Hoi An ❼. One of the key attractions of central Vietnam, it is a relaxed place of about 120,000 people, 10 percent of whom live in the Old Quarter, which has been turned into a historical showpiece for tourists. Many of the older homes, with their wooden beams, carved doors and airy, open rooms, have been turned into souvenir shops masquerading as museums. Bespoke tailor shops are found everywhere, and it's not uncommon to see tourists lugging entire suitcases filled with newly tailored suits and dresses.

About an hour west of Hoi An is the ancient Cham holy land of My Son. Once the crown jewel of Vietnam archaeology, sadly, most of it was destroyed in the war. Several temple groups remain, hinting at its once great splendour.

Hoi An Old Town

The oldest part of Hoi An is in the southern section bordering the Thu Bon River, a fascinating blend of temples, pagodas, community houses, shrines, clan houses, shop houses and homes. An admission ticket (sold by various tourist offices around the perimeter of the Old Town) gains you entry to one each of four museums, four old houses, three assembly halls, the Handicraft Workshop (with traditional music performance) and either the Japanese Bridge or the Quan Cong Temple. The complicated system is designed so that you need to purchase a total of four tickets to see everything. Most sites are open daily from 7am–6pm, unless otherwise stated.

Hoi An is one of Vietnam's must-see destinations

Le Loi Street is centrally located and a good place to start your exploration. Heading south towards the river, buy your ticket at the **ticket office** on your right as you enter the Old Quarter. Turn right on Tran Phu Street and head to the **Cantonese Assembly Hall** Ⓐ (Hoi Qun Quang Dong) at No. 176, founded in 1786. It's a pleasant spot with a fountain in the middle of the courtyard, with statues of a twisted dragon trying to devour a carp and a turtle spying from behind. Large red coils of incense hang from the ceilings, hung by worshippers as offerings. Just opposite is the **Museum of Sa Huynh Culture** (Bao Tang Van Hoa), one of the best places in the country to familiarise yourself with Vietnam's ancient past (see p. 53).

On Tran Phu Street stands one of the most remarkable architectural highlights in town, the **Japanese Covered Bridge** Ⓑ (Cau Nhat Ban/Lai Vien Kieu). Built by the Japanese community in the late 16th century and renovated several times since, it links the Chinese and Japanese quarters, and Tran Phu Street with Nguyen Thi Minh Khai Street. The bridge's curved shape and undulating green-and-yellow tiled roof give the impression of moving water.

Further up on the right, at 4R Nguyen Thi Minh Khai Street, is **Phung Hung House** (Nha Lo Phung Hung; daily 8am–5pm; free), which has both Japanese and Chinese architectural influences and is still family-owned after nearly 230 years. The family conducts guided tours and operates an embroidery shop in the back and a gift shop upstairs.

From here, turn back to the Japanese Bridge and make your way to the right on Nguyen Thai Hoc Street, continuing until you reach **Tan Ky House** Ⓒ (Nha Lo Tan Ky; daily 8am–noon, 2–4.30pm) at No. 10. This elongated house extends all the way to Bach Dang Street behind, which faces the river. Typical of the old houses in Hoi An, it is built of wood in a very refined style over two storeys.

Continue down Nguyen Thai Hoc Street to the **Museum of Folklore in Hoi An** (daily 8am–5pm; free), which occupies a large old house with a craft shop on the ground floor and an excellent museum upstairs with exhibits of artisan tools, ancient crafts and local folklore.

The **Hoi An Artcraft Manufacturing Workshop** is located in a 200-year-old Chinese merchant shop at 9 Nguyen Thai Hoc Street. Lanterns and other souvenir crafts are made and sold in the back of the shop. While there is a large selection, there's nothing here you won't find in most shops in Hoi An. The main draw is the traditional music and dance show at 10.15am and 3.15pm each day.

Continue east and make your way through the **Central Market** (Cho Hoi An), which is a great place to pick up snacks, fresh fruit and find better bargains than at most street-side shops.

Take a left on Hoang Dieu Street, then a right on Nguyen Duy Hieu Street, heading northeast to No. 157, **Chaozhou Chinese Assembly Hall** 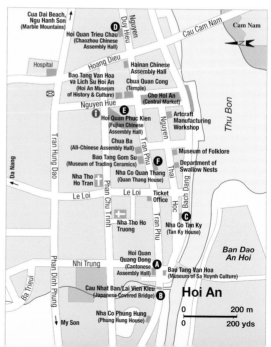 (Hoi Quan Trien Chau; daily 8am–5pm), also known as the Trieu Chau Assembly Hall. Dating back to 1776, its altars are considered to be among the finest examples of woodcarving in Hoi An. The roofs of the structure are decorated with elaborate miniature figures of soldiers, deities, dragons and mythical beasts – all made from colourful ceramic tiles.

Yaly Couture, a tailoring shop in Hoi An

Continue along Nguyen Duy Hieu Street, which, after the junction, becomes Tran Phu Street. The **Hainan Chinese Assembly Hall** (daily 8am–5pm; free) on the right at No. 10, built in 1851, is a memorial to the 107 Chinese merchants who were murdered by a rogue commanding officer in Emperor Tu Duc's navy.

Further along, at 24 Tran Phu Street, across from the market, is **Quan Cong Temple** (Chua Quam Cong), also known as Chua Ong. Built in 1653, the temple is dedicated to Quan Cong, a general from the Three Kingdoms period (AD221–65) who was deified for his loyalty and sincerity. Inside the temple is a large papier-mâché statue of Quan Cong, flanked by his general Chau Xuong and the mandarin Quan Binh.

Continue on Tran Phu Street to the **Fujian Chinese Assembly Hall** **E** (Hoi Quan Phuoc Kien). The largest and most elaborate of Hoi An's assembly halls, it dates to 1792 (the triple-arched gateway at the entrance, however, was built in 1975). Inside is a temple dedicated to Thien Hau (Tin Hau) and other minor Chinese deities.

Pass the **All-Chinese Assembly Hall** at 64 Tran Phu Street on your right. It is unmarked and empty other than a small shrine at the back. Next up is the **Museum of Trading Ceramics** at No. 80, which is set in a lovely old wooden house and contains a modest display of broken ceramics. On the opposite side, at No. 77, is **Quan Thang House** **G** (Nha Co Quan Thang), which is more than 300 years old and has been in the current family for more than six generations. It is sparsely

The Fujian Chinese Assembly Hall

decorated with two family altars and a small courtyard. The highlights are the beautiful and well-preserved carvings on the inner walls.

Cua Dai Beach

Just 5km (3 miles) from Hoi An is the broad silvery expanse of Cua Dai Beach. This stretch of sand is lined with several good beach-side resorts, including one of Vietnam's most expensive, the fabulously indulgent **Nam Hai**. The sprawling low-rise resort sits on 25 hectares (62 acres) of prime beachfront land and many of its elegant villas have their own private pools.

Some 20km (12 miles), or 25 minutes by speedboat, from Hoi An and Cua Dai Beach is **Cu Lao Cham Marine Park**, which comprises eight islands that make up the Cham Islands archipelago. The marine park is one of the finest diving spots in central Vietnam. The main Cham Island is known for its rich bounty of swallows' nests (the species in question is, in fact, German's swiftlet), used in birds' nest soup – a prized delicacy in Chinese communities all over Asia.

My Son temples

The ancient kingdom of Champa, which is thought to date back to the 2nd century AD and flourished from the 5th to 15th centuries, once occupied the central Vietnamese coast, all the way to the Dong Nai River in the south. After many struggles, Champa was conquered by the Vietnamese – but the Cham people remained. As their kingdom was swallowed piecemeal by the invading Viet (Kinh), increasing numbers of Cham fled to neighbouring Cambodia, though others chose to remain under Viet tutelage in their former homelands.

My Son ⑩ (daily 7am–4.30pm; charge), nestled under the green slopes of Cat's Tooth Mountain (Nui Rang Meo) some 50km (31 miles) from Hoi An, is the site of Vietnam's most important Cham monuments and was declared a Unesco World Heritage site in 1999. It is one of the most atmospheric locations anywhere in the

Hawkers on Cua Dai Beach

Overgrown ruins at My Son

Southern Quang Nam province

About 50km (31 miles) south of Hoi An, Highway 1A passes through **Tam Ky**, capital of Quang Nam province. Around 5km (3 miles) before reaching the town, three Cham towers dating from the 11th century rise from a walled enclosure at **Thap Chien Dang ⓫** (daily 8–11.30am, 1–5pm; charge). A small museum here has fine sculptures of creatures from Hindu mythology, as well as more everyday images of dancers, musicians and elephants.

A short distance further south is **Thap Khuong My ⓬** (daily 8am–5pm; free), another important Cham site. The temple complex here dates from the 10th century and is renowned for the richness of its decorated pillars, pilasters and arches. Both of these sites provide a sneak preview of Cham monuments yet to come, further south in Binh Dinh province.

country, with the crumbling ruins set in a verdant jungle. Chosen as a religious sanctuary by King Bhadravarman I in the 4th century, many temples and towers *(kalan)* were built in this area. There are 11 designated temple groups in My Son, and there are likely to be other groups of ruins that are either unpublicised or undiscovered.

Central Vietnam

Champa history in a nutshell

The Cham are believed to have arrived in Vietnam by sea, and their ancestors may be found in the ancient Sa Huynh Culture *(see p.53)*. The Champa empire emerged in the 6th century, with great prosperity and a culture of aesthetic excellence. In the late 8th century, Champa was attacked by Java, unsuccessfully.

A century later, the Cham were pushing westwards into Cambodia. In 1145 the Khmers reversed the tide and managed to conquer Champa, but just two years later a new Cham king pushed out the Khmers

and his successor attacked Angkor, the Cambodian capital. In the 13th century the Cham were fighting the Khmers, Vietnamese, and Mongols from China. By the late 15th century, the kingdom was crumbling, to be completely absorbed by the Vietnamese in the early 18th century.

Today, the Cham maintain a thriving matriarchal culture, and are famous for their textiles, music and art. Various communities practice different blends of religion, including Buddhism, Islam, Hinduism and Animism.

ACCOMMODATION

In Hue, Danang and Hoi An, most hotels are centred around the river fronts, although the nicest hotels in Danang and Hoi An are actually out of town, on the beach. Some of the best-value accommodation available in Vietnam is located in Hue and Danang, in terms of facilities and service for overall price.

Accommodation price categories

Prices are for a standard double room in peak season:

$ = under US$20
$$ = $20–50
$$$ = $50–100
$$$$ = $100–150
$$$$$ = over $150

Hue and environs

Hoa Hong Hotel
1 Pham Ngu Lao
Tel: 054-382 4377
Email: hoahonghotel@dng.vnn.vn
Rooms come with all the expected comforts for the price, including air conditioning and satellite TV. The spacious bathrooms have spa bathtubs and shower curtains. **$$**

Hue Heritage Hotel
9 Ly Thuong Kiet
Tel: 054-383 8111
www.hueheritagehotel.com
A fine faux-colonial style hotel with wooden floors, a rooftop swimming pool, bar and restaurant. The elegant rooms have air conditioning, satellite TV and private balconies. The spacious bathrooms have invigorating massage shower-heads. **$$$**

La Résidence Hotel & Spa
5 Le Loi
Tel: 054-383 7475

La Residence Hotel & Spa

www.la-residence-hue.com
This boutique hotel occupies the former home of the French governor. The lovely rooms have three themes: Monuments d'Egypte, Voyage en Chine and Suite d'Ornithologue. A spa and fine-dining restaurant are on site. **$$$$$**

Ngoc Binh Hotel
6/34 Nguyen Tri Phuong
Tel: 054-381 9860
www.ngocbinhhotel.com
Conveniently located in the centre of town, the staff are helpful and friendly and the facilities are disabled-friendly (with a lift system). There is free pick-up from the train and bus stations. **$**

Hotel Saigon Morin
30 Le Loi
Tel: 054-382 3526
www.morinhotel.com.vn
This legendary hotel first opened in 1901 and retains much of its old French-colonial charm. Conveniently located across the street from the Perfume River, it's within walking distance of the Dong Ba Market and Royal Citadel. **$$$$**

Danang and environs

Bamboo Green Riverside Hotel
68 Tran Phu
Tel: 0511-383 2591
www.vitours.com
Located next to the Song Han Bridge, rooms in this new addition to the Bamboo Green chain have great views, bathtubs, air conditioning and satellite TV. **$$**

Dai A Hotel
51 Yen Bai
Tel: 0511-382 7532
Located southwest of the cathedral and about a block away from the Han Market, this small, friendly hotel has great views of the cityscape and free internet access. **$**

Furama Resort Danang
68 Ho Xuan Huong, My An Beach, Danang
Tel: 0511-384 7888
www.furamavietnam.com
Furama is one of Vietnam's premier luxury resorts and is located right on China Beach. The spacious rooms are surrounded by land-scaped gardens, and there are two swimming pools and a golf driving range. **$$$$$**

Furama Resort Danang

Fusion Maia Resort
Son Tra – Dien Ngoc Coastal Street, My Khe Ward, Danang
Tel: 0511-396 7999
www.fusion-resorts.com
The Fusion resorts are a one-of-a-kind luxury experience with unlimited spa treatments included in the price. Each room comes with its own private pool, sunken black granite bathtub, fully loaded iPod and free Wi-fi.
$$$$$

Lang Co Beach Resort
Lang Co Beach
Tel: 054-387 3555
www.langcobeachresort.com.vn
This most luxurious resort in Lang Co is surrounded by lush tropical gardens and built in the style of traditional Hue wooden houses. The grounds include two large restaurants.
$$$$$

Hoi An and environs
Ha An Hotel
6–8 Phan Boi Chau
Tel: 0510-386 3126
Email: tohuong@fpt.vn
Ha An is a friendly, family-run hotel set in a quiet alley close to town. The two houses that make up the hotel are built and decorated in traditional Chinese and French-colonial styles. **$$**

Life Heritage Resort Hoi An
1 Pham Hong Thai
Tel: 0510-391 4555
www.life-resorts.com
Located on the banks of the Thu Bon River next to the Old Town, this is one of Hoi An's top resorts. The Senses Restaurant and Vienna Café serve Asian-European fusion cuisine and 'wellness' dishes designed to complement the resort's spa treatments.
$$$$

Nhat Huy Hoang Hotel
58 Ba Trieu
Tel: 0510-386 1665
Overall, Nhat Huy Hoang is the best value in a city where accommodation is generally overpriced. This small, quiet hotel has friendly, English-speaking staff, and is a few minutes from the Old Town. **$**

Vinh Hung I Hotel
143 Tran Phu
Tel: 0510-386 1621
www.vinhhungresort.com
This Chinese trading house exudes the atmosphere of old Hoi An on the outside. Only the more expensive rooms continue that theme on the inside, however. Two of the rooms were used by Michael Caine while filming *The Quiet American* in 2001.
$$$

RESTAURANTS

Hue and Hoi An both have excellent traditional Vietnamese dining options, while Danang is increasingly becoming the foreign-food destination for businessmen and expats. Hue's cuisine derives from the royal court, while Hoi An's mixes elements of French, Chinese, Cham and Vietnamese.

Restaurant price categories
Prices are for a full meal per person, with one drink
$ = under US$5
$$ = $5–10
$$$ = $10–15
$$$$ = over $15

Hue and environs

Club Garden
8 Vo Thi Sau
Tel: 054-382 6327
This eatery specialises in traditional Hue cuisine, with both à la carte and set menus. Tables are situated in a lovely garden or in air-conditioned dining rooms. **$$**

Lac Thien, Lac Thanh and Lac Thuan
06 Dinh Tien Hoang
Tel: 054-352 7348
Opened in 1965 and perhaps the most famous restaurants in Hue. The three establishments, which stand back to back, are owned by deaf siblings. The traditional Hue cuisine served is excellent and still very cheap. **$**

JASS Japanese Restaurant
12 Chu Van An Street
Tel: 054-382 8177
The menu is small but the dishes are developed to perfection. The flavours are clean and delicate. The Japanese Association of Supporting Streetchildren runs an excellent programme here to house, educate and train disadvantaged youths. **$$$**

Omar Khayyam's
22 Pham Ngu Lao
Tel: 054-381 0310
Omar's is a lively location with flashy decor and great food. The tandoori and curry is consistently excellent. Its pot of chai is a great bargain, too. **$$$**

Phuong Nam Café
38 Tran Cao Van
Tel: 054-384 9317
Despite lots of foreign customers, prices have remained normal (cheap) and the menu entirely Vietnamese, except for the many pancakes. Service is slow but friendly. **$**

Phuoc Thanh Restaurant
30 Pham Ngu Lao
Tel: 054-383 0989
Another establishment specialising in royal Hue cuisine. The set menus with seven to eight courses are very popular, and the place is often packed to the rafters. **$$$**

Danang and environs

Apsara Restaurant
222 Tran Phu
Tel: 0511-356 1409
www.apsaradanag.com
This upscale restaurant near the Cham Museum serves fresh seafood and local delicacies with a Cham theme. Nightly traditional Cham music and dance shows are scheduled from 6.30–8pm. **$$$**

Com Nieu
25 Yen Bai
Tel: 0511-384 9969
www.truclamvien.com.vn
The interior decor of this establishment is not as eye-catching as the outside, but the food is good and reasonably priced. Try the spicy beef salad and stir-fried pork and aubergine. **$$**

Garden View Café
37 Le Dinh Duong
Tel: 0511-358 2482
www.truclamvien.com.vn

Garden View has a lovely central garden with waterfalls and goldfish ponds. Prices are higher than a typical Danang café but the food is exceptional. Breakfast is the main draw. **$**

Kita Guni Japanese Restaurant
24 Le Hong Phong
Tel: 0511-356 2435
Japanese-owned and serving primarily Japanese businessmen, this eatery serves delicious traditional cuisine plus a few surprises. Try the 'Japanese pancake' and quail eggs wrapped in bacon. **$$**

Hoi An and environs
Cargo Club Restaurant and Patisserie
107–109 Nguyen Thai Hoc
Tel: 0510-391 0839
www.hoianhospitality.com
A charming and popular place with a menu of international and Vietnamese dishes, French pastries, cakes, home-made ice cream and a well-stocked wine bar. **$$**

Good Morning Vietnam
102 Nguyen Thai Hoc
Tel: 0510-391 0227
www.goodmorningviet.com
Despite no serious Italian competition in Hoi An, Good Morning Vietnam offers consistently good service and quality pastas, pizza and traditional cuisine, making it a perennial favourite. **$$$**

Mango Rooms
111 Nguyen Thai Hoc
Tel: 0510-391 0489
A bright and breezy restaurant that serves an inventive Vietnamese menu. The Vietnamese chef grew up in the US and gives a decidedly Californian spin to the dishes. **$$$**

Morning Glory
106 Nguyen Thai Hoc
Tel: 0510-224 1555
www.hoianhospitality.com
A cosy restaurant serving the best of Vietnamese street food, all conceived by its owner, Ms Vy. Housed in an elegant old French-colonial villa in the heart of the historic quarter. **$**

Omar Khayyam's
24 Tran Hung Dao
Tel: 0510-386 4538
This popular chain of Indian restaurants is located just outside the Old Town so you can walk or drive there. The menu features lots of curry, tandoori and vegetarian options. **$$$**

A dish known as *cao lau* at a café in Hoi An

NIGHTLIFE

There aren't a lot of nightlife options in Hue, but the few bars in town are well patronised and lively. Danang is relatively quiet in the evenings. Peaceful, quaint Hoi An has a surprisingly lively nightlife.

Hue and environs

B4 Bar
75 Ben Nghe
A Belgian-run bar with imported Belgian beer. Happy hours are from 4–7pm.

DMZ Bar & Café
60 Le Loi
Tel: 054-382 3414
www.dmz-bar.com
The liveliest backpacker bar in town, with very loud music.

Why Not? Bar
21 Vo Thi Sau
Tel: 054-382 4793
A small but popular corner bar owned by a couple of foreigners.

Danang and environs

Bao Nam Tran
27 Nguyen Chi Thanh
Tel: 0511-388 9889
An excellent café with a long list of cheap drinks and snacks.

Camel Club
16 Ly Thuong Kiet
Tel: 0511-388 7462
This is the only truly lively nightspot in town. The music is loud and the drinks pricey.

Paloma Café
Lot 1, Nguyen Chi Thanh
Tel: 0511-388 9833
This lively corner café has two floors and several flat-screen satellite TVs.

Hoi An and environs

Lounge Bar
102 Nguyen Thai Hoc
Tel: 0510-391 0480
Set in an old merchant house, this watering hole has a long list of drinks and a pleasant local atmosphere.

Tam Tam Café
110 Nguyen Thai Hoc
Tel: 0510-386 2212
The downstairs is a clone of the Cargo Club across the street, but upstairs has numerous private sitting areas.

Treat's Café
158 Tran Phu
Tel: 0510-386 1125
This backpacker favourite is always full, especially during the (very long) happy hours from 4–9pm.

Hoi An is well endowed with cafés and bars

ENTERTAINMENT

Although a major cultural centre during the Nguyen dynasty, there's a rather anaemic arts scene in central Vietnam these days. Hue is the most promising, followed by Hoi An. Although Danang has no regularly scheduled events, it does host travelling shows.

Hue and environs

Nha Hac Mua Roi Co Do Hue
Century Hotel, 49 Le Loi
Tel: 054-383 4779
A small outdoor theatre specialising in water puppetry. The theatre looks more impressive from the outside, but it puts on a decent show and has a small gift shop selling some of the simpler puppets. Shows are held daily at 3pm, 4.30pm and 8.30pm.

Hotel Saigon Morin
30 Le Loi
Tel: 054-823 526
www.morinhotel.com.vn
This historic colonial-era hotel has a live, traditional Vietnamese orchestra and dancers that perform all evening in the central courtyard for its dinner guests.

Royal Theatre
In the heart of the Forbidden City, the Royal Theatre gives 30-minute shows in the morning at 9.30 and 10.30 and afternoon at 2.30 and 3.30. Performances include five or six songs and dances in elaborate costumes (including lion dancers) with an 11-piece traditional orchestra. Don't bother with the de-luxe ticket – it is basically the same as the standard version but includes a cup of tea.

Tropical Garden
27 Chu Van An
Tel: 054-847 143
A four-piece traditional orchestra performs here in the restaurant courtyard from 6–9pm, nightly. Order some ice cream or drinks to enjoy the free performance.

Folk dance performance in Hoi An

Danang and environs

Le Hong Phong Cultural Performance Centre
Le Hong Phong Street
A small community centre. Performances tend to be of traditional Vietnamese opera, such as *hat treo*, *hat boi* and *cai luong*.

Nha Hat Trung Vuong
Hung Vuong Street
A local concert hall for travelling shows and live music, including traditional Vietnamese opera, pop singers from Ho Chi Minh City or Hanoi, and Western classical music.

Hoi An

Hoi An Artcraft Manufacturing Workshop
9 Nguyen Thai Hoc
Traditional costumed music and dance shows, Mon–Sat 10.15am and 3.15pm.

Traditional Arts Theatre
75 Nguyen Thai Hoc
Traditional music from the royal Nguyen court and costumed dance shows are held Mon–Sat 9–10pm.

SPORTS AND ACTIVITIES

Despite convenient access to national parks and a great surfing beach, tour operators have yet to capitalise on possible activities in central Vietnam. Below is a selection of what's available. See also the relevant Unique Experiences chapters for more on boat trips *(see p.27)*, cooking classes *(p.42)* and diving *(p.50)*.

Water sports
Karma Waters
213 Nguyen Duy Hieu Street, Hoi An
Tel: 0510-392 7632
www.karmawaters.com
Environmentally friendly kayaking, snorkelling and sailing, plus cycling and hiking tours.

Spas
Verdana Spa
Pilgrimage Village, 130 Minh Mang
Tel: 054-885 461
www.pilgrimagevillage.com
Verdana offers a full range of typical spa and massage treatments, exfoliations and wraps.

Cooking schools
The Cargo Club Restaurant and Hoi An

The Cargo Club Restaurant

Patisserie
107 Nguyen Thai Hoc
Tel: 0510-391 0489
www.hoianhospitality.com
Learn to cook a four-course meal with spring rolls, vegetables and two meat entrées.

Restaurant Du Port
70 Bach Dang
Tel: 0510-386 1786
A quick course on making spring rolls, steamed fish in banana leaves, baked squid and stir-fried morning-glory.

TOURS

Vietnam hasn't yet perfected the art of guided tours, so most continue essentially to provide transport to the most popular tourist sights, often with an English-speaking chaperone to answer occasional questions. Taking a tour is the best way to visit the Cham Islands and My Son.

Ecotours
Hoian Ecotours
7 Cua Dai Beach, Hoi An
Tel: 0510-392 7808
River tours, fishing trips and tours of the Hoi An Delta focusing on local culture, history and the traditional way of life.

Bicycle tours
Café on Thu Wheels
10/2 Nguyen Tri Phuong, Hue
Tel: 054-383 2241
Email: minhthuhue@yahoo.com
A popular company leading tours of the imperial city and tombs by motorbike and bicycle.

Sightseeing tours (general)

Camel Travel
15 Nguyen Thai Hoc, Hue
Tel: 054-384 9643
Email: phigreentravel@yahoo.com
Offers group tours of the city and the royal tombs, Perfume River boat trips, Bac Ma National Park and the DMZ.

Mandarin Café
3 Hung Vuong, Hue
Tel: 054-384 5022
Email: mandarin@dng.vnn.vn
Mandarin is another option offering mostly the same tours as Camel Travel.

Nga
22 Phan Boi Chau, Hoi An
Tel: 0510-386 3485
Email: lenga22us@yahoo.com
Nga specialises in tours to Cham Island and My Son, and boat trips. They also sell bus tickets.

Sinh Café
587 Hai Ba Trung, Hoi An
Tel: 0510-386 3948
www.sinhcafevn.com
Offers a range of tours of My Son plus boat tours of Cu Lao Cham Marine Park to visit island craft villages.

FESTIVALS AND EVENTS

Unless otherwise noted, the festivals below have highly variable dates, determined by local tourism boards. Some of the festivities are tailored to the tourist market, but the shows remain authentic and well done.

Cultural Heritage Festival
Hoi An and My Son
Quang Nam province sponsors a week-long springtime festival to highlight ancient Cham crafts, music, sculpture, temple architecture and dance. Timing and events are highly variable.

Full Moon Festival
Hoi An
During each full moon throughout the year, vehicles are banned from the Old Town, coloured lanterns are hung and music performances are held all around town. The main draw is the atmosphere rather than any particular event.

Hue City Festival
Hue
A biennial event taking place over nine days in June during even-numbered years, this is a large-scale festival that celebrates the cultural heritage of Hue. Events focus on music, food, art and performance. This is the biggest tourism festival in central Vietnam.

Nam Festival
Hue
Nam Giao is the recreation of an animist ceremony instituted by the Nguyen Kings to worship the gods of the earth and sky. Parades include costumed performers riding elephants and traditional music of the royal court.

The Cultural Heritage Festival at Hoi An

South-central coast

Some come to the northern, forested reaches of the south-central coast to get away from the tourist crowds. Others flock to the southern dunes to join them. Travellers looking for attractive coastal scenery, ancient historical monuments, great seafood and friendly locals will be happy at either end – and most areas in between.

Nha Trang

 Population: 392,000

 Local dialing code: 058 (Khanh Hoa province)

 Main post office: 02 Tran Phu Street, tel: 058-382 1002

 Main hospital: Provincial Hospital, 19 Yersin Nha Trang, tel: 058-382 0624

 Airport: Cam Ranh International Airport (tel: 058-398 9917) is located in Cam Ranh Bay, 36km (22 miles) south of Nha Trang. Vietnam Airlines (91 Nguyen Thien Thuat; tel: 058-352 6768) has 3 flights per day between Ho Chi Minh City and Nha Trang, and has daily flights to and from Danang and Hanoi. A shuttle runs between 86 Tran Phu and the airport for around $6 return or $4 one-way. The shuttle heads to the airport 2hrs before scheduled departures. Taxis make the 40-minute trip for up to $20 each way

 Taxis: Mai Linh (25 Le Loi Street; tel: 058-625 4888) is the most trusted service in Nha Trang

 Trains: The railway station is on Thai Nguyen Street, close to the cathedral. There are 7–9 daily trains to Ho Chi Minh City, and 7 to Hue and Hanoi

 Ferries: Tickets to nearby islands may be purchased from any tour office or hotel in Nha Trang. There are usually 1–2 round-trips per day

 Buses: Phuong Trang (05 Le Thanh Ton Street) is the most convenient service for transport between Nha Trang and nearby cities

Vietnam's south-central coast stretches for around 650km (400 miles) from Quang Ngai to Binh Thuan, a wonderfully undeveloped and, in parts, scenic seashore punctuated by the country's top two beach resorts at Nha Trang and Mui Ne. This part of Vietnam was the core of the ancient Champa empire, and today, the centre of the modern Cham homeland is located in Phan Rang, in Ninh Thuan Province. Binh Dinh Province has the best selection of ancient Cham temples, although ancient citadels, temple ruins and museums preserving Cham artefacts are located throughout this part of the country.

Nha Trang and Mui Ne are among the fastest-growing regions of Vietnam, with scores of new restaurants and four- and five-star hotels opening each year. Water sports are the biggest draw. While Nha Trang has had a long-standing scuba-diving industry, Mui Ne is the adrenaline capital, where any afternoon sees up to 100 kiteboarding sails across the bay.

Whale Island, near Nha Trang

Quang Ngai, Binh Dinh and Phu Yen provinces

The provinces of Quang Ngai, Binh Dinh and Phu Yen boast long stretches of pristine, white-sand beaches, undeveloped and mostly empty. This strip is largely ignored by travellers as they pass through en route to or from the tourism hubs of Hoi An and Nha Trang.

Women bring in the catch, Qui Nhon beach

Quang Ngai City and Son My (My Lai)

Quang Ngai City ❶ is located on the southern bank of the **Tra Khuc River**. Locals gather along the riverfront at sunset, when the area is transformed nightly into a long succession of stalls selling fresh seafood.

The town's most noteworthy sight is the **Quang Ngai Provincial Museum** (daily 7.30–11am, 1.30–4pm; free), at 99 Le Trung Dinh/Hung Vuong streets, which is definitely worth a visit. The ground floor has an impressive exhibit of ancient Sa Huynh artefacts, including pottery, jewellery, weapons, burial displays and a giant bronze kettle. Most of the floor, however, is devoted to cultural displays and artefacts of the Koor, H're and C'dong minority hill tribes, as well as displays of 16th-century clothing of the dominant Kinh (Viet) people.

Sitting on the northeastern banks of the Tra Khuc River, **Thien An Mountain** offers sweeping views of Quang Ngai and the surrounding valleys. Built in 1627, **Thien An Pagoda** (daily 8am–5pm; free)

is perched on the highest point. A bronze bell, more than 350 years old, sits inside the temple, while a much newer replica hangs out front. This is the oldest and most famous pagoda in the province, with an active monastery.

On 16 March 1968, Lieutenant William Calley led Charlie Company from the First Battalion of the American forces in the most infamous atrocity of the entire Vietnam War. Shortly after 7am, the soldiers attacked the My Lai and My Khe hamlets of **Son My**, killing perhaps 500 of its residents (the actual number is still in question today), half of whom were children, the elderly and pregnant women.

The **Son My Memorial Museum** ❷ (daily 7am–5pm; charge), 12km (8 miles) east after crossing the Tra Khuc Bridge, is a stark reminder of the horrors that took place here. The grounds contain a recreation of the village in cement, as it would have been just after the massacre, with several mass graves off to the side.

Just a few minutes further down the road from the Son My Memorial is a pleasant stretch of white sand – a good spot for a contemplative rest after the museum.

Vietnam's Long Wall

For several years now, a long earth and stone rampart in the mountain foothills of Quang Ngai province has been the focus of local and international researchers and archaeologists. **The Long Wall of Quang Ngai** (Vietnam's own 'Great Wall') has been dated at around 200 years old, with

roads intersecting the wall. Two sites include stone forts that predate the wall by several centuries.

It is hoped that the Long Wall will come to represent a new kind of tourism for Vietnam that, ideally, will combine visits to the monuments with wilderness treks through the countryside and the nearby H're, Ca Dong and Cor villages.

Highway 1A continues south from Quang Ngai City to the small town of **Sa Huynh** ❸ (the name means 'golden sands') on the provincial border, where the coastal estuaries have been turned into shrimp farms and salt-evaporation ponds. The town is most famous for its archaeological discoveries of the Sa Huynh culture (*see p.53*). Nearby, pristine, yellow-sand beaches are interspersed by boulder-strewn capes. Facilities are sparse.

Binh Dinh province

Situated at the southern coastal tip of Binh Dinh province, 115km (72 miles) south of Sa Huynh, the capital city of **Quy Nhon** ❹ (also spelled Qui Nhon) has held a prominent place in Vietnam's political and cultural history for nearly 1,000 years. It is surprising that with so much natural beauty and a rich history, Quy Nhon has never figured very much on the popular tourist trail. Despite its relatively large size, this inexpensive, sleepy beach town is a great place to escape the crowds of Nha Trang to the south.

Right in the middle of a busy neighbourhood is an ancient Cham temple

167

forts along it dating back further. This remarkable structure runs for 127km (79 miles) north to south from Quang Ngai to Binh Dinh provinces. It was built in alternating stretches of rock and pounded earth, and the largest sections measure 4m (13ft) high and 6m (19ft) wide.

Archaeologists believe that the construction of the wall was aided by cooperation between the H're minority (a remnant of the Champa Kingdom) and the Vietnamese, for mutual protection (incursions and raids from either side were a frequent problem) and management of trade – crossing over the wall involved passing through guarded checkpoints, at which taxes were levied.

Four archaeological sites have now been signposted along main

South-central coast

complex called **Thap Doi** (Tran Hung Dao; daily 8am–5pm; free). Built in the late 12th century, both towers have pyramidal peaks rather than the characteristic terracing found on most Cham towers.

Central Beach, the city's main beach, sprawls before Xuan Dieu Street and is one of the most popular night-time hangouts in town. At the far southern end of An Duong Vuong Street, **Queen's Beach** (Bai Tam Hoang Hau) is not actually a beach but a scenic coastal drive. The road descends to the quiet cove of **Quy Hoa**, easily Quy Nhon's finest beach.

Several Cham towers are scattered in the vicinity of Quy Nhon. The ancient Cham people could not have picked a lovelier spot for the cluster of four towers called **Thap Banh It** (daily 8am–5pm; free). It is located some 20km (12 miles) north of Quy Nhon, on a hill overlooking a river valley occupied by a quaint village and surrounded by verdant green mountains. One tower sits apart from the others, claimed by a Buddhist temple seeking to benefit from the spiritual energy of the site. On the eastern side of Highway 1A, on a hill above the river (a tributary of the Kon River), stands the solitary **Thap Phu Loc** (Golden Tower).

Some 50km (31 miles) northwest of Quy Nhon is another important Cham site, **Thap Duong Long** (daily 8am–5pm; free). The three enormous temples here are under renovation. Nearby, off Highway 19 to the south of Thap Duong Long, **Thap Thu Thien** was once a treasure trove of ancient relics, but the 11th-century tower has been greatly damaged by pillaging over the years.

There are numerous, lesser-known Cham towers dotted about the land-scape in these parts, but they are

Women haggling over seafood on its arrival at the Quy Nhon fish market

Quy Hoa Beach, Quy Nhon

interior is perfect for nature lovers and those interested in hill tribes.

Tuy Hoa ❺ is the small provincial capital. On a hilltop in the centre of town is **Thap Nhan**, a 25m (82ft) -tall Cham temple dating from the 12th century. It looks quite striking lit up each night, perched above the town.

Dai Lanh Beach ❻, 37km (23 miles) south of Tuy Hoa, is a beautiful cove nestled into coastal mountains, forming a natural harbour for the colourful fishing boats. It's sometimes used as a brief rest stop, but few people stay here given the lack of facilities. It makes a good base to explore Hon Gon, a wild peninsula nearby.

often in remote areas and, without a great deal of tourism infrastructure in place, can be difficult to find.

Past the village of Phu Phong, on Highway 19, is the **Quang Trung Museum** (Mon–Fri 8–11.30am, 1–4pm; charge), located on the site of the family home of Emperor Quang Trung who, as Nguyen Hue, was a national hero for his role in defeating the Chinese in the late 18th century. Exhibits include artefacts from the time as well as items relating to local hill tribes, with many captions in English.

Phu Yen province

Most tourists probably sleep through the entire drive across Phu Yen province since it doesn't appear on the itinerary of any major tours. This is a pity because Phu Yen has spectacular deserted beaches running its entire length, and the rugged, verdant

Nha Trang and Khanh Hoa province

Nha Trang is Vietnam's favourite party town, but has many hidden

Unravelling Kate

The Kate Festival is the most important holiday in the Cham calendar, and for this reason Vietnamese have wrongly labelled it 'Cham New Year' (assuming that the New Year must be equally important for the Cham as Tet is for the Vietnamese). Kate occurs according to the Cham calendar, and is usually observed in October. The ancient Cham temples are the focal point of this occasion, which is celebrated by Cham communities in Binh Thuan, Ninh Thuan and Khanh Hoa. Po Klong Garai, outside Phan Rang, has the largest celebration, with traditional music, dance and crowds of worshippers making offerings.

City beach, Nha Trang

charms for those who delve deeper and explore its museums, aquariums and rich ethnic culture. Within striking distance in the hinterland are several important sites where the ancient Cham culture has left its mark. What is more, Nha Trang is serviced by daily flights from Hanoi, Danang and Ho Chi Minh City, making a relaxing beach holiday within easy reach when the big cities start to grate on your nerves. The surrounding province of Khanh Hoa, however, is relatively unexplored by tourists. The attractive, hilly countryside of the interior is inhabited by Raglai, Churu and other minorities.

North of Nha Trang

North of Nha Trang is the **Hon Heo Peninsula** ❼, an idyllic world of secluded beaches and tall boulder-strewn mountains, inhabited by one of Indochina's rarest primates – the black-shanked Douc langur (*Pygathix nemaeus nigripes*). The two beaches on the peninsula have become legendary destinations themselves. The first, Jungle Beach, is on the northern side, some 40km (25 miles) from Nha Trang – about one hour's drive. The sand here is pristine and the water sparkling and clear year-round, with bioluminescent algae that magically light up when swimmers stir the water at night. The rustic **Jungle Beach Resort** (*see p.178*) occupies the prime location. On the southern side of the peninsula at Ninh Van Bay, reachable only by boat, is the second beach – an exclusive getaway for people with money to burn.

Nha Trang

Nha Trang ❽ has a stunning location, bordered by mountains on one side and a beautiful stretch of beach on the other. There are always visitors basting away in the hot sun, and a cool breeze blowing at popular beach spots fronted by bars and restaurants.

As a tourism showpiece, Nha Trang's golden sands are kept pretty clean, but the water quality can vary during the year, from clear and sparkling blue to murky and speckled with bits of garbage from the Cai River; the latter usually happens after heavy rain causes the river to run off into the bay.

On a hill above the **Cai River**, at the city's northern entrance, stands the majestic temple of the famous Cham sanctuary, **Po Nagar** (daily 8am–6pm; charge). The 25m (82ft) main tower is dedicated to the Cham goddess Po Yan Inu Nagar, the 'Holy Mother' of the Champa kingdom, and considered to be Shiva's female form. Her statue resides in the main temple, but it was decapitated during French rule; the original head now resides in the Guimet Museum in Paris. Only four of the sanctuary's original eight temples, all of which face east (symbolising life, renewal and purification with the sunrise), remain standing.

Following the Cai River west of Po Nagar brings you to the **Thap Ba Hot Springs** (15 Ngoc Son Street; www.thapbahotspring.com.vn; daily 7am–7.30pm; charge), famous for their mineral mud baths, although there are also a number of thermal pools with the water simmering at a toasty 40°C (104°F), and a swimming pool with a man-made waterfall.

Nha Trang city centre

Some of Nha Trang's most interesting French-colonial architecture and crumbling 19th-century Chinese houses can be seen around **Dam Market** (Cho Dam), near the Cai River. This former Chinese quarter is truly the most underrated part of town. The busy market sees surprisingly few foreign tourists, and is a welcome contrast to the rest of the modernised city – and a great place to snack on local food.

The **Pasteur Institute** , on the seafront at 10D Tran Phu Street, was founded in 1895 by Dr Alexandre Yersin (1863–1943), a French microbiologist, military doctor, explorer and overall Renaissance man who had worked at the Pasteur Institute in Paris, where he helped Emile Roux discover the diphtheria bacterium.

Yersin was instrumental in the development of the hill station at Dalat and was also responsible for introducing Brazilian rubber trees and establishing quinine-producing plantations in the Suoi Dau region southwest of Nha Trang.

Having discovered the link between rats, fleas and eventually the bacteria

Thap Ba Hot Mud Springs

PANDURANGA DRIVE

Take an epic two-day journey by car through the landscapes of Binh Thuan and Ninh Thuan provinces, once collectively known as Panduranga, exploring some of the oldest monuments of the Champa Kingdom.

Begin your tour at 8am at **Thap Po Sha Nu**, on a hilltop overlooking Phan Thiet, just west of Mui Ne. Here three temple towers now stand, along with vestiges of several other structures, all built in the 8th century.

A Cham woman at the Po Nagar Cham Towers, Nha Trang

Drive east along **Mui Ne Beach,** and then head northeast for 33km (20 miles) along the coast. Take the right fork along the lake and stop at the park entrance. The **White Sand Dunes** (Bau Trang) are an immense range of undulating golden and snow-white dunes. Continue driving north for 14km (9 miles) to meet Highway 1. Turn left (west) on Highway 1 and drive for 5km (3 miles) before taking the first right on the dirt road going north to enter Song Luy Town.

Song Luy (meaning 'River Fortification') is the site of **Ban Canan** (Bal Canar), the ancient imperial capital of Panduranga and last capital city of the Champa empire. It is likely to have been Panduranga's capital for the better part of a millennium. In 1822 the Vietnamese emperor Minh Mang sacked the city and Ban Canan fell into obscurity. The citadel with built on the south banks of the **Luy River**. The ruined walls now stand 1–6m (3¼–20ft) high, with a total circumference of around 4km (2½ miles).

From Song Luy, backtrack and drive east on Highway 1 for 4.4km (2¾ miles. You'll pass through the town of Luong Son. As the road veers left,

Tips

- Day 1: 150km (93 miles)
- Day 2: 50km (31 miles)
- Phan Thiet (Mui Ne) is accessible from Ho Chi Minh City by train and bus
- Travel on this tour is best undertaken by car or motorbike, with a knowledgeable guide

Po Ro Me Cham Tower, near Phan Rang

on a hilltop to your right, overlooking the river, you will see the 17th-century **Thap Po Klong M'hnai**, a temple complex dedicated to one of the last kings of Champa.

Heading another 13km (8½ miles) east on Highway 1, you'll come to a crossroads in the middle of the town of **Cho Lau**. On the northeast corner is the new **Binh Thuan Museum of Cham Culture**. The museum contains replicas of statuary and items of worship, costumes, musical instruments, baskets and pottery, as well as replicas of the royal wardrobe and crowns.

It's another 80km (50 miles) north to the city of **Phan Rang**, the capital of Ninh Thuan province, and the focal point of the modern Cham homeland. Spend the night here, rising early in the morning for breakfast at the Central Market, before heading south on Highway 1 to the town of Phuoc Dan. Head north through Nhuan Duc village. About 15km (10 miles) south of Phan

Rang, on a hilltop, sits the temple-tower of **Thap Po Ro Me**. The tower is one of the last built by the Cham, in the early 17th century. From Po Ro Me backtrack, heading north on road 703. Turn west, driving another 7km (4 miles) toward Dalat on Highway 27. You'll see the three 14th-century towers, known as **Po Klong Garai**, standing on an arid hill.

For more information on the Cham culture see p.55–59.

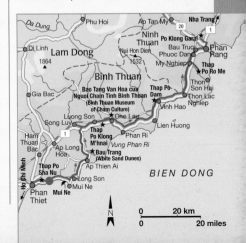

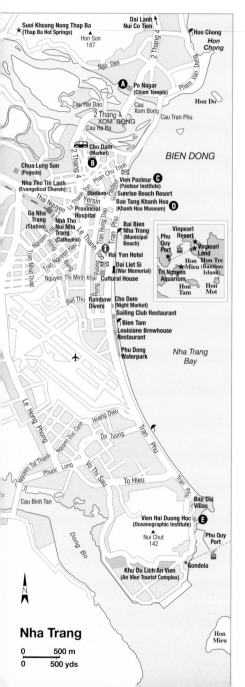

Nha Trang

0   500 m
0   500 yds

that cause bubonic plague (later renamed *Yersinia pestis* in his honour), Yersin built a laboratory to manufacture the serum for the disease, and the lab later became an official branch of the Pasteur Institute.

The small **Alexandre Yersin Museum** (Mon–Fri 7.30–11am, 2–4.30pm; charge) attached to the institute displays many of his personal effects, furniture, documents and antique laboratory equipment (including an enormous telescope). Many of his old books are still kept in the library.

A few doors down from the Pasteur Institute is the small **Khanh Hoa Museum** **D** (Bao Tang Khanh Hoa) Tue–Fri 8–11am, 2–5pm; free) at 16D Tran Phu Street. The museum's left wing contains relics from the Xom Con (about 3,000 years old), the Dong Son (*c.*2,000BC–AD200) and Cham cultures. The most unusual item is the ancient musical instrument similar to a marimba which is estimated to be 3,000 years old.

Beside Cau Da Port, to the south of the city, is the **Oceanographic Institute** **E** (Vien Hai Duong Hoc; daily 6am–6pm; charge), founded in 1923 and housed in a large French-colonial complex. The institute has a dozen large, open tanks – most notable are the prowling sharks, inquisitive rays and the seemingly oblivious sea turtles.

Nha Trang's islands

From Nha Trang Beach, the outline of large **Hon Tre** (Bamboo Island) in the distance is clearly visible. The island is dominated by the **Vinpearl**

Vinpearl cable car, Nha Trang

Land Amusement Park (www.vinpearlland.com; daily 8am–10pm; charge) and **Vinpearl Resort**. A cable car (charge) departs from **Phu Quy Port** and delivers visitors 3,320m (10,892ft) across the bay to the centre of the amusement park. If you find the idea of a 10-minute cable-car ride daunting, take the ferry instead (20 minutes) from Phu Quy Port. The park contains a number of rides and a roller-coaster, a games area, water park, a shopping centre and several restaurants.

The crowning feature of the park is the modern **Underwater World**, with more than 20 fresh- and seawater tanks of varying sizes, including an impressive walk-through wraparound tank featuring sharks, rays and moray eels.

From Phu Quy Port, visitors can also take a 20-minute boat ride to **Hon Mieu**, where the large **Tri Nguyen Aquarium** (daily 8am–5pm; charge), designed to look like a tall ship that has sunk and been fossilised, is located. The facility also serves as a fish and crustacean hatchery.

Several other islands are located in the vicinity of Nha Trang, including **Hon Mun** (Ebony Island), **Hon Yen** (Bird's Nest Island), **Hon Ong** (Whale Island) and **Hon Lao** (Monkey Island). Most of these islands, as well as beaches on Hon Mieu and Hon Tre, are easily visited on a boat tour. Tours include snorkelling at various reef spots.

Ninh Thuan and Binh Thuan provinces

Once a great empire occupying most of Central Vietnam, the Cham Balamon (Hindu Cham) are now restricted to the provinces of Ninh Thuan and Binh Thuan. Together known as Panduranga, these provinces were the last stronghold of the Champa state, which was finally dissolved in the early 1800s. Mui Ne Beach, near the city of Phan Thiet in Binh Thuan Province, is Vietnam's fastest-growing resort destination.

The town of **Phan Rang** ❾ and its

sister city **Thap Cham**, 7km (4 miles) to the west, are co-capitals of Ninh Thuan province, and the modern cultural centre of the Cham people. Local residents often walk about in surrounding villages wearing traditional dress. The towns are located in an extremely arid landscape dotted with menacing-looking cacti and poinciana trees. Outside the city are a number of Cham villages and the two ancient temples of **Po Ro Me** and **Po Klong Garai**. A three-hour drive south from Phan Rang leads through rocky desert landscape and sand dunes.

Further southwest is **Phan Thiet ⑩**, around 200km (125 miles) from Ho Chi Minh City on the **Ca Ty River**, once a sleepy little fishing port known only for its pungent *nuoc mam* (fish sauce) and dragon fruit. As tourism developed on the nearby beach of Mui Ne, however, the economy of Phan Thiet quickly grew. The river front is a lovely place to walk both day and night, offering the best views of colourful wooden fishing boats in the harbour and **Tran Hung Dao Bridge**. The **Phan Thiet Water Tower** – at the eastern end of Le Hong Phong Bridge – designed by Prince Souphanouvong of Laos in the 1930s, is the symbol of both the city and the province.

Ta Kou Mountain Nature Reserve ⑪ (Vuon Quoc Gia Nui Ta Kou; Mon–Fri 6.30am–5pm, Sat–Sun 6.30am–6pm; charge) towers high above the town of Ham Tan, about 30km (19 miles) west from Phan Thiet, along Highway 1A. Take a ride on the cable car to the top, or hike the forest trail for a better glimpse of the local birdlife. The temple is surrounded by a cluster of stupas (relic shrines), a trio of smaller Buddha statues and – the main attraction – Vietnam's largest reclining Buddha, some 49m (161ft) long.

Further down the coast is the **Khe Ga Lighthouse ⑫**, located on a small island off **Tien Thanh Beach**, the longest continuous beach in the province. This is the tallest lighthouse in Vietnam, built by the French in 1897. It's still a beautiful spot, with large orange-and-red boulders jutting out from enormous windswept dunes.

In 1995, when it was declared to be the best spot in Vietnam to view the solar eclipse, **Mui Ne ⑬**, 11km / 7 miles from Phan Thiet and reached by bus, taxi or *xe om*, caught the attention of resort developers looking for fresh territory to stake out. Within a few

Phan Thiet tower

Kiteboarders on Mui Ne Beach

years, this obscure little fishing community had morphed into the premier beach-resort capital of Vietnam, and the centre of kiteboarding and windsurfing for the region.

While the beach itself is the main draw in Mui Ne, there are a few other sights worth visiting. The three Cham temple-towers of **Thap Po Sha Nu** (daily 8am–5pm; charge), at the 5km (3-mile) marker on Nguyen Thong Street, were built in the 8th century to honour Shiva. The primary tower (usually locked) contains a pair of phallic linga-yoni. The tower beside

is devoted to Agni, the fire deity, and the smallest tower to Nandi, the bull deity. The site offers the best view of Phan Thiet City, the Phu Hai River and Song Len Mountain.

The **White Sand Dunes** (also known as Bau Trang or 'White Lake') are an immense Saharan-like series of gold-and-snow-white dunes, located around 45 minutes' drive, 30km (19 miles) northwest of Mui Ne village. Nestled in the dunes are two large reservoirs and a series of smaller lakes, which offer excellent opportunities to observe local birdlife.

The whale-worshippers

In coastal communities of southern Vietnam the festival known as Lang Ca Ong is part of an ancient whale-worshipping cult practised by local fisherman. During the festival, fishermen pray to whales and dolphins, asking their spirits to watch over them in the coming year. During the festival there is a parade with performers in flamboyant traditional costumes, stilt-walkers, musicians and dragon dancers. Dates vary between communities, but most festivities take place around the middle of the 3rd lunar month.

When a whale or dolphin dies and is washed ashore, there is an elaborate funeral to welcome its spirit. The remains of the creatures are buried at the local fishermen's temple near the beach. After five years, the bones are exhumed, shrouded and carried around the town in a similar procession until finally returned to the temple to be worshipped.

ACCOMMODATION

The stretch of coastline from Quang Ngai to Binh Thuan offers perhaps the broadest accommodation selection to be found in Vietnam, ranging from five-star to backpacker. Nha Trang has by far the best choice of hotels, although Mui Ne is developing fast.

Quang Ngai, Binh Dinh and Phu Yen provinces

Kim Thanh Hotel
19 Hung Vuong, Quang Ngai
Tel: 055-382 3471
www.langcobeachresort.com.vn
This small, family-run hotel is located right across from the town square. The large rooms here are the best value in town, with hot water, air conditioning, fridge and satellite TV. **$**

Saigon-Quy Nhon Hotel
24 Nguyen Hue, Quy Nhon
Tel: 056-382 8235
www.saigonquynhonhotel.com.vn
This government-run hotel is the nicest spot in town. Facilities include a rooftop swimming pool, spa and gym overlooking the beach. Disability-friendly, with an elevator. Free Wi-fi throughout. **$$**

Vinh Thuan Hotel
227 Highway 1A, Tuy Hoa

The Six Senses Hideaway Ninh Van Bay

Tel: 058-383 8483
This no-frills hotel is located, in the centre of town next to the bus station, and has an on-site restaurant. Owned by a bus company, it's nothing if not convenient. **$**

Nha Trang and Khanh Hoa province

Jungle Beach
Ocean Road, Ninh Phuoc Village
Tel: 058-362 2384
www.junglebeachvietnam.com
Rates include three meals and refreshments. It's possible to view the local douc langur monkeys from the grounds. The water on the private beach is calm and crystal clear, with bioluminescent algae at night. **$$**

Novotel Nha Trang
50 Tran Phu Street
Tel: 058-625 6900
www.accorhotels.com
Though taken for granted in the West, Novotel has many great safety and security features uncommon in Vietnam. Wheelchair-accessible rooms available. Most rooms are non-smoking. There's also a rooftop swimming pool. **$$$$**

Sao Mai Hotel
99 Nguyen Thien Thuat, Nha Trang
Tel: 058-352 6412
Email: Saomai2ht@yahoo.com
A family-run guesthouse owned by an award-winning photographer and guide. Large, tidy rooms have fan or air-conditioning, hot water, a refrigerator and a TV. All have balcony entrances. **$**

Six Senses Hideaway Ninh Van Bay
Ninh Van Bay, Ninh Hoa
Tel: 058-352 4268
www.sixsenses.com
Perhaps Vietnam's priciest resort, accesssed only by boat. Five villa types to chose from, each with their own butler. Every private villa, with its own pool, feels entirely isolated. **$$$$$**

Ninh Thuan and Binh Thuan provinces
Ho Phong Hotel
363 Ngo Gia Tu Street, Phan Rang
Tel: 068-392 0333
Email: hophong@yahoo.com
Just off the main drag, on the south side of town. A lovely hotel, with friendly staff and clean, spacious rooms. Complimentary internet access is provided. **$**

Mia Resort Mui Ne (Sailing Club)
24 Nguyen Dinh Chieu Street, Ham Tien (Mui Ne), Phan Thiet
Tel: 062-384 7440
www.sailingclubvietnam.com
Private bungalows on the best stretch of Mui Ne's beach, hidden among tropical gardens with a beachside pool and bar. Xanh Spa, Sandals Restaurant and Storm Kiteboarding are all located on site. **$$$**

Mui Ne Backpackers (Vietnam-Austria House)
Km 13.5, Ham Tien (Mui Ne), Phan Thiet
Tel: 062-384 7047
Email: jdajenkins@hotmail.com
The place has changed its name many times but remains a budget favourite. Dorms, private rooms and bungalows on the beach are all on offer, with a swimming pool out front. **$**

RESTAURANTS

Both Nha Trang and Mui Ne have plentiful dining options, with tourist-orientated restaurants serving Vietnamese, French, Indian, Italian, American and Spanish fare. The other destinations in this section have little to offer other than street food and very basic diners serving only local dishes.

Restaurant price categories
Prices are for a full meal per person, with one drink
$ = under US$5
$$ = $5–10
$$$ = $10–15
$$$$ = over $15

Quang Ngai, Binh Dinh and Phu Yen provinces
Barbara's 'The Kiwi Connection'
102 Xuan Dieu, Quy Nhon
Tel: 056-389 2921
Barbara offers a light menu of family recipes and Western favourites. She's a traveller's best friend, with lots of tips. **$$**

Cung Dinh Restaurant
Lo 127 Truong Dinh, Quang Ngai
Tel: 055-381 8555
Dine on Vietnamese haute cuisine and local specialities in gazebos overlooking the Tra Khuc River. Service is fast and friendly and English is spoken by many of the staff. **$$$**

Pho Nuong
Highway 25 (off Highway 1A), Tuy Hoa
Tel: 057-389 9466
This open-air barbecue restaurant serves grilled meat of all sorts, best accompanied by cold beer. Avoid any exotic meats, which may be locally sourced and illegal. **$$**

Nha Trang and Khanh Hoa province
Louisiane Brewhouse
Lot 29, Tran Phu, Nha Trang
Tel: 058-352 1948
www.louisianebrewhouse.com.vn
This expensive but lovely beachside restaurant with swimming pool offers mostly

Vietnamese seafood, with some steaks, burgers, pizza and sushi thrown in for variety. The home brews are excellent. **$$$**

Da Fernando
96 Nguyen Thien Thuat, Nha Trang
Tel: 058-352 8034
Italian favourites – pizza, pasta, gnocchi and risotto – but also some delightful surprises. Anchovies, sun-dried tomatoes and highly refined olive oil are signature ingredients. **$$**

La Mancha
78 Nguyen Thien Thuat, Nha Trang
Tel: 091-456 9782
This excellent tapas restaurant, attractively centered around a fountain, has a great atmosphere and lively Spanish music. Free fresh bread keeps coming throughout the meal. Try the stewed Spanish sausages. **$$**

Ninh Thuan and Binh Thuan provinces

Forest Restaurant (Rung)
67 Nguyen Dinh Chieu, Ham Tien (Mui Ne), Phan Thiet
Tel: 062-384 7589
www.forestrestaurant.com
The Forest Restaurant resembles a ruined Cham temple reclaimed by the jungle. Live Cham music and dance shows go on all evening. The menu includes traditional Vietnamese favourites and seafood. **$$$**

Joe's Cafe
139 Nguyen Dinh Chieu, Ham Tien (Mui Ne), Phan Thiet
Tel: 062-374 3447
The only local venue open 24 hours, offering Italian coffee, pizzas, burgers, pasta, a wide selection of sandwiches and breakfast. Live music is performed every night after 8pm. **$**

Phan Rang Street Food
Roundabout at Le Loi and Ngo Gia Tu Intersection and Central Market on Thong Nhat Street
Phan Rang has great street food: local specialities include *com ga* (chicken and rice), *banh xeo* (seafood pancakes), *sup cua* (crab soup), *banh canh* (noodle soup with fish cakes) and *banh cuon* (fresh spring rolls). **$**

NIGHTLIFE AND ENTERTAINMENT

The nightlife and entertainment scene along the southern coast consists solely of beach bars, some of which have occasional live music or DJs. Live music tends to be Filipino bands, Cham ethnic dancing or travelling rock singers, mostly in Mui Ne and Nha Trang.

Krazy Kim's
19 Biet Thu, Nha Trang
Tel: 058-352 3072
Popular backpacker bar with great pizzas, themed party nights and a wide selection of drinks.

The Sailing Club
72–74 Tran Phu, Nha Trang
Tel: 058-382 6528
www.sailingclubvietnam.com
Orange stucco walls, thatched roofs with wooden pillars and spacious seating: it feels more like a resort than a bar and restaurant.

Sankara
78 Nguyen Dinh Chieu, Ham Tien (Mui Ne)
Tel: 062-374 1122
www.sankaravietnam.com
This new million-dollar bar is a destination in itself, leading the wave of new upscale establishments in Mui Ne.

Snow
109 Nguyen Dinh Chieu, Ham Tien (Mui Ne)
Tel: 062-374 3123
Bountiful selection of drinks. Classy white and blue decor. The only restaurant with air conditioning.

SPORTS AND TOURS

Water sports constitute the main activities in this region, although there are a few very good tour providers as well. In Mui Ne visitors can enjoy kiteboarding, windsurfing and sailing. Nha Trang is the boating and diving capital.

Diving
Rainbow Divers
90A Hung Vuong, Nha Trang
Tel: 058-352 4351
www.divevietnam.com
Vietnam's top dive centre, and the only National Geographic centre in the country. PADI certification available.

Kiteboarding and windsurfing
Storm Kiteboarding Center
Mia Resort (Sailing Club), 24 Nguyen Dinh Chieu, Ham Tien (Mui Ne)
www.stormkiteboarding.com
Experienced one-to-one instruction in a relaxed atmosphere.

Sailing
MANTA Sail Training Centre
108 Huynh Thuc Khang, Mui Ne Village, Phan Thiet
Tel: 090-840 0108
www.mantasailing.org

Recreational sailing, dinghy rental, sail training, racing and beach-side accommodation.

Tours
Barbara's Kiwi Connection
19 Xuan Dieu, Quy Nhon
Tel: 056-389 2921
Tours to various nearby Cham temples and pagodas.

Mai Loc
Sao Mai Hotel, 99 Nguyen Thien Thuat, Nha Trang
Tel: 090-515 6711
Motorbike tours around Nha Trang, the central coast, and up into the central highlands.

Mr Binh Sahara Tour
81 Huynh Thuc Khang, Ham Tien (Mui Ne)
Tel: 098-929 7648
Highly knowledgeable motorbike tour guide for off-the-beaten-track tours.

FESTIVALS AND EVENTS

Most of the festivals on the south-central coast revolve around the local fishing communities, Chinese merchant communities and the Cham.

April–May
Po Nagar Festival
Nha Trang
Cham temple festival celebrated by local Vietnamese residents, honouring the goddess Po Nagar.

May–June
Whale Festival
Phan Thiet
Occurs during odd-numbered years, with parades of costumed performers, dragon dancing and whale bones.

August–September
Nghinh Ong Festival
Phan Thiet
Occurs during even-numbered years, with costumed performers, lion dancing, stilt walkers, musicians and Vietnam's largest *ky lan* (a green dragon-like creature) dance.

September–October
Kate Festival
Phan Thiet and Phan Rang
Most important festival of the Cham calendar, celebrated at ancient temples.

Southern Highlands

As you ascend from the coastal plains into the cool, green mountains of the Southern Highlands, steamy jungles and palm groves give way to temperate pine forests, cut by tall waterfalls and inhabited by hill tribes. The delightful city of Dalat, established as a hill station by the French, makes the perfect base from which to explore.

Dalat

Population: 207,200

Local dialling code: 063

Main post office: 14–16 Tran Phu, tel: 063-382 2586

The cool, temperate climate of the highland region around Dalat, Buon Ma Thuat, Pleiku and Kon Tum is a welcome relief from the steamy coast of Vietnam. The French found it much to their liking, establishing a large hill station and sanatorium at Dalat over a century ago. Further underpinning the feeling of being in a separate country from the rest of Vietnam, the Southern Highlands are still the domain of numerous ethnic minorities, with the Vietnamese themselves only arriving in large numbers in the area at about the same time as the French. What's more, some of the hill tribes have a very independent streak: due to periodic political uprisings, some of the more remote areas, particularly along national borders, are still off limits to visitors.

This part of Vietnam is characterised by pine forests interspersed with vegetable and flower gardens, and vast tea and coffee plantations. The people also cultivate rubber trees, strawberries, mushrooms and silkworms. The area surrounding Dalat is Vietnam's primary cool-weather agricultural zone.

Dalat and environs

The largest and by far the most 'touristed' town in the Central highlands, **Dalat ❶** is the capital of Lam Dong province. The bracing, cool mountain

View over Dalat

climate that Dalat enjoys at an altitude of 1,500m (4,920ft), its large open spaces, picturesque waterfalls, colonial architecture and incredibly fresh produce provide respite for those wishing to escape the heat and humidity of Ho Chi Minh City and the lowlands of southern Vietnam. Annual temperatures range between a comfortable 16°C (61°F) and 24°C (75°F), making the city Vietnam's most popular fair-weather retreat – and its top honeymoon destination.

It is easy to see why the French were so enamoured of Dalat during the colonial days and why it was the favourite getaway for the last emperor,

Xuan Huong Lake, Dalat

Bao Dai. During the American war, the city remained a haven of peace, and as a result, Dalat's beautiful colonial architecture has been preserved as nowhere else in Vietnam. It is a wonderful city to explore on foot. Although largely assimilated now, local ethnic minorities can still be seen walking to the market in quasi-traditional dress, with baskets and large jars hanging on their backs.

Central Dalat

Dalat's **Central Market** Ⓐ (Cho Da Lat; daily 6am–10pm) is one of the largest in the country, set in the deep hollow of a hillside and surrounded by rows of cafés and shops selling wine and candied fruit. The food is the highlight here. The second floor of the middle building is devoted entirely to food stalls. The ground floor of the market offers a peek into the great diversity of produce grown in the surrounding region: tomatoes, avocados, asparagus, strawberries and just about any other fruit you can think of, as well as flowers in abundance.

Xuan Huong Lake Ⓑ (Ho Xuan Huong), formerly part of the town's golf course before it was flooded,

XQ embroidery

About 6km (4 miles) north of Dalat is the XQ Historical Village. Although run as a commercial enterprise, with the primary aim being to sell high-quality Vietnamese embroidery, it offers an entertaining and informative experience, engaging all the senses in a way that few other tourist attractions in Dalat can match.

XQ's embroidery is one of Vietnam's success stories. The company has a presence in every major city in Vietnam – but it goes far beyond mere shops. Most of these include live-music shows, serve inexpensive but delicious local cuisine at in-house restaurants, and have extensive art galleries of embroidery works, which are not for sale. Its outlet in Dalat includes all of this plus a fine museum on the culture of embroidery, as well as local minority handicrafts. A cluster of gift shops and a café (in addition to the restaurant) await customers at the end of the village tour.

extends through the heart of Dalat. The surrounding hills, French-style villas and pine forests provide a lovely backdrop, although the water itself is muddy with red clay after the rains. Drivers offer rides in horse-drawn carts along the edge of the lake.

On the northern banks of the lake, the golf course – originally built for the last emperor, Bao Dai – has been expanded into the **Dalat Palace Golf Club** **G**. The 18-hole championship course is a sister club to the **Ocean Dunes Golf Club** in Phan Thiet.

In the southern part of town, at the intersection of Tran Phu and Le Dai Hanh streets, is the large, pink **Dalat Cathedral** **D** (Nha Tho Con Ga; also known as the Rooster Church), dating from 1942, with stained-glass windows made by Louis Balmet, in Grenoble, France.

For anyone travelling with children, or those who have played in tree-houses themselves as children, **Hang Nga's Crazy House** **E** (daily 7am–6pm; charge), at 3 Huynh Thuc Khang Street, will surely appeal. This is a whimsical and inspiring piece of architecture that is guaranteed to delight. The never-completed house is continuously being added to, with tunnels, stairways and halls meandering into secret rooms and towers, and reading nooks occupied by statues of giant kangaroos, giraffes, eagles and bears.

Tucked away under pine trees on a hill about 1km (½ mile) from Nga's Crazy House, at Trieu Viet Vuong Street, is the **Summer Palace of Bao Dai** **F** (Biet Dien Quoc Truong; daily 7.30–11am, 1.30–4pm; charge). This Art Deco-influenced abode of Vietnam's last emperor was built between

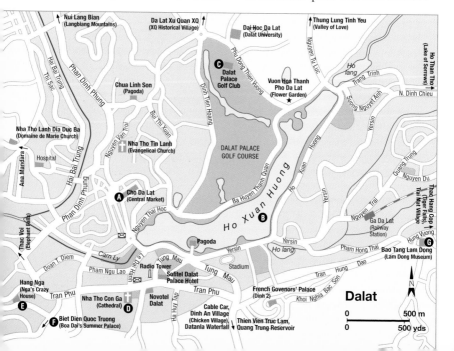

Inside the Crazy House

1933 and 1938. Also referred to as Dinh III, it is actually one of three palaces (the others being Dinh I and Dinh II, neither of which is currently open to the public) belonging to Bao Dai in Dalat. It's said that all three are connected by tunnels so that the emperor could secretly visit his mistresses in each one. Although guides will say that the furnishings and artefacts in the house were used by Bao Dai, it is a well-known fact that many of his belongings were carted away in the early years. Outside the mansion, a carnival-like atmosphere prevails, with souvenir vendors, pony rides and Disney characters. To appreciate the villa better, visit it right after it opens in the morning, or just before lunch.

Dalat and the Southern Highlands transport

 Airport: Vietnam Airlines (2 Ho Trung Mau; tel: 063-833 499) has daily flights connecting Ho Chi Minh City and Hanoi from Lien Khuong Airport (tel: 063-843 373), 30km (19 miles) south of Dalat. The airport shuttle leaves the terminal and arrives at 40 Ho Tung Mau. The shuttle returns to the airport from that location, 2hrs before each flight. Taxis to or from the airport will run up to $20, and motorbike taxis up to $10

 Taxis: A taxi ride for quick trips around Dalat will normally cost under $5. Mai Linh (tel: 063-511 511) is one of the more reputable local companies

 Bicycles: Dalat can be a fun place to ride a bicycle, although casual riders may find it more than challenging due to the many hills, some of which are rather steep. Rent a bike from any hotel for a few dollars, if they don't provide them for free. All adventure tour companies also lead bicycle tours around the city

Motorbikes: Motorbikes can be rented for $5-10 per day. A *xe om* (motorbike taxi) ride for short distances around the city will cost about $2. For information about Easyrider motorcycle tours through the Highlands, *see p.192*

 Buses: Phuong Trang (11A/2 Le Quy Don, Dalat; tel: 063-585 858) is one of the best bus services in the country, with air-conditioned vehicles and free bottled water for their customers. Ticket prices for all neighbouring cities range between $4 and $8, depending on the particular bus company used

On Hung Vuong Street is the **Lam Dong Museum** ⑥ (Bao Tang Lam Dong; daily 7.30–11.30am, 1.30–4.30pm; charge), an excellent museum that has been recognised by the United Nations for its extensive collection of musical gongs used by the local K'ho, Ma and Churu minorities. Other exhibits include an impressive taxidermy collection of local wildlife; ancient relics from the Champa empire excavated near Cat Tien National Park, with others from recent excavations throughout the province; and full-sized Ma and K'ho tribal longhouses, decorated with musical instruments, weapons and common household items.

Around Dalat

Outside of the main town centre are several sights in the surroundings of Dalat that can be easily visited on half- or full-day trips. It is best to hire a car, taxi or motorbike (see p.185) to get to these places.

The **Dalat Cable Car** ⑧ (Cap Treo Da Lat; Tue–Fri 7.30–11.30am, 1.30–5pm, Mon 7.30–11.30am only; charge) is located about 3km (2 miles) south of town. The cable-car ride extends over 2km (1¼ miles) and offers lovely panoramas of villages and mountain forests, all the way to the **Bamboo Forest Meditation Centre** ① (Thien Vien Truc Lam). This Zen-style Buddhist monastery was built in 1993 and has about 100 monks and 80 nuns in residence. The temple is said to benefit from perfect feng-shui placement, with **Pin Haat Mountain** (Nui Pin Haat) behind and **Quang Trung Reservoir** (Ho Tuyen Lam) below. Beneath the monastery is a picnic area with tables and chairs that overlooks the tranquil

Traditional K'ho musical instrument

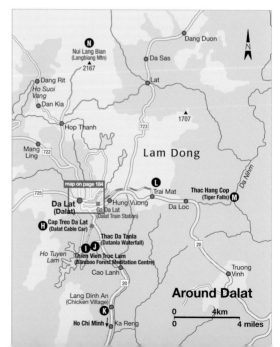

Around Dalat

Dalat railway station

reservoir. The artificial lake was created in 1980 and is now a recreational area with rowing-boats and canoes for hire.

The turn-off for **Datanla Waterfall**  (Thac Da Tanla; daily, daylight hours; charge) is about 5km (3 miles) south of Dalat, just a few hundred metres past the turn-off for the Bamboo Forest Meditation Centre. A gauntlet of souvenir shops must be run at both ends of the 10-minute walk through rainforest, down to the falls below (allow 20 minutes for the return walk). The waterfall makes for great photos, if you can overlook the kitsch pony rides, girls in fake minority costumes and men in bear suits. The new mechanised toboggan run (extra charge) down to the falls and back is the most enjoyable aspect of the commercialism that has taken root here.

Once a favourite stop for tourists wishing to see the K'ho ethnic minority, **Lang Dinh An** (more popularly known as Chicken Village), 17km (11 miles) south from Dalat on Highway 20, today resembles most other villages in Dalat's environs, with one exception. Its unique focal point is a giant concrete chicken, subject of a local legend. Shops around the chicken statue sell lovely hand-woven blankets, handbags, tablecloths and other items with bright tribal patterns that prominently feature horses and elephants (but no chickens, oddly enough).

The picturesque colonial-style **Dalat Train Station** (Ga Da Lat), at Quang Trung Street, opened in 1932 and was once the terminus of a train service that ran all the way to Phan Rang, just east of Nha Trang on the coast. The track, however, was damaged during the American War and never repaired. The only line that exists today is a short 7km (4-mile) stretch that carries a small diesel-run train transporting tourists to **Trai Mat village**, east of the city. There are five daily departures at 8am, 9.30am, 11am, 2pm and 3.30pm;

minimum six passengers required. The ride takes 30 minutes and passes thorough some lovely countryside.

There isn't much to see in Trai Mat for the moment, save for the grandiose **Linh Phuoc Pagoda** (Chua Ling Phuoc; daily 8am–5pm; free). Built in 1952, the imposing seven-tiered structure is just a few hundred metres from the train station, on the other side of the street. The pagoda has almost been eclipsed by the enormous new **Cao Dai Temple**, visible about 1km (½ mile) further up the hill. The temple serves a very large Cao Dai community in Dalat and its size rivals that of the main Cao Dai Temple in Tay Ninh *(see p.220)*.

Tiger Falls  (Thac Hang Cop; daily, daylight hours; charge) is the grandest waterfall in the Dalat area, and thankfully the least visited or developed, largely because of the long drive down a poor road and a further walk down a very steep hill. The falls are an ideal outing for nature lovers who wish to indulge in some adventure trekking, following the stream as it crashes among the boulders in the rainforest canyon below. Tiger Falls is 14km (9 miles) east of Dalat, past Trai Mat village, where there is a signposted turning on the left.

The 12km (7-mile) drive from Dalat to **Langbiang Mountain** (Nui Lang Bian) passes through quaint **Lat Village**, inhabited by K'ho, Lat and Ma minorities. The villagers make a meagre living from the squash, tobacco, coffee, tea and cotton that they grow on the hillsides. Visitors can explore Langbian Mountain's hiking trails on their own, but hiring a guide offers more options. The mountain is a favourite trekking

Langbiang Mountain

location for adventure-tour companies such as Groovy Gecko and Phat Tire *(see p.196–7)*. There are breathtaking vistas of the countryside, and the surrounding pine forests are said to harbour a few surviving bears, deers, leopards and boars. The government-run Vietwings *(see p.197)* offers climbing, camping and paragliding activities.

Around the Southern Highlands

Outside Dalat and further into the highlands, visitors encounter the most spectacular scenery: dramatic waterfalls, lush forests and numerous ethnic minorities living traditional lifestyles. The cities of Buon Ma Thuot and Pleiku, together with the national parks of Cat Tien and Yuk Don, form the bases to explore it all.

West of Dalat

The town of **Di Linh** ❷ lies at the heart of an area of tea and coffee

Although tourism contributes to a significant portion of the Central Highland's economy, some 60 percent is actually based on agriculture, thanks to rich soils, heavy rainfall and mild temperatures. Vegetables grown here – cabbages, carrots, yams, potatoes, artichokes (made locally into tea called *tra atiso* or *actiso*), as well as edible mushrooms – supply the whole country. Dalat wine, available in red or white, is one of Vietnam's staple products, as are the plethora of dried and candied fruits. Every conceivable fruit, as well as a few vegetables and flowers, are candied and shipped to tourist markets such as Ben Thanh in Ho Chi Minh City, and special night markets across the country for Tet. Strawberries are another signature Dalat product, whether candied, turned into jam, concentrated, fermented into wine or blended into tasty fruit shakes.

plantations and is a major stop on the highway for Vietnamese tourists to buy green tea. Nearby, the town of **Bao Loc** ❸ is another tea and coffee centre. It also serves as a base to visit the lovely **Dambri Falls** (charge). The 90-metre (295ft) waterfall is one of the highest in Vietnam. Take the cable car to the summit, or negotiate the steep trail through the forest.

About halfway between Ho Chi Minh City and Dalat lies **Cat Tien National Park** ❹ (Vuon Quoc Gia Cat Tien; www.cattiennationalpark. org; daily, daylight hours; charge), one of Vietnam's best areas for wildlife. The large expanse of forest shelters some 105 species of mammal, 360 species of bird and 120 species of reptile and amphibian. There are significant populations of yellow-cheeked gibbon, civet, sambar deer and gaur, as well as a few tigers, elephants, Asian black bears and sun bears. Sadly, it is believed the last remaining Javan rhinoceros in mainland Southeast Asia may have been killed by poachers here in May 2010.

The park has 14 excursions and hiking trails, with more under development. The crown jewel of the park is Crocodile Lake (Bai Sau). Getting here involves a drive and a long trek, but it's well worth it for the chance to see some of the park's wildlife, including the Siamese crocodiles that were reintroduced in 2000.

A Lat woman in Lat Village

Southern Highlands

North of Dalat

About a day's drive north of Dalat, the shores of **Lak Lake ❺** (Ho Lak) are inhabited by displaced members of the M'nong tribe. The M'nong (see p.32) have been famed elephant catchers for hundreds of years, although their elephants are now used for tourist rides rather than dragging logs from the forest. A number of villages can be visited by boat. Another local minority group, the Ede, are closely related to the Jarai and were once part of the

Southern Highlands

Champa Kingdom. Today they live in small villages of wooden longhouses (see also page 32). The best Ede village to visit is **Buon Tur**, while **Buon Jun** is inhabited by M'nong. Villagers live in tall longhouses.

Originating from Cu Yang Sin Mountain, the three waterfalls of **Dray Sap, Dray Nur and Gia Long** (daily 7am–5pm; charge) form a 100m (330ft) -wide cascade. They are particularly stunning in the wet season, although Dray Sap and Dray Nur are impressive even in the drier months.

Two hours east of the falls is **Buon Ma Thuot ❻**, the capital of Dak Lak province, as well as the capital of Vietnam's coffee production (For more on the drive from Dalat to Buon Ma Thuot see p.193). Just south of the town centre, on the corner of Le Duan and Y Nong streets, is Dak Lak's **Museum of Ethnology** (Tue–Sun 7.30–11am, 2–5pm; charge), which has one of the country's finest collections of Central Highlands hill-tribe crafts and relics. The collection includes intricate costumes, rice-wine jars, musical instruments and baskets of the K'ho, Ede, Ma, Jarai, S'tieng and Bahnar peoples.

A few **Ede villages** lie at the outskirts of town, such as Ako Dhong, and are worth visiting. Around Ly Thuong Kiet Street are some of the only **craft shops** in Vietnam where authentic crafts of the Central Highlands hill tribe can be purchased.

Drive another hour west and spend the evening inside **Yok Don National Park ❼**, (Vuon Quoc Gia Yok Don, Buon Don District; charge). This 115,545-hectare (285,520-acre) wildlife reserve contains at least 63 species

Dray Sap Waterfall

of mammal and 250 species of bird. More than 15 of these animals are listed as endangered. There are known to be around 50 Asian elephants (including rare white elephants), 10 tigers, giant muntjac, sambar deer, golden jackals, leopards and green peafowl living in the park. Rise early the next morning for an elephant and boat ride. Elephant rides cost $40 for 2hrs and river-boat rides are $20 for 1hr (trekking in the park is also available with a guide, at $15 for 3 hrs). For more on Yok Don, *see p.48*.

Foreigners are not allowed to venture outside the capital, **Pleiku** ❽, or off Highway 14 without signing up for an official bus tour, complete with permit and guide. Most won't spend the night here unless they have an interest in the war-era history (Pleiku hosted an American military base and major battles were fought here). Just north of town, on the east side of the highway, is **Sea Lake** (Ho Bien), a volcanic crater that forms a lake.

Kon Tum ❾ is the capital of the province of the same name, and the most northern city of the Central Highlands. The suburbs are filled with the stilt homes of ethnic Banhar and S'tieng, the thatched roofs of their communal *rong* houses towering above the villages. There are several points of interest in the city, besides the obvious cultural richness, including the beautiful wooden cathedral, French seminary and provincial museum.

Wicker baskets for carrying food to market

🚗 HIGHLAND ROAD TRIP

Spend a couple of days exploring Vietnam's mountainous interior, populated by hill-tribe minorities. With a mild climate and scenery quite unlike the coast of Vietnam, the Central Highlands are well suited to travel by motorbike.

Leave early in the morning from **Dalat**. The first day of driving 156km (96 miles) north on Highway 27 is mostly about enjoying the mountainous scenery through tea and coffee plantations.

Elephant Falls (Thac Voi), 30km (19 miles) southwest of Dalat, is a favourite stop for most tours. It's a bit of a climb down to the bottom of the falls, but natural-looking stairs have been skilfully built into the rocks to make the way easier. A shop above the falls sells attractive hand-woven K'ho blankets and crafts, all made on site.

On your way to your next destination at Lak Lake, you will pass many different kinds of farm specialising in roses and other flowers, mushrooms, silk and black pepper. There are also coffee and tea plantations, and rice-wine distilleries. To visit the latter, it is essential to have a guide as they are not signposted and do not have their own guides to provide tours.

Try to arrive at **Lak Lake** (Ho Lak) in time for dinner at **Lak Resort Floating Restaurant**. This area is inhabited by the M'nong tribe. Spend the night in one of their immense wooden longhouses on the lake (the tour will arrange this). Sleeping is on a mat on the floor, under a mosquito net, and bathrooms are a communal outhouse.

Elephant Falls, near Dalat

Tips

- Distance: 260km (162 miles)
- Time: 2 days
- Start in Dalat, end in Buon Ma Thuot
- The trip may be taken by car or motorbike, ideally with a guide. Dalat's 'Easyriders', is a loose association of motorbike guides (see p. 196). Just stand on the street above Dalat's Central Market and one will find you
- The roads between Dalat and Buon Ma Thuot are not too bad, but watch out for potholes. Petrol stations are frequent, though your guide will probably take care of that for you
- It's a good idea to bring a poncho
- If you are an inexperienced rider, we strongly advise that you get some practice in Dalat before you embark. If you are riding pillion, have your driver do a practice run in town to make sure that you feel comfortable

Ducks at market, Buon Ma Thuot

Rise early the next morning and explore the lake by dugout – a great way to admire the mountain scenery and watch the village kids riding their water buffalo as they swim across the lake. A number of villages can be visited by boat. The best Ede village to visit is **Buon Tur**, while **Buon Jun** is inhabited by M'nong.

After a quick lunch, drive north on Highway 27. At the 22km marker, south of Buon Ma Thuot, take route 690 west to Highway 14. Continue 8km (5 miles) south, then take the marked left turnoff 3km (2 miles) to the entrance of **Dray Sap, Dray Nur and Gia Long waterfalls**. There are toilets and a café at the entrance. Their waters originating from Cu Yang Sin Mountain, the three waterfalls form a 100m (330ft) -wide cascade.

Drive two hours east and arrive at **Buon Ma Thuot**, the centre of Vietnam's coffee production. Have a late lunch at **Thang Loi Restaurant** at 1 Phan Chu Trinh Street.

If travelling with a guide or guides, they will take the motorbike off your hands. If you drive yourself, there will be a pre-arranged drop-off point where you can collect your deposit. Most people doing this tour will take their bags with them (rather than leaving them for collection on return to Dalat).

Longer tours from Dalat (and Buon Ma Thuot) head north through the hills to Pleiku, Kon Tum, Quang Ngai, Quy Nhon, Hoi An and beyond.

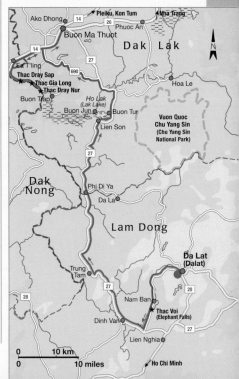

ACCOMMODATION

Dalat has a fine selection of luxury hotels and budget backpacker guesthouses. Most are situated in close proximity to the Central Market or the lake. Elsewhere in the highlands, the selection is limited. Buon Ma Thuat has some larger hotels but other destinations have mainly guesthouses and small, spartan hotels.

Dalat and environs

Evason Ana Mandara Villas Dalat
Le Lai Street
Tel: 063-355 5888
www.mandara-resort.com
The most luxurious resort in Dalat is set in an unlikely, secluded neighbourhood on the southwest side of town. The resort's take on rustic elegance is not lost on the 17 beautifully restored French-colonial villas dating from the 1920s and 1930s. **$$$$$**

Dalat Palace
12 Tran Phu
Tel: 063-382 5444
www.dalatpalace.vn
Dalat's original luxury hotel is the best choice if you want to be transported back to the time of the French colonials. The hotel originally opened in 1922 and, although it was completely renovated in 1995, it still drips with old-world charm and elegance. **$$$$$**

An Evason resort villa

Dreams Hotel
151 and 164B Phan Dinh Phung
Tel: 063-383 3748 and 063-382 2981
Unmatched comfort on the cheap. The natural-wood floors and double-panelled windows (to block off street noise), along with a rooftop jacuzzi, sauna and steam room, make this hotel an incredible bargain. **$$**

Golf 3 Hotel
4 Nguyen Thi Minh Khai
Tel: 063-382 6042
www.vilagolf.vn
Spacious rooms have sunken bathtubs, wood or tiled floors, satellite TV with DVD players, and Wi-fi. The top-floor Sky View Café offers panoramic vistas of the lake and market area. **$$**

Hotel Du Parc
7 Tran Phu
Tel: 063-382 5777
www.hotelduparc.vn
The Du Parc became Dalat's second hotel when it was built in 1932. Located across the street from the Café de la Poste, it offers package deals with the Dalat Palace Golf Club, and shares a number of amenities with the Dalat Palace. **$$$**

Phuong Thanh
65 Truong Cong Dinh
Tel: 063-382 5097
This cosy, family-run hotel is attached to the Groovy Gecko Adventure Tours company and is located in Dalat's backpacker area. The tidy rooms are mostly downstairs and have satellite TV and hot water. **$**

Saigon-Dalat Hotel
2 Hoang Van Thu
Tel: 063-3545 6789
www.saigondalathotel.com
One of the newest upscale options, the government-owned Saigon-Dalat is also one of the city's largest buildings. There are two in-house restaurants and a bar, plus the Moulin Rouge Restaurant across the street. **$$$**

Around the Southern Highlands
Bao Dai Villa
30 Au Co, Lien Son Town (Lak Lake)
Tel: 0500-358 6184
www.daklaktourist.com.vn
Despite being an old vacation home of the last emperor, all six rooms in the Bao Dai Villa have modern comforts and bathtubs. If available, try for the massive King's Room with the monarch's own portraits hung on the walls. **$$**

Damsan Hotel
212–214 Nguyen Cong Tru
Tel: 0500-385 1234
www.damsanhotel.com.vn
Damsan is one of the nicest hotels in town, with a pool, tennis court and large

The Dalat Palace Golf Course

restaurant. Service is good, as is the staff's level of English, and rooms are comfortable. **$$**

Indochine Dong Duong Hotel
30 Bach Dang, Kon Tum
Tel: 060-386 3335
Email: indochinevn@kontumtourism.com
Indochine is perhaps the best hotel in town. The views of the Dak Bla River and mountains from the hotel are fantastic. The rooms are spacious and well appointed. **$**

RESTAURANTS

With a tiny expat community and more domestic than foreign tourists, Dalat has fewer outstanding restaurants catering to foreigners than other tourist destinations in Vietnam. Some of the best street food can be bought in and around the Central Market.

Restaurant price categories
Prices are for a full meal per person, with one drink
$ = under US$5
$$ = $5–10
$$$ = $10–15
$$$$ = over $15

Dalat and environs
Bluewater Restaurant (Thanh Thuy)
2 Nguyen Thai Hoc
Tel: 063-353 1668
Serving a large selection of Chinese and Vietnamese dishes, the food is generally good but most of your money goes towards paying for the restaurant's romantic

atmosphere and excellent service. **$$$**

Café de la Poste
Tran Phu
Tel: 063-382 5444
Set between the Dalat Palace and Hotel Du Parc, this charming French-style café serves a select menu of sandwiches, pasta, Asian

and French entrées. Service is friendly and meals are prepared with great care. **$$$**

Café Nam Huy
26 Phan Dinh Phung
Tel: 063-352 0205
Walking distance from the backpacker district but also frequented by locals looking for bargains, this cosy café has lots of comfortable nooks. Serves great street dishes like *pho* and beef curry. **$**

Dalat Palace Golf Club
Phu Dong Thien Vuong
Tel: 063-382 1201
www.vietnamgolfresorts.com
Set in the original colonial clubhouse, the restaurant serves an eclectic mix of Tex-Mex, Korean, Japanese, Thai and Vietnamese specialities. The home-made chips and salsa, buffalo wings and chicken fingers are all top-notch. **$$$**

Phu Dong
1A/1B Quang Trung
Tel: 063-354 2222
www.nhahangphudong.com.vn
Ambience is the main draw here in this French-style castle. The beautiful stonework, mosaic floors and fountains offer a romantic departure from typical run-of-the-mill Vietnamese restaurants. **$$**

XQ Historical Village
258 Mai Anh Dao
Tel: 063-383 1343
www.xqhandembroidery.com

Fresh food at Dalat Market

Enjoy an exquisite three-course meal of traditional Hue and Dalat dishes for less than US$2. A separate café in the complex serves pastries and desserts. Another XQ restaurant on the top floor of the Dalat Central Market is open on Fridays. **$**

Around the Southern Highlands
Lak Resort Floating Restaurant
Lien Son village, Lak Lake
Tel: 0500-358 6184
In a scenic location on Lak Lake, the restaurant is an ideal spot for lunch or to watch the sunset over a beer or two. The menu includes Vietnamese and a few backpacker favourites. **$$**

Thang Loi Restaurant
Thang Loi Hotel, 1 Phan Chu Trinh, Buon Ma Thuat
Thang Loi is located on the ground floor of the eponymous hotel, overlooking Liberty Square. The menu has a good selection of international and Vietnamese cuisine. **$**

SPORTS, ACTIVITIES AND TOURS

Dalat has some of the best opportunities for adventure activities in the country, including trekking, mountain biking, rock climbing, abseiling and paragliding. Always ask questions before you engage in any risky activity.

Adventure
For road trips through the Southern Highlands, *see p.192*.
'River' Vietnam Easyrider; tel: 098 925-3394; www.vietnameasyrider.com and 'Long', Vietnam Easyriders; tel: 090 920-1075; www.vietnam-easyriders.com.
(Long and River are the names of the guides)

Groovy Gecko Adventure Tours
65 Truong Cong Dinh
Mobile tel: 091-824 8976
www.groovygeckotours.net
Trekking adventures on Langbiang Mountain, mountain-biking, canyoning, abseiling, rock climbing and treks to minority villages.

Phat Tire Ventures
109 Nguyen Van Troi
Tel: 091-843 8781
www.phattireventures.com
Offers many of the same activities as Gecko, with more experience and higher prices.

Vietwings
Mobile tel: 090-382 5607
www.vietwings-hpg.com

Vietwings offers rock climbing, camping and paragliding on Langbiang Mountain.

Golf
Dalat Palace Golf Club
Phu Dong Thiet Vuong
Tel: 063-382 1201
www.dalatpalacegolf.vn
An 18-hole, par-72 championship course.

Tours
Sinh Café Travel
4A Bui Thi Xuan
Tel: 063-382 2663
www.sinhcafevn.com
Tours of local sights around Dalat, as well as 2–4-day trips through the Central Highlands.

FESTIVALS AND EVENTS

Dominated by hill tribes, many of the Central Highland's festivals have ethnic themes or revolve around agriculture and work animals such as elephants and buffalo. Because the region is so ethnically diverse, special events derive from a variety of traditions.

Year-round
Buffalo-Stabbing Festivals
Hill-tribe villages
A festival of ritual sacrifice with music and dance. Check with local tour companies for dates. *(See also p.34)*

Winter–spring
Coffee Festival
Buon Ma Thuat
A food and beverage festival with live shows, celebrating the economic staple of Vietnam's coffee capital.

March–April
Elephant Race Festival
Ban Don Village,
Dak Lak Province
Elephant races are a traditional event for the M'nong tribe. Ethnic music, dancing and drinking of *ruou can* are all part of the festivities.

November–December
Flower Festival
Dalat
This is a week-long festival with parades, street food, games, live music and endless flower markets and flower exhibits.

The Ban Don Village elephant race

★ TEA AND COFFEE

A quintessential Vietnamese experience is to order a baguette and sit down to enjoy some locally produced coffee or tea. You may sit in tiny plastic chairs at a curbside coffee stall watching motorbikes whizz down Saigon's boulevards, or recline on a couch in a chic, new air-conditioned Wi-fi café overlooking rice paddies and water buffalo. Either way, you'll be taking part in a cultural institution dating back to the colonial days.

Coffee and tea are not only a vital part of Vietnam's culture, but also the economy. The country is the world's second-largest exporter of coffee, after Brazil. Its coffee industry is a gift from the French, but it's unclear whether tea growing was bestowed by India or China. Vietnam's Central Highlands, particularly around Buon Ma Thuat, is the primary region for production due to the mild temperatures, rich volcanic soil and high rainfall.

Three coffee beans are grown locally: mocha, robusta and arabica. Beans are allegedly slurred in a mix of rum, fish sauce and butter before roasting, giving them the trademark Vietnamese taste. *Ca phe chon*, a speciality of the highlands, is coffee that has passed – remarkably enough – through the digestive system of civet cats, which removes the outer casing of the beans and instils a rich, earthy taste. The real thing is rare and very expensive.

Café life in Hanoi

Only one type of plant produces all the tea grown in the Central Highlands. Flavours are changed by varying fertiliser, the time of year the leaves are harvested, and the mix of final herbal additives. To make the most expensive brew – Oolong tea – plantation owners use a fertiliser of eggs, honey and fresh milk. At the other end of the price scale, iced tea is an accompaniment to most street food. It's often free, although there may be charges at restaurants, particularly if customers don't order other drinks. It is also offered in cafés, with unlimited free refills, in addition to the ordered drink. Hot, exceptionally bitter tea is offered to guests visiting homes. Green tea is sipped without sugar or milk, although Western-style Lipton tea is served in cafés with a concoction of herbs, spices, citrus and dried, salted fruit.

Cafés serving *café sua da* (iced coffee with sweetened condensed milk) or *café den* (black coffee, usually iced as well) form the centre of Vietnamese social life. It is common, particularly for Vietnamese men, to visit a café at least once a day, even during work hours. Cafés are not just a place for casual social encounters. Business meetings are conducted there, birthday parties celebrated, adulterous love affairs flaunted, and hours spent watching American movies on half-a-dozen different widescreen TVs or surfing the internet. Free Wi-fi in Vietnam's rural cafés became the norm several years before it caught on in the West.

Tea picker at a plantation near Thanh Son, Phu Tho province

Tea and coffee

A group of men enjoy chatting and drinking tea in Hanoi

Ho Chi Minh City and environs

Brasher, more dynamic and younger than the more traditional Hanoi, Ho Chi Minh City is Vietnam's most exciting and sophisticated metropolis, defiantly embracing consumerism and capitalism, but without forsaking its Saigonese charm. Outside the city are the amazing Cu Chi Tunnels and the seaside appeal of Vung Tau.

Population: 7,162,850

Local dialling code: 08

Local tourist office: 23 Le Loi, District 1; tel: 08-3822 5874

Main police station: 161 Nguyen Du, District 1; Dial 113

Main post office: 2 Cong Xa Paris; tel: 08-3829 6555

Main hospital: HCMC Family Medical Practice, Diamond Plaza, 34 Le Duan; tel: 08-3822 7848

Local newspapers/listings magazines: *The Word* Ho Chi Minh City, *Tuoi Tre*

Compared with other cities in Vietnam, **Ho Chi Minh City ❶** (Thanh Pho Ho Chi Minh) is relatively young, celebrating its 300th anniversary only in 1998. It's a loud, vivid, chaotic and mesmerising place, and a highlight of any visit to Vietnam.

Until the 17th century, the site of the present-day metropolis was a thinly populated area of forest and swamps. The settlement of Saigon was officially established in 1698 as a territory and governmental base of Gia Dinh Prefecture. Due to its strategic riverside location, it developed as a trading centre for foreign merchants. Then, over the coming years, Saigon suffered from poor leadership, corruption, demonstrations and coups.

During the American War, Saigon became the nerve centre of US military operations, a place notorious for its sleazy nightlife and rampant corruption. When US troops withdrew in 1973, the chaos escalated. The city came under Communist rule, with the capital in Hanoi, and was renamed Thanh Pho Ho Chi Minh in 1976, after the founder of the modern Vietnamese state.

Only after the late 1980s' *doi moi* ('economic renovation') did the city's fortunes turn. Dynamic and increasingly cosmopolitan, Ho Chi Minh City has wasted no time catapulting itself into the 21st century and is now – by a distance – Vietnam's commercial and economic hub.

The city centre

Although the pain of its strife-torn past remains embedded in the city's psyche, Ho Chi Minh City still clings to its impressive colonial architecture and romantic Gallic-oriental charm, as well as its unique Saigonese identity. Sprawling across 2,090 sq km (807 sq miles), with a population of more than 7 million, this is Vietnam's largest city. The central districts form one of the most densely populated urban areas on earth. The city is divided into 19 urban districts (Quan) plus five outer districts, although the main points of interest are mostly found in Districts 1, 3 and 5.

District 1 is, unsurprisingly, the city centre, where most of the main shops, hotels, restaurants, bars and tourist attractions are located. It contains the original French Quarter, dissected

Night skyline, Ho Chi Minh City

by the city's main tourist magnet, Dong Khoi Street. North and west of District 1, the more sedate **District 3** offers more colonial architecture, parks and wide, tree-lined boulevards interspersed with a few dining and shopping diversions. To the southwest

Mopeds on Nguyen Trai Street

Sundowners

Ho Chi Minh City has some great rooftop bars at which to take in the sunset and while away the evening. Try these two classics after a day of tours:

Rex Rooftop Garden Bar (Rex Hotel, 141 Nguyen Hue Street; tel: 08-3829 2185) has a fifth-floor open terrace that offers bird's-eye views of downtown, and its giant crown, illuminated at night, is one of the city's best-known landmarks. The historic bar is a favourite of expats and visitors alike.

Saigon Saigon Bar (Caravelle Hotel, 19 Lam Son Square; tel: 08-3823 4999) is a rooftop bar that boasts one of the best downtown views in the city. During the American War, it was home to numerous US press corps and was an infamous 'centre of operations' for many war correspondents.

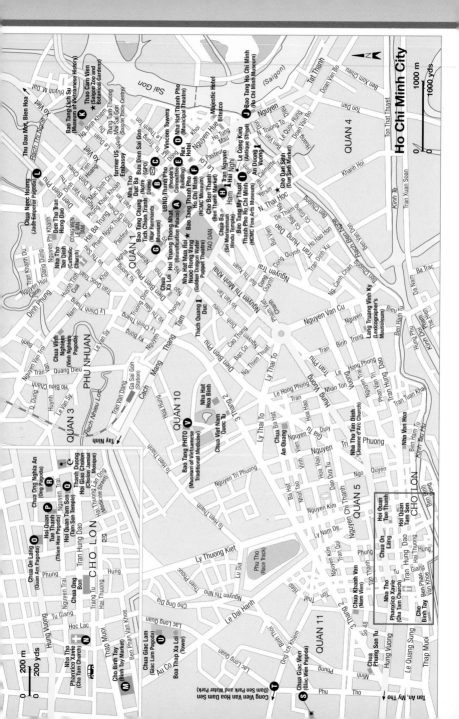

Ho Chi Minh City

Thu Dau Mot, Bien Hoa

Chua Ngoc Hoang
(Jade Emperor Pagoda) **L**

Thao Cam Vien
(Saigon Zoo and
Botanical Gardens) ★

Bao Tang Lich Su
(Museum of Vietnamese History) ★

Sai Gon
(Saigon)

Nha Hat Thanh Pho
(Municipal Theatre)

Majestic Hotel

Bao Tang Ho Chi Minh
(Ho Chi Minh Museum) **K**

Bitexco

QUAN 4

Vincom Towers

Nha Tho
Duc Ba
(Notre
Dame)

Bao Tang Chung
Tich Chien Tranh
(War Remnants
Museum) **G**

UBND Thanh Pho
(People's
Committee
Building) **A**

Bao Tang Thanh Pho
Ho Chi Minh
(HCMC Museum) **F**

Cho Ben Thanh
(Ben Thanh Market) **H**

Hex
Hotel **E**

Bao Tang My Thuat
Thanh Pho Ho Chi Minh
(HCMC Fine Arts Museum) **I**

An Duong
Vuong

Le Cong Kieu
(Antique Street)

Chua Ba
(Sri Mariamman
Hindu Temple)

TAO DAN

Nha Hat Mua Roi
Nuoc Rong Vang
(Golden Dragon Water
Puppet Theatre)

Thich Quang Duc

QUAN 1

Chua Vinh
Nghiem
(Vinh Nghiem
Pagoda)

PHU NHUAN

Ga Sai Gon
(Station)

QUAN 3

Tay Ninh

Lang Truong Vinh Ky
(Lexicographer's
Mausoleum)

Nha Tho Tan Dinh
(Jeanne d'Arc Church)

Nha Hat
Hoa Binh

Chua Viet Nam
Quoc Tu

Bao Tang PHITO

Bao Tang Vietnamese
Traditional Medicine)

QUAN 10

Chua
An Quang

QUAN 5

Nha Van Hoa

CHO LON

Ben Binh
Dong

Hoi Quan
the Thanh

Hoi Quan
Tam Son

Chua On
Lang

Nha Tho
Phanxico Xavier
(Cha Tam Church)

Cho
Binh Tay

QUAN 11

Chua
Phung Son Tu

Chua Giac Vien
(Giac Vien Pagoda) **S**

Cong Vien Van Hoa Dam Sen
(Dam Sen Park and Water Park)

T

Tan An, My Tho

Chua Giac Lam
(Giac Lam Pagoda) **U**

Boa Thap Xa Loi
(Tower)

Nha Tho
Phanxico Xavier
(Cha Tam Church) **M**

Cho Binh Tay
(Binh Tay Market) **N**

Chua On Lang
(Quan Am Pagoda) **O**

Chua Ong
Bon

CHO LON

Hoi Quan
Tue Thanh
(Thien Hau Pagoda) **P**

Hoi Quan Tam Son
(Tam Son Temple) **Q**

Chua Ong Nghia An
(Chua Ong Pagoda) **O**

Thanh Duong
Hoi Giao Cholon
(Cholon Jamil
Mosque) **C**

Medicine Street

0   200 m
0   200 yds

0   1000 m
0   1000 yds

Airport: Tan Son Nhat International Airport is just 7km (4 miles) from the city centre, but the ride into town can take up to 40 minutes. Your best option is an airport taxi, outside both Terminal 1 and Terminal 2. There are no fixed rates, so be sure to establish the fare before departing (expect to pay around US$15 for downtown)

 Taxis: Most are air-conditioned and fares are relatively cheap. The usual flag-fall rate is VND15,000 for the first 1.5km (1 mile), followed by VND9,000 for each additional kilometre travelled. Popular companies include: Mai Linh Taxis (tel: 08-3822 2666); Saigon Tourist (tel: 08-3845 8888); Vina Taxi (tel: 08-3811 1111; Vinasun, tel: 08-3827 2727); and SASCO Airport Taxis (tel: 1800-1565)
Motorbike taxis: The more adventurous may opt for motorbike taxis, known locally as *xe om*. Drivers invariably hang round at most street corners and call out 'Motorbike?'. Most are friendly and speak basic English, although increasingly, many are from the countryside and do not. *Xe om* are a cheap, quick and adrenalin-packed means to beat the traffic jams, but they are more susceptible to accidents

 Cyclos: These were officially banned by the city authorities in 2008, although a few still ply the streets in the backpacker area, Cholon and Ben Thanh Market. It's worth being on your guard – organised rip-offs and thefts are common

 Trains: The main station is at 1 Nguyen Thong, District 3. The ticket office is open daily 7.15–11am and 1–3pm. There are six daily departures to Hanoi

 Boats: A high-speed hydrofoil operates twice daily to Can Tho from the pier at the end of Ham Nghi Street for about US$12. Hydrofoils operating between Ho Chi Minh City and Vung Tau (around 80 minutes) terminate and depart from the Passenger Quay (Ben Tau Khach Thanh Pho), 2 Ton Duc Thang, District 1. Vina Express (tel: 08-3821 4948; www.vinaexpress.com.vn) and Greenlines (tel: 08-3821 5609; www.greenlines.com.vn) operate six departures daily from both cities, 6am–5pm

 Buses: Buses carry a flat-rate ticket of VND3,000 that take you anywhere in the city. The main bus station for local routes is Ben Thanh Bus Station opposite Ben Thanh Market. Useful routes include No. 1 (Binh Tay Market and Cholon Bus Station, Cholon); No. 13 (Cu Chi); No. 45, No. 49 and No. 96 (Cholon); and No. 152 (airport)

Ho Chi Minh City and environs

of the centre is the sprawling **District 5** (which runs into Districts 6, 10 and 11), incorporating bustling Chinatown (Cholon), with its vibrant markets, pagodas and temples, and authentic Chinese restaurants. **District 7** is the most upwardly mobile area of the city, replete with luxurious shopping centres, elite residential areas, expensive boutiques, foreign fast food, and is the favourite playground of Vietnam's rich and famous.

Central District 1
Prominently located in the centre of District 1, at 135 Nam Ky Khoi Nghia Street, is the former Presidential Palace of South Vietnam, now named

The Reunification Palace dates from 1966

the **Reunification Palace**  (Hoi Truong Thong Nhat; daily 7.30–11am, 1–4pm; charge includes guide). To the Communists, this piece of ostentatious excess – sometimes referred to as the Independence Palace – will forever symbolise the decadence of the Saigon regime. In truth, the building itself is a bit of an eyesore – inside and out – and tours are rather lacklustre.

Surrounded by extensive gardens, this concrete monolith stands on the site of the Governor-General of Indochina Residence, or Norodom Palace, which dates back to 1871. The present-day building was inaugurated in 1966 and combines modern and traditional oriental architecture. It functioned as the headquarters of South Vietnam's President Nguyen Van Thieu from 1967 to April 1975.

The building opened as a museum and 'historical relic' in 1990; its multiple floors and nearly 100 rooms resemble a time capsule, with everything left largely unchanged from the moment the North Vietnamese tanks crashed through the front gates, as captured in the iconic photograph seen around the world.

The fascinating bombproof basement yields an eerie warren of tunnels and rooms, including a war command room with original war maps, a communications room and the president's combat-duty bedroom.

Heading northeast and walking across the park, you'll come to Cong Truong Cong Xa Paris (Paris Commune Square) and one of Ho Chi Minh City's most iconic landmarks, **Notre-Dame**  or Cathedral of Our Lady (Nha Tho Duc Ba; 8–11am, 3–4pm; Mass at 5.30am and 5pm Mon–Sat, seven Masses on Sun; free). The French-colonial architect Pavrard designed the neo-Romanesque structure to represent the glory of the French empire and mirror the original Notre-Dame de Paris. Inaugurated in 1880, making it the oldest brick cathedral in Vietnam, this was one of France's most ambitious projects in Indochina at the time; bricks used in the construction were shipped all the way from Marseille.

Adjacent to the cathedral, at 2 Cong Truong Cong Xa Paris, is the **General Post Office** ● (Buu Dien Sai Gon; daily 7am–10pm), an impressive salmon-hued colonial-era building. Also known as Saigon Central Post Office, this is a tourist attraction in its own right, and certainly the loveliest place in Ho Chi Minh City to post a letter or postcard. This classic colonial building appears little changed since its completion in 1891, with green wrought-iron work and arched ceilings.

Running about 1km (½ mile), from Le Duan Street to the Saigon River,

through the heart of District 1, **Dong Khoi Street** (Duong Dong Khoi) is the city's main commercial drag. This wide, tree-lined boulevard is lined with shops, galleries, cafés, luxury hotels and a scattering of historic sights. During French colonial times, it was known as rue Catinat, the elegant epicentre of colonial life. Today, despite its international designer boutiques and upmarket shopping malls, the street still projects a distinctly languid, amiable air.

At the junction of Le Loi and Dong Khoi streets, at **Lam Son Square** (Cong Truong Lam Son), stands the **Municipal Theatre** ● (Nha Hat Thanh Pho). Also called the **Opera House**, it was designed by French architect Ferret Eugène and features a grandiose, neoclassical pink facade, white classical statues and a domed entrance. It was opened in 1899 to keep the French expats entertained. Restored to its former glory to celebrate the 300th anniversary of Ho Chi Minh City in 1998, it received a complete facelift, modern lighting and sound systems, a rotating stage and an 800-seater hall.

Lam Son Square is sandwiched between two historic hotels. The first is the **Hôtel Continental**, dating from 1880. In the early 20th century, this was where the cream of French high society gathered. In the 1950s, the British novelist Graham Greene resided in Room 214, where he wrote much of *The Quiet American*; the hotel and its surrounds find their way on to the pages *(see p.210–11)*.

The General Post Office

Shopping around Dong Khoi Street

The area around Dong Khoi Street in District 1 is great for shopping. Here are a few highlights:

The **Bookazine** (28 Dong Khoi; tel: 08-3829 7455) specialises in rare first-editions, out-of-print books, and original maps from around Indochina. Most books are written in French, but there are also editions in English and Vietnamese.

Khai Silk (107 Dong Koi; tel: 08-3829 1146) is Vietnam's premier silk fashion brand and its most successful boutique chain. The owner is a celebrity designer and mogul of a large empire of shopping centres, resorts and restaurants.

Mystere (141 Dong Khoi; tel: 0084-8382 39615) is no ordinary handicraft shop. Owner Dirk Salewski travels to remote villages, procuring fine garments, bags and textiles with hand-woven designs, unique to each tribe. Rare items include Burmese lacquer, embroidered Laotian quilts, and baskets made by Central Highland hill tribes.

On the opposite side is the extensively rebuilt and glitzy five-star **Caravelle Hotel**. The hotel's older 10-storey wing was home to the offices of the Associated Press, NBC, CBS, the *New York Times* and the *Washington Post* during the American War. The rooftop bar (now the Saigon Saigon Bar) was the favourite watering hole of many war correspondents, some recording the action without ever vacating their bar stools.

Further south down Dong Khoi Street, at the junction of the waterfront Ton Duc Thang Street, stands the aptly named **Majestic Hotel**. Built in 1925 by the French, the Majestic counts as one of Southeast Asia's classic colonial hotels. Despite several extensive renovations and the fact that it is now state-run, the elegant building still radiates an old-world colonial charm.

Situated on Nguyen Hue Street and overlooking both plazas, the

The legendary Rex Hotel

The People's Committee Building, with a statue of Uncle Ho in the foreground

legendary **Rex Hotel** (Khach San Rex) is part of Saigon history. Originally a French garage and American Cultural Centre, it became the headquarters of the US Information Service and home to billeted US servicemen during the Vietnam War. The US military also hosted daily press briefings here, which came to be known as the 'Five o'Clock Follies'. The building only opened as a hotel in 1976, after reunification. The fifth-floor Rooftop Garden Restaurant and Bar, with its amazing views, is a popular tourist haunt, especially for sunset cocktails, while its emblematic giant crown, illuminated at night, is one of the city's best-known landmarks. The Rex was recently upgraded to five-star status.

If the Reunification Palace symbolises the former South Vietnam regime, then the **People's Committee Building** 🇪 (UBND Thanh Pho), at the northern end of Nguyen Hue Street, is one of the strongest symbols of colonial rule. The *hôtel de ville* was completed in 1908, after 16 years of wrangling over its structure and style. Its Baroque yellow-and-white facade encloses an equally ornate interior of crystal chandeliers and wall-sized murals. Now the headquarters of the Ho Chi Minh City People's Committee, visitors are not permitted inside. It is one of the city's loveliest landmarks, and beautifully illuminated at night.

One block west of the People's Committee Building, at 65 Ly Tu Trong Street, is the **Ho Chi Minh City Museum** 🇫 (Bao Tang Thanh Pho Ho Chi Minh; www.hcmc-museum.edu.vn; daily 8am–5pm; charge). Unfortunately, the contents don't do any justice to its magnificent architecture. Completed in 1890, the neoclassical grey-and-white building combines Western and oriental styles. Its faded interiors feature high ceilings, a sweeping staircase and chandeliers. Previously the Revolutionary Museum, its numerous former guises include the

My Lai Massacre exhibit at the War Remnants Museum

Cochinchina Governor's Palace, Gia Long Palace and the Supreme Court; Ngo Dinh Diem stayed here briefly in February 1962 following an air raid on the Presidential Palace.

Spread over two floors, the displays cover aspects of Ho Chi Minh City and southern Vietnam, including natural history, culture, archaeology, economics and history, plus the obligatory revolutionary struggles (1930–75). Underneath lies a network of reinforced bunkers, built by Ngo in 1962. The underground shelter comprises six rooms with 1m (3ft) -thick walls, including a living room and communications centre.

Two blocks north of the Reunification Palace, at 28 Vo Van Tan Street, is the **War Remnants Museum** Ⓖ (Bao Tang Chung Tich Chien Tranh; daily 7.30am–noon, 1.30–5pm; charge). A

Saigon: what's in a name?

When the newly formed Socialist Republic of Vietnam compelled Saigon to take the name of Ho Chi Minh City in 1976, it was like rubbing salt into the wounds of its inhabitants. Yet most locals still defiantly refer to their city as Saigon as a matter of principle (and prefer to call themselves Saigonese). At the very least, people use the name Saigon for downtown District 1, one of the first sectors of the city to be built and the original French Quarter.

Although great measures have been taken – even to this day – to eradicate the Saigon name in most official capacities (some publications, for example, are not allowed to use the Saigon title), it is still, confusingly, allowed to be used in some forms: notably, the river winding its way around the city remains Saigon River, the main city newspaper is the *Saigon Times* and the city's state-owned tour company is Saigontourism. Place names such as Saigon Zoo and Saigon Railway Station are still in use, and the three-letter ticket code for Tan Son Nhat International Airport is SGN.

visit here is a sobering reminder of the heavy toll of war. Occupying the former US Information Agency, this was hurriedly opened as the Museum of American War Crimes after reunification in 1975. Its controversial name was changed in 1997 as part of conditions dictated by the US government over trade pacts.

A series of numbered exhibition halls display the horrors of both the French and American wars; these include graphic photographs, bell jars containing deformed foetuses to show the effects of US-sprayed chemical defoliants, plus a guillotine used by the French and a mock-up of the notorious 'tiger cages' *(see p.139)*. Although the exhibits are distressing to see, this is one of the city's biggest tourist attractions; it's also arguably the quietest, as visitors generally move around in stunned silence.

Southern District 1

A few blocks southeast, at the intersection of Ham Nghi, Le Loi, Le Lai and Tran Hung Dao streets, is the city's well-known **Ben Thanh Market** ⓗ (Cho Ben Thanh; daily 6.30am–6.30pm). Opened in 1914 by the French and covering some 11,000 sq m (118,400 sq ft), its distinctive pillbox-style clock over the main entrance tower on Le Loi Street has become a well-known city emblem. Under one roof is practically every conceivable product, sold at countless stalls located along narrow alleys leading off a main central aisle.

Predominantly still a market for locals, selling basic necessities such as household wares, fabrics and foodstuffs, Ben Thanh is increasingly geared towards the lucrative tourist market, with some specialist goods on sale.

Ho Chi Minh City and environs

Ben Thanh Night Market

THE QUIET AMERICAN

Relive some of the sights, smells and sounds of Graham Greene's classic novel, *The Quiet American*. The contrast between 1950s Saigon, as depicted in the book, and the modern city makes for an excitingly diverse walking tour.

Read *The Quiet American* before setting out. Begin at the **Majestic Hotel** (1 Dong Khoi Street). In the early 1950s, covering Vietnam's struggle for independence from France, British war correspondent Graham Greene lived in Suite R404, where he wrote a significant proportion of the novel.

Turn left out of the Majestic and walk up **Dong Khoi Street**, away from the river. In the early 1900s this boulevard was known as rue Catinat, edged with

fashionable boutiques, cafés and theatres. It's still the city's main commercial thoroughfare. Running across it is **Mac Thi Buoi Street**, previously Rue d'Ormay, where one of the notorious opium dens of which Greene's protagonist, Fowler, was so fond was to be found.

Continuing up Dong Khoi, you'll arrive at Lam Son Square (Cong Truong Lam Son), on the corner of Le Loi Boulevard. Formerly place Garnier, this was the setting of General Thé's terrorist bombing in *The Quiet American*. Opposite was the Girval Café, where Greene's Phuong stopped for her 'elevenses', or afternoon tea. The entire block is now under renovation to become a new shopping centre.

On the northern side of the square, the colonial **Hôtel Continental** no longer has the famous Continental Shelf Café, where Fowler sipped vermouth cassis. Graham Greene wrote much of *The Quiet American* here, residing in Room 214.

Continue up Dong Khoi Street and you'll pass the sparkling **Vincom Towers** shopping plaza. Straight ahead is the **Notre-Dame Cathedral** (Nha Tho Duc

Praying at night, Notre-Dame Cathedral

Tips

- Distance 5.7km (3½ miles)
- Time: A full day
- Transport by taxi and motorbike is available, as well as cyclo (though the last is not recommended for safety)
- While on the street, beware of bag-snatching thieves and 'friendly' strangers (con artists) inviting you for coffee or dinner at their house

The view from the Rex Hotel Rooftop Bar towards the People's Committee Building

Ba), described by Greene as 'the hideous pink Cathedral' in the aftermath of the bombing at place Garnier. The salmon-hued building to the right is the **General Post Office** (Buu Dien Sai Gon), another impressive colonial-era edifice.

Head back to Lam Son Square and look to the northern end of Nguyen Hue Street for the lavish **People's Committee Building** (UBND Thanh Pho). Formerly the French administrative headquarters, this is one of the city's loveliest landmarks.

Turn into **Nguyen Hue Street**, then right into Hai Trieu and continue until you reach the former **American Legation**, on the corner of Ham Nghi and Ho Tung Mau streets. This block was where the character Pyle conducted his nefarious affairs close to Mr Muoi's bomb factory. On the other side of Ho Tung Mau is the new **Bitexco Financial Tower**. At 68 storeys, it is currently the tallest building in Vietnam. Be sure to take the elevator to the top for spectacular 360°

views of the cityscape.

Further up on your right, **Ton That Dam Street** was originally the location of Greene's 'Thieves Market'. Now, this neighbourhood is a centre for the burgeoning trade in pirated DVDs and electronics. Finally, round off the day with a cocktail back at the **Rex Hotel Rooftop Garden Bar**.

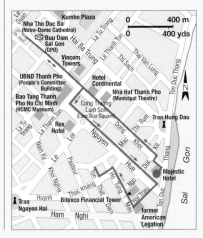

Thanh Pho Ho Chi Minh; Tue–Sun 9am–5pm; charge). It is divided into three sections: the ground floor features a changing collection of contemporary works by Vietnamese and foreign artists, while the first floor has a permanent collection of Vietnamese art, mostly oils, charcoal drawings and lacquer works, plus bronze sculptures – many with war themes. An open balcony displays several statues. The second floor features ceramics (19th–20th century), carved wooden funeral statues (early 20th century), plus sculptures from the Champa (7th–16th century) and Oc Eo (4th century BC to 7th century AD) civilisations.

Across from the Fine Arts Museum, narrow **Le Cong Kieu Street** (Duong Le Cong Kieu) has long been known as 'Antique Street'. One of the city's most atmospheric streets, the row of narrow, open-fronted dwellings along this small stretch are devoted to selling a

Once the main market shuts for the day, the **Ben Thanh Night Market** springs into action, operating until late along the streets immediately surrounding the building. The main attraction is the open-air makeshift food stalls serving authentic and inexpensive Vietnamese fare.

On the other side of the intersection, at 97A Pho Duc Chinh Street, is the **Ho Chi Minh City Fine Arts Museum ❶** (Bao Tang My Thuat

Yesterday and today

During colonial times, Cholon was a dangerous area, rife with gangsters and Communist revolutionaries. Some, though, found it a glamorous, fascinating place; Graham Greene spent time here, allegedly sampling the opium dens. Today it is an atmospheric blend of ancient Chinese temples, 19th-century shop-houses, busy markets and a few modern developments.

With France's departure in 1954, rue Catinat was renamed Tu Do (Freedom Street) and during the Vietnam War,

degenerated into a sleazy street lined with raucous bars and clubs. Following unification in 1975, the street was renamed Dong Khoi (Popular Uprising).

Cholon has changed a great deal but it's still wise to exercise caution here. Be wary of anyone who casually approaches you on the street and invites you for coffee or to their home to meet their family. The dangers may seem obvious, but a local mafia stalks tourist dollars at attractions in this part of the city.

chaotic jumble of Vietnamese, Chinese and Cham 'relics' and 'antiques' (most of which are reproductions), furniture and home-decor items.

The striking **Ho Chi Minh Museum**  (Bao Tang Ho Chi Minh; Tue–Sun 7.30–11.30am, 1.30–5pm; charge) is easily visible just across the bridge in District 4, where Ben Nghe Canal (Rach Ben Nghe) enters the Saigon River. Oriental dragons slithering across the rooftop explain its alternative name, Dragon House (Nha Rong). One of the first buildings constructed by the French in Cochinchina (the French designation for the southern third of Vietnam, with Saigon as its capital) in 1863, this was originally the head office of a French shipping company. It was from this wharf that Ho Chi Minh, using his real name, Nguyen Tat Thanh, left Vietnam in 1911 on a French merchant ship for 30 years of self-imposed exile. Fittingly, in 1979, the renovated building became a museum dedicated to the life, revolutionary activities and legacy of Vietnam's first president. There are over two floors of photographs, documents, artefacts and Ho's personal items.

Northern District 1

At the end of Le Duan Street, along Nguyen Binh Khiem Street, is the **Museum of Vietnamese History**  (Bao Tang Lich Su; Tue–Sun 8–11.30am, 1.30–5pm; charge), housed in another stunning example of French-Chinese hybrid architecture, with a distinctive pagoda-style roof. Formerly the Musée Blanchard de la Brosse under French rule, the museum today gives an excellent

Ho Chi Minh City and environs

Antique store, Le Cong Kieu Street

The Jade Emperor Pagoda

introduction to Vietnamese history and culture from prehistory to the founding of the Democratic Republic in 1945.

A small, attached outdoor theatre, **Saigon Water Puppets** (Mua Roi Nuoc Saigon; Tue–Sun; charge) presents six half-hourly water performances. There is also a museum on site.

One of the city's most colourful and captivating places of worship is the **Jade Emperor Pagoda** ❶ (Chua Ngoc Hoang; daily 8am–5pm; free), located on Mai Thi Luu Street, on the northern fringes of District 1. Built in 1909 by Cantonese Buddhists who settled in Saigon, its unique interior architectural style is heavily influenced by southern Chinese elements. A dense fog of smoke from spiral incense coils suspended from the rafters envelops a fascinating array of weird and wonderfully elaborate statues – some Buddhist, others Taoist-inspired. The ornately robed Jade Emperor surveys the main sanctuary

from his central altar. To the left, the Hall of Ten Hells features intricately carved wood reliefs portraying the fate awaiting those sentenced to the diverse tortures found in the 10 levels of hell. The front courtyard has a pond containing numerous tortoises, explaining the pagoda's other name, **Tortoise Pagoda** (Phuoc Hai Tu).

Cholon (Chinatown) and beyond

About 5km (3 miles) west of downtown, Ho Chi Minh City's sprawling Chinatown, or Cholon, is infused with a subtle Chinese ambience, given a unique twist by the scattered remnants of French colonial architecture. 'Cho Lon' translates as 'big market', and commerce is what still drives this frenetically industrious district today – a hive of non-stop retail and wholesale activity. The area is undergoing considerable change and, unfortunately, some historical Chinese shop-houses and colonial edifices are being demolished. Nonetheless, it is still a fascinating and authentic working and living area, offering the visitor bustling markets and commerce, excellent Chinese food and richly decorated Chinese temples and pagodas.

Central Cholon

Binh Tay Market (Cho Binh Tay; daily 6am–7pm), at 57A Thap Muoi Street, is Cholon's biggest market and epitomises the vibrant commercialism of the neighbourhood. Built in 1928, its exterior is a fine example of early 20th-century Chinese-influenced French architecture: oriental-style multi-tiered roofs stalked by serpentine dragons blend with distinctive French mustard-yellow walls and a clock tower with four clock faces. Although predominantly a wholesale market, Binh Tay is far less commercialised than Ben Thanh Market, and thus offers a more authentic cultural experience. Spread over a vast 17,000 sq m (183,000 sq ft) on two levels, the market is divided into organised sections, with more than 2,300 stalls.

Several blocks northeast of the market, at 25 Hoc Lac Street, is the Catholic **Cha Tam Church** (Nha Tho Phanxico Xavie; daily 8am–6pm; free). Although built in classic French style, it has a pagoda-style entrance gate. Cha Tam is infamous as the place where the Catholic president of South Vietnam, Ngo Dinh Diem, and his brother took refuge on 1 November 1963 after fleeing Gia Long Palace during a coup sanctioned by the US government. Having surrendered, they were assassinated on their way to central Saigon. A small plaque on a rear pew indicates where Ngo awaited his fate before being escorted away.

The adjacent **Tran Hung Dao Street** is the main artery linking Cholon to the city centre. This street's western section is known as 'garment district' due to its continuous

Ho Chi Minh City and environs

Binh Tay Market

Thien Hau Pagoda

succession of open-sided garment workshops and wholesale warehouses stacked with rolls of fabric.

Heading east along Tran Hung Dao Street and then north along Luong Nhu Hoc Street takes you to **Quan Am Pagoda** ⑨ (Chua On Lang or Chua Quan Am; daily 8am–5pm; free), located on minuscule Lao Tu Street. This is one of the city's most visually stunning pagodas. Built in 1740 by Chinese Fukien immigrants, it's also probably the oldest.

Dedicated to the Goddess of Mercy (Quan Am), not surprisingly, the two statues of Quan Am dominate. In fact, a total of 16 deities are worshipped here, many festooned with flashing fairy lights in the large open court-yard area at the back. Constantly busy with worshippers, the burning paper votive offerings and hanging spiral incense coils result in a permanent smoky haze. The pagoda is a heady riot of red and gold, with decorative details and striking relief murals. The show-stopper is the entrance, its ridged roof and wall edged with exquisite ornamental glazed-ceramic figurines and sculptures.

South along Nguyen Trai Street, at No. 710, is **Thien Hau Pagoda** ⑩ (Hoi Quan Tue Thanh; daily 8am–5pm; free), one of Cholon's most important pagodas. Cantonese immigrants established this temple-pagoda in 1760, dedicating it to Thien Hau (Tin Hau), the Goddess Protector of Seafarers, and giving thanks for a safe passage across the perilous East Sea (Bien Dong). Images of the temple's patron are found throughout, but mainly at the back of the second open-air courtyard, where three statues of Thien Hau stand one behind the other.

A festival in Thien Hau's honour is held here in March, on the 23rd day of the lunar calendar. Thien Hau is also known as the **Women's Pagoda** (Chua Ba) because local women make offerings and prayers to Me Sanh, the Goddess of Fertility, and Long Mau, the Goddess of Mothers and Babies, statues of whom are displayed on other altars.

Diagonally across from Thien Hau, at 118 Trieu Quang Phuc Street, is the **Tam Son Temple** Ⓠ (Hoi Quan Tam Son; daily 8am–5pm; free). Built by Fukien migrants in the 19th century, this temple is far less elaborate in terms of architecture and sees fewer tourists. It is noteworthy for attracting a constant flow of women, who come here in search of blessings to improve their chances of conceiving children.

Back on Nguyen Trai Street, at No. 678, is Thien Hau Pagoda's counterpart, **Ong Pagoda** Ⓡ (Chua Ong Nghia An; daily 8am–5pm; free), also known as the Men's Pagoda. An intricately carved wooden boat stands over its entrance and a statue of Quan Cong (a famous Chinese military general), with a ruddy face, long black beard and ornate regalia, presides over the main altar.

The almost minimalist blue-and-white **Cholon Jamial Mosque** (Thanh Duong Hoi Giao Cholon; daily 8am–5pm; free), nearby at 641 Nguyen Trai Street, contrasts sharply with the area's riotously decorative Chinese pagodas and temples. It was built by Tamil Muslims, most of whom fled the country around 1975. This is one of only eight mosques in the city.

Head south down Trieu Quang Phuc Street to get to **Hai Thuong Lan Ong Street**, or 'Medicine Street'. This lengthy street is named in honour of Lan Ong, an 18th-century physician, mandarin and master of Vietnamese herbal medicine. Shops specialising in traditional Chinese and Vietnamese medicine have long proliferated here; nowadays they are mostly concentrated in the eastern section of the street. The old, open-fronted shophouses, some of which date back to French colonial times, are stocked full of curious concoctions purported to cure all sorts of ailments.

Further west and north

From Cholon head north to District 11, where a bright red-and-yellow entrance gate at 247 Lac Long Quan Street will lead you down a long alley to the **Giac Vien Pagoda** Ⓢ (Chua Giac Vien; daily 8am–5pm; free). Built

French-colonial buildings in Cholon

in 1803, within its dimly lit and cluttered interiors, enveloped in a joss-stick haze, are 153 beautifully carved wooden statues, with many Buddhist and Taoist deities located on the multi-tiered altar in the main sanctuary. The front hall has rows of old dark-wood tables, flanked by funerary tablets and time-worn photographs of the deceased. The pagoda has a refreshingly tranquil feel and does not see too many tourists.

Bordering Giac Vien Pagoda, and in complete contrast to it, lies the enormous **Dam Sen Park** ❼ (www.damsenpark.com.vn; daily 7.30am–10pm; charge). One of the largest theme parks in Vietnam, it covers 50 hectares (124 acres) of landscaped parkland and offers an array of attractions for families, including a roller-coaster and giant Ferris wheel. There is also a boating lake, crocodile farm, and bird and animal enclosure.

Part of the sprawling grounds is given over to **Dam Sen Water Park** (03 Hoa Binh, District 11; www.damsenwaterpark.com.vn; Mon–Sat 8.30am–6pm, Sun 8am–7pm; charge; access at a separate main entrance next to Dam Sen Park). It offers a multitude of exhilarating water-based fun rides and slides, including the Kamikaze Ride and Black Thunder.

Heading further north into Tan Binh District, about 7km (4 miles) from downtown, at 118 Lac Long Quan Street is **Giac Lam Pagoda** ❿ (Chua Giac Lam; daily 8am–6pm; free). It is recognised as the city's second-oldest pagoda and an important

historical site. Dating from 1744 and reconstructed in 1909, Giac Lam's design reflects the typical architectural style of pagodas in south Vietnam. The large complex incorporates several sections, including monks' living and study quarters. Although larger than Giac Vien and receiving more visitors, there are many similarities between the two mustard-hued pagodas. Giac Lam is supported by 98 carved ironwood pillars, inscribed with gilded Nom characters. Among its dark, well-worn interiors are around 113 statues, some over 250 years old.

Heading east, back towards the city centre, at 41 Hoang Du Khuong Street in District 10, is the **Museum of Vietnamese Traditional Medicine** ❦ (Bao Tang FITO; www.fitomuseum.com; Mon–Sat 8.30am–5.30pm; charge), a refreshing alternative to the usual war- and Ho Chi Minh-themed offerings. The building alone is worth a visit, a remarkable replica of a traditional northern house, complete with dark-wood interiors and authentic furnishings. Over six floors and 18 exhibition rooms, the origins and chronology of time-honoured traditional Vietnamese medicine are explained.

Outside Ho Chi Minh City

The area surrounding Ho Chi Minh City encompasses a variety of landscapes and some worthwhile sights. To the northwest are the flat plains that contain the tunnels of Cu Chi and the town of Tay Ninh, the birthplace of the Cao Dai cult. The coastline to the east is lined with sandy beaches, extending from Vung Tau through Phan Thiet.

The Cu Chi tunnels and Tay Ninh

Located 70km (44 miles) to the northwest of Ho Chi Minh City is **Cu Chi** ❷ (daily 7am–5pm; charge), famous for its extensive network of underground tunnels. The tunnels were first used by the Viet Minh against the French in the 1940s, and later became hide-outs for the Viet Cong, who reportedly extended the labyrinthine network until it reached beneath the Mekong Delta headquarters of the US Army's 25th Division.

From these hiding places, the Viet Cong were able to spring devastating surprise attacks on their enemies. The earth through which the tunnels burrowed is red clay, well suited to this kind of excavation. To avoid detection, the soil that had been removed was often dumped in bomb craters, rice fields or the Saigon River. The Americans often used trained dogs to sniff out the tunnels, but the Viet Cong would deflect them by scattering pepper at the tunnel entrances and vents. It is said that they would even use the same soap as Americans to confuse the dogs. The tunnels are a

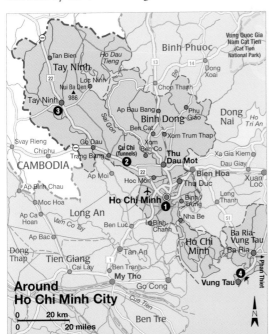

Squeezing into the Cu Chi Tunnels

vivid testament to the ingenuity and perseverance that eventually helped to win the war against the vast technical superiority of the Americans.

Further to the northwest, Highway 22 passes through Tay Ninh province before continuing on to Cambodia. From 400BC to AD600, this area belonged to the powerful Funan Empire, before being absorbed into the Chen La kingdom, the forerunner of the Khmer kingdom. In the early 18th century, the Nguyen Lords defeated the last of the Champa people here and assumed control.

During the war against the French, Tay Ninh was a hotbed of anti-colonial sentiment, and in the 1950s, a hero of the armed resistance forces made Black Lady Mountain (Nui Ba Den) his hide-out. The mountain went on to become an important strategic point of bloody confrontations in the war against America.

Tay Ninh's greatest attraction is found approximately 100km (60 miles) northwest of Ho Chi Minh City, in the township of **Tay Ninh** ❸ itself. Here, in all its resplendent gaudiness, stands the **Cao Dai Great Temple** (Thanh That Cao Dai). Founded in 1926 by Ngo Minh Chieu, Cao Dai followers believe that all major world faiths offer pieces of the truth, but that Cao Daism arose in a third age to unite them all. While Cao Dai borrows saints and divinities from other religions and philosophies, it is principally a repackaging of Buddhism, Confucianism and Taoism, with a new liturgy and leadership hierarchy.

Most tours arrive at the temple for the noon prayer ceremony, though there are also daily ceremonies at 6am, 6pm and midnight. Followers in their colourful ceremonial gowns cut striking figures in their

Worshippers at the Cao Dai Holy See

The Jesus statue above Vung Tau

star-studded vaulted ceiling and dragon-entwined pillars. The ceremony is usually completed in less than 30 minutes, after which visitors are free to explore the temple.

South to Vung Tau

The port city of **Vung Tau** ❹ is situated 125km (80 miles) southeast of Ho Chi Minh City, on a peninsula straddling two mountains, **Nui Nho** (Small Mountain) and **Nui Lon** (Big Mountain), with some of the most stunning coastal scenery anywhere in Vietnam. It's a popular weekend getaway, despite falling out of favour in the past decade with foreign visitors, who prefer the charms of Phan Thiet further down the coast.

At the far end of the peninsula, perched on top of Nui Nho, is a 30-metre (100ft) **statue of Jesus**, arms outstretched to the sea and reminiscent of the Christ the Redeemer statue in Rio de Janeiro, Brazil. The statue was erected by the Americans in 1971. Park your vehicle

procession towards the altar, entering from opposite sides. On the outside, a large eye symbolising the religion guards the entrance. The interior is fantastical, with a blue,

Ho Chi Minh City and environs

The Cao Dai Holy See

In the 1920s, Ngo Van Chieu formed the Cao Dai religion, following a revelation of 'The Way' in a dream. In 1926, one of his followers, Le Van Trung, deserted with 20,000 disciples, crowned himself 'Pontiff' and built the Cao Dai Temple at Tay Ninh, north of Saigon. Graham Greene described the temple as 'a Walt Disney fantasia of the East'. Seven years later, Le Van Trung was deposed for embezzling the temple funds.

Cao Daism seeks to create the ultimate religion by fusing Buddhist, Taoist, Confucian and Catholic beliefs into a synthesis of its own. Today, around 3 million Vietnamese still follow the Cao Dai way, but sermons by 'planchette' – séances that used to be held to contact 'saints' such as Sun Yat Sen and Victor Hugo – are no longer practised. Tourists flock to the bizarre cathedral, and the 'joke gone too far' (according to Greene) seems set to endure.

at the foot, on Ha Long Street, and hike up the path for about 30 minutes for incredible views of the coast.

Many locals enjoy an evening stroll up the other side of Nui Nho via Hai Dang Street (across from the wharf) for unmatchable views of **Front Beach** (Bai Truoc), **Back Beach** (Bai Sau) and the cityscape between. Back Beach is the only sizeable sandy beach around the city. It is largely denuded of trees but is still a pleasant – albeit somewhat urban – place to swim and sunbathe.

Taking both left-hand forks on Hai Dang Street will lead about 1km (½ mile) to the very top of the mountain and the blinding-white **Vung Tau Lighthouse** (daily 7am–5pm; free), originally built by the French in 1910. Taking the left and then a right fork will lead you to an **abandoned military bunker** dating from the same period. You can freely explore the crumbling fort (at your own risk). Tree roots have begun to tear away at the walls like a mini version of Ta Prohm at Angkor.

A popular evening hike leads you up Big Mountain via Vi Ba Street, past numerous Buddhist and Daoist temples, as well as another devoted to Cao Dai. Big Mountain's top landmark is **Villa Blanche** (Bach Dinh; Tran Phu Street; daily 7am–5pm; charge), built at the end of the 19th century by French Governor-General Paul Doumer. Emperor Thanh Thai was held there for some time before his exile to Reunion Island in 1909. Later it became the residence of presidents Ngo Dinh Diem and Nguyen Van Thieu. Set above a forest of frangipani, today it houses ceramics and other items recovered from a Chinese junk, shipwrecked off the Con Dao Islands in 1690.

Like many coastal towns in southern Vietnam, Vung Tau has a fishermen's temple devoted to whale worship, **Lang Ca Ong** (also referred to as Dinh Than Thang-Tam, the Whale Temple; daily 8am–5pm; free). Dating from 1911, it is situated on the corner of Hoang Hoa Tham and Xo Viet Nghe streets, halfway between Front and Back beaches.

In this region, whales are revered by local fishermen, who see the mighty creatures as man's saviour from the perils of the high seas. Whales are depicted in beautiful murals with dragons and sea monsters, and skeletons of beached whales are displayed in glass cases.

Looking east from Big Mountain, Vung Tau

ACCOMMODATION

Ho Chi Minh City's District 1 has a staggering number of hotels, with many in the international 5-star category. At the other end of the spectrum, budget-priced accommodation is mostly concentrated in the backpacker neighbourhood surrounding De Tham, Pham Ngo Lao and Bui Vien streets.

Central Ho Chi Minh City

Caravelle Hotel
19 Lam Son Square
Tel: 08-3823 4999
www.caravellehotel.com
The 5-star Caravelle is one of the city's most celebrated hotels. A glitzy 24-floor edifice, the original low-rise wing was famously home to foreign press corps during the American War. **$$$$$**

Hotel Continental Saigon
132–134 Dong Khoi
Tel: 08-3829 9201
www.continentalvietnam.com
The antithesis of Ho Chi Minh City's slick and modern downtown hotels, the charming, historic Continental has a to-die-for location. Today state-run, this 1880s colonial-era hotel seems to have scarcely changed since Graham Greene was holed up in Room 214.
$$$$$

Elios
233 Pham Ngu Lao
Tel: 08-3838 5585
www.elioshotel.vn
Located in the heart of the backpacker district, this 3-star hotel has slightly higher standards than others in this price category. The rooftop restaurant-bar offers good views. Elios also has a gym, meeting rooms and a lift. **$$**

Lavender Hotel
208–210 Le Thanh Ton
Tel: 08-2222 8888
www.lavenderhotel.com.vn
A much-needed new boutique hotel in this price category, the Lavender Hotel has established itself as a firm favourite for its stylish, intimate ambience and great pricing. All of the rooms are nicely decorated. **$$$**

Hotel Majestic
1 Dong Khoi
Tel: 08-3829 5517
www.majesticsaigon.com.vn
This 1925-built historic landmark is one of Southeast Asia's classic colonial hotels. State-run, it still radiates an old-world charm, with dapper bellboys, violinists serenading at afternoon tea and a grand marbled lobby with chandeliers and stained-glass skylights. **$$$$$**

Hotel Metropole
148 Tran Hung Dao
Tel: 08-6295 8944
www.metropolesaigon.com
The Metropole is one of the most reliable and popular 3-star options in Ho Chi Minh City, with the added benefit of friendly service. Features include a gym, conference centre, small rooftop pool and snooker room. **$$$**

Ordinary Bed and Breakfast
25 Dong Du
Tel: 08-3824 8262
Email: info@ordinaryvn.com
The innovative creation of a Vietnamese-American owner-designer, this is anything but ordinary. A boutique hotel in a narrow five-storey townhouse, it seamlessly blends Indochinese furnishings with modern comforts such as a pleasant coffee bar and well-appointed rooms. **$**

Park Hyatt Saigon
2 Lam Son Square
Tel: 08-3824 1234
www.parkhyattsaigon.com
Overlooking the Municipal Theatre, this
5-star hotel boasts some of the best service
standards in Vietnam. The rooms feature
colonial touches such as four-poster beds
and modern amenities such as huge flat-
screen TVs. **$$$$$**

Renaissance Riverside Hotel Saigon
8-15 Ton Duc Thang
Tel: 08-3822 0033
www.renaissancehotels.com/sgnbr
Located downtown along the river, this
Marriott-managed 5-star offers high
standards with a boutique-style vibe and
exceptionally friendly service. Highlights
include the 22nd-floor rooftop-terrace
pool, elegant 5th-floor Atrium Lounge and
excellent Chinese restaurant. **$$$$**

Sheraton Saigon Hotel and Towers
88 Dong Khoi
Tel: 08-3827 2828
www.sheraton.com/saigon
The original 23-floor hotel has consistently
been an award-winning favourite. The
25-floor Grand Tower next door has 112
sophisticated studios and suites serviced by
a personal butler. **$$$$$**

Sofitel Plaza Saigon
17 Le Duan
Tel: 08-3824 1555
www.sofitelplazasaigon.com
Opened in 1998, this is one of the city's
newest 5-star establishments. Stylish, contemporary flair extends from the stunning
atrium-style lobby to the sleek rooms and
suites. Facilities include a rooftop pool, plus
a an excellent fitness centre and ground-
floor Martini bar. **$$$$**

Chinatown/Cholon and around
Windsor Plaza Hotel
18 An Duong Vuong
Tel: 08-3833 6688
www.windsorplazahotel.com

Sheraton Saigon Hotel and Towers

Marking Cholon's boundary, this 25-floor
4-star offers an astounding array of facilities including a casino, Vietnam's largest
nightclub, a three-floor shopping plaza and
several food and beverage outlets, including
a rooftop restaurant-cocktail lounge with
spectacular views. **$$$$**

Outside Ho Chi Minh City
Hoa Binh Hotel
210D 30/4 Street, Tay Ninh
Tel: 066-382 7306
Right in the centre of town, this Soviet-era
concrete place has simple but clean rooms
with air conditioning, hot water and TV.
Walking distance from the Cao Dai Temple. **$**

Grand Hotel
2 Nguyen Du, Vung Tau
Tel: 064-385 6888
www.grand.oscvn.com
A bar, restaurant, café and nightclub are all
on site, and a buffet breakfast is included
in the rate. The apartments are perfect for
small families. **$$$**

Rex Hotel
01 Le Quy Don, Vung Tau
Tel: 064-385 2135
www.rexhotelvungtau.com.vn
The Rex offers immaculate rooms with
beautiful wooden furniture and some of the
best views of Front Beach. Rooms include
whirlpool bathtub, air conditioning and
satellite TV. **$$**

RESTAURANTS

Ho Chi Minh City is indisputably Vietnam's culinary capital, with a diverse range of both Vietnamese and international cuisines served at its many restaurants. The city's economic boom and growing expat population has created the demand for a cosmopolitan range of culinary choices and chic eateries in which to sample them.

Central Ho Chi Minh City

Banh Xeo
46A Dinh Cong Trang
Tel: 08-3824 1110
The house speciality is *banh xeo* – crispy folded pancakes stuffed with pork, bean sprouts and shrimp – cooked over open fires out front. Other Vietnamese dishes are served, too. This place is wonderfully animated at night-time. **$**

Barbecue Garden
135A Nam Ky Khoi Nghia
Tel: 08-3823 3340
www.barbecuegarden.com
Clay pots with coals are set on each table so that you can barbecue your own skewered meats (pork, beef, chicken and seafood) and vegetables, best eaten wrapped in ricepaper with fresh herbs. **$$$**

Ben Thanh Night Market
Phan Boi Chau and Phan Chu Trinh streets
Makeshift eateries are assembled at this open-air night market outside Ben Thanh Market to serve up a huge selection of good-value Vietnamese fare. Dishes include noodle soups, seafood crêpes and fruit salads. **$–$$$**

Black Cat
13 Phan Van Dat
Tel: 08-3829 2055
Black Cat is a sanctuary of Western comfort food, and particularly renowned for its excellent burgers. The menu also features pizza, Indian and Tex-Mex food and their famous fruit shakes made from local and hard-to-find imported fruits and sorbets. **$$**

Com Nieu Saigon
6C Tu Xuong
Tel: 08-3932 6388
Com Nieu is popular for its clay-pot fragrant rice (*com nieu*) and the entertaining spectacle of waiters smashing pots and throwing the extracted contents across the room. **$$$**

Quan An Ngon
138 Nam Ky Khoi Nghia
Tel: 08-3825 7179
Quang An Ngon is popular with both local Vietnamese and expats. At around 5pm, folding tables and chairs roll out on to the pavement to create a temporary smorgasbord of Vietnamese seafood and popular cuisine and ice-cold beer. **$$**

The Refinery
74 Hai Ba Trung
Tel: 08-3823 0509
This period French-style bistro is housed in a restored opium refinery, set off the street behind the Opera House. The menu is contemporary European and includes homemade ice-creams and excellent weekend brunches. **$$$$**

Sandals Restaurant and Bar
93 Hai Ba Trung
Tel: 08-3827 5198
Part of the Sailing Club empire in Vietnam, Sandals provides intimate and elegant dining in an oasis amid the clamour and bustle of downtown Saigon. The interesting menu has seafood and Vietnamese fusion dishes as well as some Middle Eastern specialities. **$$$$**

Square One
Mezzanine, Park Hyatt Saigon,
2 Lam Son Square
Tel: 08-3520 2357
www.saigon.park.hyatt.com
The menu includes simple yet top-notch
Western and Vietnamese dishes that are
grilled, steamed and wok-fried in front
of diners. Steaks and seafood are house
specialities. After dinner, head to the
Hyatt's classy 2 Lam Son Bar.
$$$$

Temple Club
29–31 Ton That Thiep
Tel: 08-3829 9244
Housed within a former Hindu pilgrim
guesthouse, the refined interiors evoke old
Saigon. This is a good restaurant to head to
for a special occasion requiring a romantic
atmosphere. **$$$$**

Xu Restaurant-Lounge
71–75 Hai Ba Trung
Tel: 08-3824 8468
www.xusaigon.com
Ultra-sleek Xu serves contemporary Vietnamese fusion cuisine, true to its roots yet
with an international twist, such as tuna
spring rolls with mango salsa. The menu
also includes traditional Vietnamese and
Western dishes. **$$$$**

Wrap & Roll
62 Hai Ba Trung
Tel: 08-3822 2166
www.wrap-roll.com
Vietnamese street food in somewhat
sanitised and tourist-friendly surroundings.
Vietnamese spring rolls (ready-made or
roll-your-own) are the house speciality, plus
salads, hotpot meals and the sweet bean
desserts called *che*. **$**

Chinatown/Cholon and around

La Camargue
191 Hai Ba Trung
Tel: 08-3520 4888
Renowned French fine-dining venue with
a romantic ambience. Expect classic
French and Mediterranean cuisine with
Asian accents – think duck confit samosas
with balsamic and shallot dipping sauce.
Extensive wine selection and immaculate
service. **$$$$**

Tib
187 Hai Ba Trung
Tel: 08-3829 7242
www.tibrestaurant.com
This cavernous restaurant specialises in
authentic imperial Hue cuisine, such as
tiny rice pancakes with shredded shrimp.
Decorated in traditional imperial style and

Xu Restaurant-Lounge

set in a colonial villa. Reservations are essential. **$$$$**

Outside Ho Chi Minh City
Good Morning Vietnam
6 Hoang Hoa Tham, Vung Tau
Tel: 064-385 6959
www.thegoodmorningvietnam.com
Expect consistent quality from the original outlet of a chain of authentic Italian restaurants. Pizzas are its claim to fame, but its breads (free with every meal), pastas and meat dishes are exceptional, too. **$$**

Ma Maison
Petro House, 63 Tran Hung Dao, Vung Tau
Tel: 064-385 2014

www.petrohousehotel.com.vn
Billed as a gourmet restaurant but really serving American comfort food. The pizza, burgers, soups and salads are all good. The setting, in an elegant house, helps to make Ma Maison a favourite of expats and businessmen. **$$$**

Sea Song
163 Thuy Van, Imperial Plaza, Vung Tau
Tel: 062-362 6888
This rooftop restaurant, complete with its own garden and stream, overlooks Back Beach from the new Imperial Plaza. Specialises in seafood, but the *bo xao mi* (stir-fried beef with egg noodles) is the best ever. **$$**

NIGHTLIFE

Downtown Ho Chi Minh City has many hip, cosmopolitan bars that keep the burgeoning ranks of expats, business travellers, tourists and moneyed locals happy. Its club and bar scene is getting better every day, although very fickle, with clubs opening, closing and losing favour on a regular basis.

Apocalypse Now
2B Thi Sach, District 1
Tel: 08-3825 6124
This long-running institution is by turns adored, despised – and occasionally shut down.

Bounce
4/F, Parkson Saigontourist Plaza, 35–45 Le Thanh Ton, District 1
Tel: 08-3824 8555
Resident DJs play the latest sounds, including hip-hop, to keep dancers happy on the compact dance floor.

Gossip Club
79 Tran Hung Dao, District 1
Tel: 08-3824 2602
Located near the backpacker district, this is the city's largest, most popular dance club.

Lush Saigon
2 Ly Tu Trong, District 1

Tel: 08-3824 2496
The most cosmopolitan of Saigon's dance clubs, the lower-level hip-hop-, R&B- and House-fuelled dance floor is always crowded.

Q BAR
7 Lam Son Square, District 1
Tel: 08-3823 3479
www.qbarsaigon.com
Ensconced in the Opera House, the long-established, cavernous Q Bar features Renaissance-inspired murals, contrasting leopard-print couches and ultraviolet-lit bars.

2 Lam Son
Park Hyatt Saigon, 2 Lam Son Square, District 1
Tel: 08-3824 1234
Intimate booth seating is available for small groups, or luxurious lounging for larger groups on the balcony above.

ENTERTAINMENT

Ho Chi Minh City is the centre of modern Vietnamese pop culture but has a much smaller traditional arts scene than the political and cultural capital, Hanoi. The majority of venues in Ho Chi Minh City are located in District 1 and have irregular performance schedules.

Sax n' art club

Performing arts venues
Ho Chi Minh City Conservatory of Music
112 Nguyen Du, District 1
Tel: 08-3824 3774
www.hbso.org.vn
Southern Vietnam's centre for classical (Western) music training; occasional classical-music concerts are hosted here.

IDECAF
31 Thai Van Lung, District 1
Tel: 08-3829 5451
www.idecaf.gov.vn
Ho Chi Minh City's French Cultural Centre hosts a variety of performing-arts events.

Sax n' art
28 Le Loi, District 1
Tel: 08-3822 8472
www.saxnart.com
This premier jazz and blues club is a suave, intimate venue.

Traditional Vietnamese theatre
Tran Huu Trang
136 Tran Hung Dao, District 1

Tel: 08-3836 9718
Traditional Vietnamese theatre integrates music, singing, dance, recitation and mime, and here's where to enjoy it.

Water puppetry
Saigon Water Puppets
History Museum, 2 Nguyen Binh Khiem, District 1
Tel: 08-3823 4582
www.saigonwaterpuppets.com
Part of Vietnam's cultural heritage, this is a delightful must-see, especially for children. Performances (25 minutes) Tue–Sun 9am, 10am, 11am, 2pm, 3pm and 4pm.

Cultural dinner shows
Binh Quoi Tourist Village
1147 Binh Quoi, Binh Thanh District
Tel: 08-3556 6020
www.binhquoiresort.com.vn
Riverside gardens are the venue for a show of song and dance from a traditional wedding plus an elaborate Vietnamese dinner.

TOURS AND ACTIVITIES

City-based tour operators (and some hotels) in Ho Chi Minh City all offer standard half-day city tours that take in the key sites, plus day tours that cover the historic Cu Chi Tunnels and Cao Dai Temple. Other organised activities are somewhat limited.

Speciality tours
Art Discovery Tours
Tel: 08-3898 6835
www.helenehagemansfineart.com

Resident art historian Helene Hagemans leads small group tours (maximum 10) to galleries, museums and artists' studios.

Mekong Delta Cruises, Bassac Boat (TransMekong)
Tel: 071-382 9540
www.transmekong.com
Operates two large, luxurious wooden boats designed like rice barges, with en suite cabins and all mod cons.

Mekong Eyes Cruise
Tel: 071-546 0786
www.mekongeyes.com
Two-day boat cruises on a traditional rice barge, with en suite cabins.

Vespa Tours
169a De Tham St, District 1
Tel: 012-2299 3585
www.vietnamvespaadventures.com
This American-owned outfit runs personalised, small-group five-day tours on classic Vespas through southern Vietnam.

Golf
Vietnam Golf and Country Club
Long Thanh My Ward, District 9
Tel: 08-6280 0103
www.vietnamgolfcc.com
Vietnam's first 36-hole golf club; two challenging, championship 18-hole courses.

Water parks
Dam Sen Water Park
3 Hoa Binh, District 11
Tel: 08-3858 8418
www.damsenwaterpark.com.vn
Ho Chi Minh City's premier water park, with numerous exhilarating water slides, including Kamikaze Ride and Twister Space Bowl.

FESTIVALS AND EVENTS

Since Ho Chi Minh City is the centre of commerce and culture in the south, it is also one of the best places to observe national festivals, both religious and secular. Exclusively local festivals feature prominently Buddhist and Chinese themes.

January–February
Nghia An Hoi Festival
Ho Chi Minh City
Celebrated by ethnic Chinese, the festival honours Quan Cong, an ancient hero.

Nui Ba Den Festival
Tay Ninh
A pilgrimage festival to the Buddhist temple on Ba Den Mountain, just outside Tay Ninh.

April–May
Thien Nau Festival
Ho Chi Minh City
Celebrated by ethnic Chinese on the birthday of Thien Hau at her eponymous temple.

Whale Festival
Known as both *Lang Ca Ong* and *Cau Ngu*, it is celebrated in Vung Tau and other southern fishing communities around the middle of the third lunar month.

September–October
Le Van Duyet Tomb Festival
Ho Chi Minh City
A pilgrimage festival honouring a military leader who served under the Nguyen Dynasty.

A procession during Tet

⭐ FRENCH INFLUENCE

It is difficult to overstate the importance of French influence in the development of Vietnam. The most obvious legacies include cuisine and architecture, but the French have also had a large part to play in the development of language, religion, law, medicine and education, and the preservation of ancient Champa art and monuments. Their final, crucial contribution has been to help to create the concept of Vietnamese national unity.

The unmistakably French veneer that makes this corner of Southeast Asia so distinctive is perhaps most immediately apparent in the food. As well as pâté and baguettes, the French introduced tea and coffee, and the culture that surrounds them *(see p.198)*. Furthermore, they bestowed Vietnam's appetite for dairy products (unique at the time for Southeast Asian countries), in the form of butter, yoghurt, ice cream, condensed milk and custard tarts. They also brought potatoes, a key ingredient in Vietnamese curries and stews.

Sadly, French-colonial architectural treasures are quickly disappearing, as older monuments are torn down due to the Vietnamese love of all things new. Still, Ho Chi Minh City, Hanoi, Dalat, and the old quarters of many river towns and sea ports have a few remaining French villas, shop-houses and administrative buildings.

The French introduced and perpetuated Catholicism in Vietnam, which has had a significant impact on both the ethnic Vietnamese and the hill tribes. Catholic-Buddhist tensions were a significant political motivator during the war, and current land-rights issues continue to erupt under the banner of Catholicism.

Grand Theatre, Haiphong – a fine example of French-colonial architecture

It was a French Jesuit priest, Alexandre de Rhodes, who developed the first Portuguese-Vietnamese-Latin dictionary in 1651, and in its course, he is credited with developing the modern Vietnamese script in current use today (the Vietnamese previously used modified Chinese characters).

Perhaps most importantly, however, it was the colonisation by the French that drove Vietnam towards national unity. Before they arrived, the country was a divided nation of warlords, but the colonisers helped to bring the final Nguyen Dynasty to power, and in so doing unified north, central and southern Vietnam for the first time. The Mekong Delta had previously been Khmer territory, and until that time, the provinces of Dong Nai, Binh Thuan and Ninh Thuan were the last vestiges of Cham autonomy. The French performed a similar role in neighbouring Cambodia and Laos, over which Vietnam continues to exert considerable influence.

Unification was also furthered by the French exploration of the Central Highlands, hitherto the exclusive domain of hill tribes. Alexandre Yersin *(see p.171)*, a French doctor, is credited with founding the city of Dalat. It was Yersin who discovered the cause of the bubonic plague, and he was instrumental in medical advances to treat tropical diseases in Vietnam, particularly malaria.

Of course, the French, through their imperialism, inspired a final reactionary push towards national unity and revolt against the French, under the banner of Communism.

Baguettes on sale in Danang (the city known as Tourane by the French)

French influence

Notre-Dame Cathedral, Ho Chi Minh City

The Mekong Delta

Known as 'Vietnam's rice bowl', the Mekong Delta is a region of stunningly green fields, orchards, sleepy villages and colourful floating markets, interspersed by countless canals fed by the mighty Mekong. It's a wonderful place to explore by boat. With Cambodia to the west, local life is strongly influenced by Khmer culture.

Mekong Delta transport

 Getting around the Mekong Delta is simple enough, but there are no large, regional transport companies, unlike the open tour-bus operators that cover the rest of Vietnam. Many travellers get nervous about the absence of a well-developed transport infrastructure and thus opt for 2-day and 3-day package tours, arranged with tour companies in Ho Chi Minh City. Yet it really is very easy to travel independently in the Delta

 Airports: Both Phu Quoc and Con Dao have small airports. Flights normally connect via Ho Chi Minh City

 Ferries: Almost every town has a dock or port of some kind where ferry tickets can be purchased to other localities along the river. All of the destinations in this chapter will have local agents (often working at the front desks of hotels and guesthouses) who can also book these tickets for guests

 Buses: Most towns in the delta have a bus station serviced by small buses and vans, situated near the central market. Vehicles – regular buses and privately-run minibuses – arrive and depart regularly throughout the day

The vast **Mekong Delta** is formed as the Mekong River fans out and deposits alluvium along its many smaller channels, creating a fertile, watery landscape of vivid green padi fields punctuated by scattered small towns. The Vietnamese name for the Mekong is Song Cuu Long, the River of Nine Dragons, in reference to the nine principal tributaries that make up the delta.

This mighty waterway descends from its source in the arid heights of the eastern Tibetan Plateau and follows a 4,500km (2,800-mile) course through China, Myanmar (Burma), Laos, Thailand, Cambodia and southern Vietnam before emptying into the sea. The delta region covers almost 40,000 sq km (15,400 sq miles) and is populated by Khmer, Chinese and Cham, as well as Vietnamese people, all of whom practice different faiths.

An improving road network serves the delta's 13 provinces. Until recently, the locals largely relied on ferries to get around, but these days only a handful remain. Even so, the river and its network of tributaries carry a busy and greatly varied flow of traffic, and exploring some of the narrow waterways by boat is a key part of any trip to the delta *(see p.27–9)*.

The Southeastern Delta

The southeastern quarter of the delta – encompassing the provinces of Tien Giang, Ben Tre, Vinh Long, Tra Vinh, Can Tho and Soc Trang – is renowned for its floating villages and island orchards. One of the most enjoyable ways to experience this part of the country is to take an evening boat trip through the many canals, and enjoy fried fish, frog's legs and other local cuisine, all at the laid-back pace of the Mekong lifestyle.

My Tho to Ben Tre

A two-hour drive some 70km (43 miles) south from Ho Chi Minh City will bring you to **My Tho ❶**, the

Rural scene near Ba Chuc, near Chau Doc and the Cambodian border

The morning market at My Tho

sleepy capital of **Tien Giang province**. Situated on the left bank of the My Tho River (Song My Tho), the northernmost branch of the Mekong, the town was founded in 1680 by political refugees fleeing China at the end of the Ming dynasty. My Tho's busy **Central Market** on Trung Trac and Nguyen Hue streets is a great place to flex your bartering skills and haggle over succulent fruits plucked fresh from the trees.

Criss crossed by many small canals, **Ben Tre province** has perfect conditions for rice-growing, but is also prone to flooding during the rainy season – the pancake-flat area is only 1.25m (4ft) above sea level. Competing with the extensive rice fields are coconut plantations: more coconut palms are grown in Ben Tre than in any other province in the country. The provincial capital, **Ben Tre ❷** ('Bamboo Boat Port'), is 10km (6

The Mekong Delta

miles) from the My Tho ferry dock on the Ham Luong tributary, and is named after the little wooden vessels that used to dock there. A boat trip along the Ba Lai–Ham Luong waterway is the ideal way to get a feel of everyday life on the river. Beehives and orchards are scattered around and can be reached by the network of small canals that incise the landscape.

Vinh Long to Tra Vinh

West of Ben Tre province and 66km (41 miles) from My Tho is Vinh Long ❸, one of the better-known towns in the delta. The main reason people come here is to explore the nearby islands. Boats leave regularly from in front of the Cuu Long Hotel for trips to **Cai Be Floating Market** and the islands of **An Binh** and **Binh Hoa Phuoc** (*see p.29*). One of the appealing experiences of a boat trip is visiting the small villages with their gardens and orchards, and sampling the variety of luscious tropical fruit that they produce.

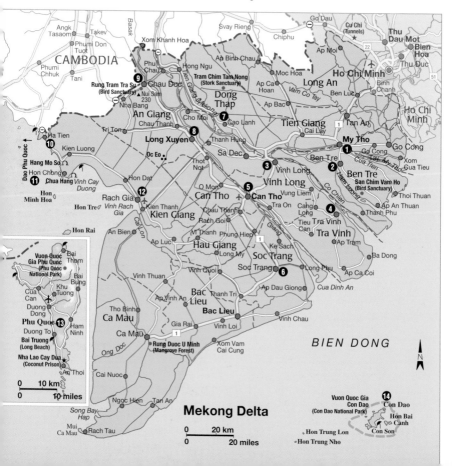

Cai Rang floating market, near Can Tho

Situated around 40km (25 miles) southwest of Ben Tre, **Tra Vinh province** is bordered by the Tien and Hau rivers and over 65km (40 miles) of coastline. Well removed from the tourist trail, leafy, sleepy **Tra Vinh** ❹ is arguably the delta's prettiest town, locally nicknamed Go Do, the 'City in the Forest', in reference to its ancient trees. Around a third of Tra Vinh's 96,000-strong population are ethnic Khmer, who make their living from farming. There are a total of 140 Khmer pagodas dotted around the province.

Can Tho to Soc Trang

Can Tho ❺ is the capital of the eponymous province and the largest and most modern city in the delta, with a population of 1.2 million. Situated 34km (21 miles) southwest of Vinh Long, on the banks of the Hau River (Song Hau), this is an important commercial centre and river port, bustling with energy.

As the hub of the Mekong Delta, Can Tho is a prosperous and vibrant city, and an enjoyable place to stroll around and soak up the atmosphere, although there are few sights of interest. The city's **Central Market** is the largest fruit market in the Mekong Delta region, and although the main building is at the intersection of Hai Ba Trung and Nam Ky Khoi Nghia streets, the market hustle stretches the length of Hai Ba Trung Street. Several restaurants on the waterfront serve specialities of the region: frog, turtle, snake and many kinds of fish. The **Can Tho Museum**, at 1 Hoa Binh Street (daily 8–11am, 2–5pm; free), has exhibits detailing local history.

Boat trips on the Hau River are one of the highlights of Can Tho, and it's probably the best place in the Mekong Delta to do a tour of the fascinating floating markets. *(For more on boat trips, see p.29).*

To the south of Can Tho, **Soc Trang province** is home to around 300,000

The Mekong Delta

Kh'leng Pagoda, Soc Trang

Khmer people. Its capital, **Soc Trang** ❻, has a number of interesting Khmer temples and pagodas, the most striking of which is the luridly painted **Kh'leng Pagoda** (daily 8am–5pm; charge). Originally built more than 400 years ago, it was reconstructed in 1907 and is richly decorated on the outside with carved griffins, snakes and statues of dancing maidens. Inside, a gilded bronze statue of Sakyamuni Buddha presides over the main altar. There are about two dozen monks in residence and 170 monks attending the Buddhist College on the premises. The ancient dharma (Buddhist scripture), written on palm leaves, is one of the pagoda's most treasured relics.

The Northern and Western Delta

The western delta offers a chance to explore the way of life of local Khmer and Muslim Cham communities. There are also several notable beaches on the west coast, popular with domestic tourists. International visitors are more likely to fly direct from Ho Chi Minh City to Phu Quoc Island, with its beautiful beaches and lush forests, just off the coast from Hon Chong.

Dong Thap province

Bordering Cambodia in the north, **Dong Thap province** is one of the three provinces lying in the marshy area known as **Dong Thap Muoi** ('10 Tower Field'). The province takes its name from the 10-storey **Thap Muoi** tower that was built in ancient times in the commune of An Phong. The tower, which no longer stands today, was used as a lookout by the resistance forces against the French during colonial times. The area is populated primarily by people of Chinese, Khmer, Cham and Thai origin.

The provincial capital of Dong Thap province, **Cao Lanh** ❼ has

Ethnic and political tensions tend to make it something of a taboo subject in Vietnam, and one that the state is keen to gloss over, but the Mekong Delta once belonged exclusively to the Khmers.

The ethnic Vietnamese are something of an outsider community in the region. Besides the Khmers and Chinese (or Hoa), the Cham are the other common minority in the Mekong. The Cham Bani of the Mekong practice an ancient form of Islam blended with indigenous traditions of their cousins, the Cham Balamon of Binh Thuan and Ninh Thuan provinces. The Cham Islam culture of the Mekong is more recent, with modern influences from communities in Malaysia, Indonesia and the Middle East.

some interesting sights around it. About 1km (½ mile) south of the town is the **grave of Nguyen Sinh Sac**, Ho Chi Minh's father. About 20km (12 miles) southeast, and accessible only by boat, is **Rung Tram**, a forested area that harboured an underground Viet Cong camp called **Xeo Quit Base** (daily 7am–5pm; charge) during the American War. For nearly 15 years, key Viet Cong personnel lived here in underground bunkers while planning strategic attacks against the American forces.

An Giang province

To the west, **An Giang province** ('Splitting River') borders the Cambodian province of Takeo. Here, the Mekong splits into two branches, forming the Tien and Hau rivers, which every year deposit millions of cubic metres of alluvial soil in the adjacent areas.

This prosperous region, intersected by numerous natural canals and small rivers, is rich in natural resources and fertile land, and produces many varieties of fruit tree

Waterway near Long Xuyen

★ FESTIVALS

Festivals in Vietnam are a time of fun and plenty. In fact, the country is a great place for festival lovers. Colourful celebrations, most with a strong Chinese cultural influence, take place throughout the year, although the most interesting are in spring and autumn. Common elements in traditional festivals include temple visits, offerings to ancestors or tutelary gods, costumes, dragon and lion dancing, music, parades – and lots of food.

Vietnam has a vast number of traditional religious and cultural festivals. Some are celebrated across the country, but each province, and often each village or temple, may have its own unique calendar of events. All traditional Vietnamese festivals occur according to the lunar calendar (a gift from the Chinese), and a few dates may be altered according to messages from sacred oracles (or the local Communist 'People's Committee' governing board).

Cham and Khmer groups, as well as many hill tribes, set festivals according to their own lunar calendars as well.

The biggest and most important celebration of the year, Tet Nguyen Dan, usually shortened to 'Tet', heralds the start of the Vietnamese Lunar New Year. The first three days of the new year are the most important, although ceremonially the holiday lasts for two weeks. The whole country shuts down for about a

A street vendor sells lanterns in Hanoi during the Mid-Autumn Festival

The Vietnamese light incense and votive paper money to honour their ancestors

week. Everyone returns home for the holidays, including many overseas Vietnamese. The most interesting time for visitors is actually the week prior to the holiday, when night markets are even more animated than usual, and candy, flower and lantern vendors are much in demand. Tet eve is celebrated with fireworks and dragon and lion dancing.

The best time to observe village festivals is just after Tet. During the first two lunar months (February and March), most villages organise a fête of some sort. Families will visit the village pagoda and light incense to local deities and their ancestors. Youngsters play games, swinging on giant bamboo swings or playing 'human chess' with people or metre-high models moving between squares marked on a courtyard.

Villages near the Red River, in northern Vietnam, send boats to collect ceremonial water to offer to the water god, Ha Ba. The most spectacular of these traditions is the lion dance, when young men don elaborate costumes and dance energetically among the revellers to the sound of beating drums. One of the most popular of these occasions is the Quan Ho festival at Lim village, near Hanoi. Here, young couples sing love songs to each other in a fertility rite to welcome the spring, a tradition that goes back to ancient times.

For a long list of festivals (including many region-specific events) and precise dates, check www.vietnamtourism.com; see also p.14–15.

Performing a lion dance

and crops of rice, soya bean, tobacco, groundnut and mulberry. It is also known for its silk industry.

An Giang province's capital, **Long Xuyen** , located in the east of the province 190km (118 miles) from Ho Chi Minh City and just 45km (28 miles) from the Cambodian border, is a thriving commercial town, the streets lined with cafés and chock-a-block with motorbikes. The town's name refers to the shape of the river and literally means 'dragon running through'. Home to over 300,000 people, the predominant industries here are rice production and the processing of fish (mainly catfish) for export, which have made the town the second-most prosperous town in the delta after Can Tho.

At 77 Thoai Ngoc Hau Street is the small **An Giang Museum** (Bao Tang An Giang; daily 7.30–10.30am, 2–4.30pm; charge). Displayed here are a few exhibits on the ancient city of Oc Eo (*see p.55*), as well as personal effects of Ton Duc Thang, the first president of the Socialist Republic of Vietnam) and pictures of the town in the 1930s. The site of **Oc Eo** is around 40km (25 miles) southwest of Long Xuyen but there is very little to see.

A stone's throw from the Cambodian border, Long Xuyen is situated on the right bank of the **Hau Giang River** (Song Hau Giang) and is the usual entry or exit point for people doing a boat tour between Ho Chi Minh City and the Cambodian capital Phnom Penh via Chau Doc.

With a population of 100,000, **Chau Doc** , close to the Cambodian border, has a lively feel and there is plenty to see and do on day trips from the town. It is also

Fish-farm house, Chau Doc

must obtain their visa (in Ho Chi Minh City, not at the border) before entering Cambodia. Forests, plains, offshore islands and a 200km (125-mile) coastline make Kien Giang the delta's most geographically diverse and scenic province.

Nestling in a bend of the **Gian Thang River** (Song Gian Thang), close to where it enters the Gulf of Thailand, is the town of **Ha Tien ⑩**, with a diverse population of 120,000 ethnic Vietnamese, Cham, Khmer and Chinese. Only 10km (6 miles) from the Cambodian border, the lovely beaches and karst outcrops attract many visitors on their way to or from Cambodia.

To the east of Ha Tien, scenic **East Lake** (Ho Dong) – actually a sea

renowned for its quaint floating villages. Living in houses built over empty metal tanks to keep them afloat, many villagers make a living from fishing. Nearby is the Buddhist pilgrimage site of **Sam Mountain** (Nui Sam), surrounded by the tranquil bird sanctuary of Rung Tram Tra Su *(see panel, right)*.

Kien Giang province

Kien Giang province, in the southwest of the Mekong Delta, shares a common border in the northwest with Cambodia, with the warm waters of the Gulf of Thailand to the west. The border crossing from Ha Tien into Kampot in Cambodia is now open, but would-be travellers

241

The Mekong Delta

Sam Mountain

The focal point of the 230m (755ft) -high Sam Mountain (Nui Sam) is the temple of Ba Chua Xu, dedicated to the 'Lady of the Region'. According to legend, a young woman had a vision of the Buddha here, instructing her to build a temple at the site. Buddhist and Taoist shrines scatter the slopes, visited by ethnic Chinese and pilgrims from Vietnam and abroad. The vast bird sanctuary of Rung Tram Tra Su, covering 845 hectares (2,088 acres), is along the road to Sam Mountain, around 30km (19 miles) southwest of Chau Doc. This area around the Hau River is a protected forest reserve, home to over 70 species of bird, notably the Indian crane, which is exceptionally rare.

inlet – is the first sight to greet visitors arriving from Cambodia. The town itself is renowned for its fresh seafood and trademark black-pepper plantations.

The road from Ha Tien southeast to the provincial capital, Rach Gia, is generally good, and passes many small farms and picturesque villages. About 20km (12 miles) from Ha Tien, a detour off the main road in Ba Hon leads to the appealing seaside town of **Hon Chong** ⓫, in an area studded with impressive limestone towers. The best beach in the area is **Duong Beach** (Bai Duong), which takes its name from the *duong* (casuarina) trees growing beside it. It's a pleasant place, with clear water and attractive surroundings.

Kien Giang's provincial capital, **Rach Gia** ⓬, about 100km (60 miles) southeast of Ha Tien, is an active fishing port with a population of around 220,000, and is bordered by marshlands, many of which have been drained for rice cultivation. Well known for its seafood, Rach Gia has a few interesting temples and pagodas, but does not offer as much as other delta towns; it's mainly used as a jumping-off point for travellers taking the ferry or plane to Phu Quoc Island.

The Islands

Of all of Vietnam's Islands, Phu Quoc and the Con Dao Archipelago have the greatest potential for tourism. While Phu Quoc has begun to

see some activity and development, Con Dao remains pristine and relatively undeveloped.

Phu Quoc

Vietnam's largest island, **Phu Quoc** ⓭ lies about 45km (28 miles) west of Ha Tien and forms part of Kien Giang province. In 1869, the French occupied the island, establishing rubber and coconut plantations, and also a notorious prison. During the American War, the South Vietnam government reopened the penal centre and incarcerated nearly 40,000 Viet Cong between 1969 and 1972.

For tourists the principal reason for visiting is the island's almost uninterrupted fringe of beautiful white-sand beaches washed by clear waters. **Dai Beach** (Bai Dai) in the northwest

The beach at Hon Chong, looking out to a limestone pinnacle characteristic of the area

Long Beach, Phu Quoc

offers the perfect vantage point to enjoy the sunset, while remote **Thom Beach** (Bai Thom) in the northeast is usually deserted. **Long Beach** (Bai Truong) runs 20km (12 miles) along the western side of the island and is where most of the resorts are located. Other paradisiacal stretches of sand are found on **Star Beach** (Bai Sao) and **Cream Beach** (Bai Khem), 25km (16 miles) from Duong Dong town on the far southeastern coast.

Established in 2001 in the hilly northeastern part of the island is **Phu Quoc National Park** (Vuon Quoc Gia Phu Quoc). The highest of the 99 peaks on the island, **Pagoda Mountain** (Nui Chua) is part of the nature reserve. Little, however, is yet known about the biodiversity of the park's 37,000 hectares (91,427 acres) of lowland evergreen forest, which covers two-thirds of the island. Check with your hotel about jungle trekking tours of the reserve.

Con Dao

Once a feared prison known as 'Devil's Island', **Con Son Island**, the largest of 15 islands that make up the **Con Dao Archipelago** ⓮, is now the heart of a national park famous for its hawksbill and green marine turtles, as well as the dugong, a distant aquatic relative of the elephant. Few tourists make it out here, but it is well worth the effort. Con Son is mountainous and covered in rainforest, with great hiking trails for viewing the local wildlife. The best information source is the **National Park Headquarters** (www.condaopark.com.vn; 7–11.30am, 1.30–5pm) at 29 Vo Thi Sau Street. There are several beautiful beaches on Con Son – such as **Bai Dat Doc Beach** and **Bai Nhat Beach** – and also on some of the smaller islands, like **Bai Canh**, which is also an important nesting area for turtles between May and September.

ACCOMMODATION

Most of the accommodation in the Mekong consists of small, independent hotels and family-run guesthouses. However, a few luxury hotels do exist, namely the Victoria hotels and resorts and the Saigon Tourist chain establishments on Phu Quoc and Con Dao islands.

Accommodation price categories

Prices are for a standard double room in peak season:

$ = under US$20
$$ = $20–50
$$$ = $50–100
$$$$ = $100–150
$$$$$ = over $150

The Southeastern Delta

Cuu Long Hotel
02 Phan Bui Chau, Vinh Long, Vinh Long
Tel: 070-382 3656
www.cuulongtourist.com
Comprises two blocks, A and B: the latter is newer. All rooms are spacious with modern facilities and en suite bathrooms, and command views over the river. **$$**

Ham Luong Hotel
200C Hung Vuong, Ben Tre
Mobile tel: 090-812 0818
www.hamluongtourist.com.vn
New hotel with comfy rooms tastefully decorated in cream and wood. The open roof commands great views of the river, and there is a swimming pool. Also has billiards table and karaoke. **$**

Ngoc Suong Hotel
Km 2127, 1A Road, An Hiep, My Tu, Soc Trang

Tel: 079-361 3108
This 3-star hotel is Soc Trang's most upscale option, with well-appointed rooms, an inviting restaurant serving local and foreign food, and a large, clean swimming pool. **$**

Tra Vinh Palace
3 Le Thanh Ton, Tra Vinh
Tel: 074-386 4999
Modelled on a French villa, this pink-painted property is Tra Vinh's best option. The main building comprises 10 spacious, high-ceilinged rooms, with another 12 in a nearby annexe. **$**

Victoria Can Tho
Cai Khe Ward, Can Tho
Tel: 071-0381 0111
www.victoriahotels-asia.com
This elegant colonial-style resort lies on the banks of the Hau River. Located close to town but tucked away from the action, all the well-appointed rooms feature furnishings that blend traditional handicrafts with colonial-style design. **$$$$$**

The Northern and Western Delta

Dong Xuyen
9A Luong Van Cu, Long Xuyen
Tel: 076-394 2260
www.angiangtourimex.com.vn
Located in the centre of town, these are Long Xuyen's most upscale lodgings, and a favourite of travelling businesspeople. Bright and modern, all the rooms have en suite bathrooms, air conditioning and satellite TV. **$$**

Victoria Can Tho

Ha Tien Hotel
36 Tran Hau, Ha Tien
Tel: 077-385 1563
Centrally located near the market and waterfront, this is the town's most modern and smart hotel. Rooms have carpeted floors, tasteful wooden furnishings and soft lighting. **$**

Victoria Chau Doc
1 Le Loi, Chau Doc
Tel: 076-386 5010
www.victoriahotels-asia.com
Built in the traditional French, low-rise architectural style, with tastefully decorated wooden-floored rooms. The swimming pool, restaurant and spa are excellent, and most rooms have river views. **$$$$**

The Islands
Mango Bay
Ong Lang Beach, Phu Quoc
Tel: 077-398 1693
www.mangobayphuquoc.com
Mango Bay is a truly back-to-nature experience. There is no air conditioning, TV or telephone in its bungalows, which are made of packed earth. The resort occupies a

Mango Bay

sprawling site, with two splendid beaches and protected forest at its doorstep. **$$$**

Saigon-Con Dao Resort
18 Ton Duc Thang, Loi Voi Beach, Con Dao Islands
Tel: 064-383 0155
www.saigoncondao.com
A low-rise building overlooking Loi Voi Beach and well-tended gardens. Rooms are clean, spacious and comfortable, and all have air conditioning. Restaurant and tennis court on site. **$$$**

RESTAURANTS

The vast majority of restaurants in the Mekong serve local food only, either Vietnamese or dishes typical of the local Chinese and Khmer communities. Some rural establishments try their hand at Western favourites like pizza and burgers, with rather mixed results. For better Western food, dine at the better hotels, such as those of the Saigon Tourist and Victoria hotel chains.

Restaurant price categories
Prices are for a full meal per person, with one drink

$ = under US$5
$$ = $5–10
$$$ = $10–15
$$$$ = over $15

The Southeastern Delta
Bach Tung Vien
171B Anh Giac, My Tho
Tel: 073-388 8989
Not far from Vinh Trang Pagoda, this open-sided, thatched-roofed eatery is popular in the afternoon with tour groups day-tripping from Ho Chi Minh City, before it turns into a more local haunt at night. **$**

Spices Restaurant
Victoria Can Tho Hotel, Cai Khe Ward, Can Tho
Tel: 071-381 0111
www.victoriahotels-asia.com

A beachside restaurant on Phu Quoc

The Victoria's French chef, David Lacroix, rustles up the best fare that the Mekong Delta has to offer. Try his speciality 'gazpacho' of Vietnamese blue crab. Indoor and outdoor seating available. **$$$**

The Northern and Western Delta

Bassac Restaurant
Victoria Chau Doc, 01 Le Loi, Chau Doc
Tel: 076-386 5010
www.victoriahotels-asia.com
Local chef Pham Van Quang has spent 20 years cooking in 5-star hotels, and a spot on the river-bank terrace is the best place to enjoy his Vietnamese specialities from across the country. **$$$$**

Hien
07 Duong Dan Cau, Ha Tien
Tel: 077-385 1850
Hien is a basic eatery that prides itself on dishing up fresh seafood plucked straight from the sea. It can rustle up pretty much any Western or Vietnamese speciality. **$$**

Long Xuyen Hotel
19 Nguyen Van Cung, Long Xuyen
Tel: 076-384 1659
On the ground floor of the hotel, with both indoor and streetside seating, this lively place is popular with local families keen to feast on fresh seafood in big portions. **$$**

Thuan Loi
18 Tran Hung Dao,
Chau Doc
Tel: 076-386 5380
A delightful, bamboo-screened floating restaurant on the river. Choose your delicious Khmer and Vietnamese dishes à la carte or fresh from the tank. You can be sure they will be served with a smile and friendly conversation. **$**

The Islands

Le Bistro
Bo Resort, Ong Lang Beach,
Phu Quoc Island
Tel: 077-398 6142
www.boresort.com
This delightfully simple alfresco restaurant on the beach dishes up fresh local produce and seafood with a French touch. Tree-slung hammocks are perfect for enjoying this secluded little slice of paradise. **$$**

Peppertree Restaurant
La Veranda Duong Dong Beach,
Phu Quoc Island
Tel: 077-398 2988
www.laverandaresort.com
The Peppertree is Phu Quoc's most upscale restaurant and dishes up the best in Vietnamese, Asian fusion and international fine dining – with an emphasis on fresh local produce. **$$$**

SPORTS, ACTIVITIES AND TOURS

The vast majority of travellers see the Mekong as part of a package tour, usually in a 2-, 3- or sometimes 5-day loop. Travel agents and most hotels in Ho Chi Minh City readily book these tours.

General tours

Buffalo Tours
Suite 601, Satra House, 58 Dong Khoi, District 1, Ho Chi Minh City
Tel: 08-3827 9169
www.buffalotours.com
Quality scheduled and customised tours.

Exotissimo Travel Vietnam
20 Hai Ba Trung, District 1, Ho Chi Minh City
Tel: 08-3827 2911
www.exotissimo.com
Long-established tour operator offering upmarket, tailor-made trips.

Cruises

Mekong Delta Cruises
Bassac Boat (TransMekong)
Tel: 071-382 9540
www.transmekong.com
This French company operates two large, luxurious wooden boats.

Mekong Eyes Cruise
Tel: 071-546 0786
www.mekongeyes.com
Can Tho-based local company operating two-day boat cruises on a traditional rice barge.

FESTIVALS AND EVENTS

Festivals in the Mekong Delta stem from its diverse mix of traditions, from Buddhist Vietnamese, Chinese and Khmer, to Muslim Cham. All run according to lunar calendars, but since the Vietnamese, Khmer and Cham all have their own, it's very difficult to plan anything.

May–June
Xu Lady Festival
Tay An Pagoda, Sam Mountain (Chau Doc)
One of the most popular pilgrimage festivals in the Mekong, Vietnamese devotees worship the statue of a local saint and deity.

June–July
Ramawan Festival
Cham communities throughout the Mekong
The Cham version of the Muslim Ramadan incorporates lavish offerings of fruit and desserts to ancestors, without the fasting or pilgrimages to Mecca.

November–December
Dolta Festival
Khmer communities throughout the Mekong
A quiet ancestor-worship festival mostly observed in private homes.

Ooc-om-bok Festival
Khmer communities, particularly Soc Trang
A moon-worshipping festival with dragon-boat racing. Lanterns are set on the river at night and offerings laid out, and special poles are decorated with flowers.

The Ooc-om-bok festival at Soc Trang

PRACTICAL ADVICE

Accommodation

A good range and standard of accommodation is available in Vietnam, although outside of major tourist destinations (particularly in the highlands and the Mekong Delta), it is often limited to basic guesthouses and budget hotels. During the school holidays (June–August) the beaches get very crowded, and during the annual Tet festival (in late January or early February), buses and trains are packed with domestic travellers. Hotel rates also spike during the Christmas and New Year periods. If you are making a trip during any of these times, it's a good idea to book ahead. Prices in high season can double. Reservations are required in Nha Trang and Mui Ne, and in many of the upmarket hotels across the country, during peak periods.

ACCOMMODATION OVERVIEW

Hotel development in the country is flourishing and visitors are spoilt for choice. International chains, with service standards and prices to match, can be found in all the major cities. Luxury hotels and resorts with business centres, Wi-fi, and spas and fitness centres are all par for the course these days, but there is also plenty of choice in the budget lodgings category, where a room can cost about US$10 a night.

The easing of restrictions on foreign investment has resulted in a boom in upmarket accommodation in particular. The Hyatt, Sheraton, Hilton and

Sofitel chains are well represented in Ho Chi Minh City and Hanoi, and along the coast, the Six Senses, Amandara, Life Resorts, Maia and other hotel groups have opened luxury establishments in Vietnam.

Hotel staff are generally friendly and helpful, and adequate English is spoken in the major tourism and

The Sheraton Towers Saigon offers all the benefits of five-star luxury

business centres. In more remote areas, communication in English can be a problem. State-run hotels tend to have indifferent staff and low standards of service, which is a pity because some of Hanoi's and Ho Chi Minh City's most atmospheric historic hotels are state-run enterprises.

Legal requirements

Archaic Communist-era Vietnamese laws insist that all hotel guests be registered with the local police. This could mean leaving your passport with the reception for the duration of your stay or just overnight. In Hanoi and Ho Chi Minh City, the practice is either to make a photocopy or to record details from your passport and landing card.

Note also that it is illegal for unmarried Vietnamese and foreigners of the opposite sex to share a room. Interestingly, it's no problem for people of the same sex.

HOTELS AND RESORTS

Vietnam offers many types of hotel, including guesthouses, mid-range hotels, boutique and luxury hotels. There are no official, reliable grading systems for accommodation in Vietnam. Though the government applies 'stars', the system is extremely corrupt and should never be given credence.

Hotels all come with cable or satellite TV, hot water, air conditioning, bathtub, Wi-fi, and usually serve breakfast. Higher prices get you better locations and views, newer renovations and a better atmosphere.

Vietnam doesn't have a clear definition of 'resort' (and the term

A church and a guesthouse at Lang Son, close to the Chinese border

Accommodation

'eco-resort' is almost never correctly applied). If you are paying less than US$70, it's just a glorified hotel in a desirable location. Closer to US$100 and above, expect an on-site spa, a bar and a restaurant or two, swimming pool, beach access and other amenities. Vietnam does have an increasing number of very good luxury resorts with international standards now, and for these, prices can be US$1,000 or more per night.

When booking your accommodation, always check the hotel website first to see what are the best rates on offer. If it's a smaller outfit without a website, call directly to ask for the best rates. The published rates listed here should only be taken as a guide, as actual prices can be quite elastic, depending on seasonal discounts. Higher-end hotels usually charge a 10 percent tax and 5 percent service

Holistic spa treatment at
La Residence Hotel in Hue

charge in addition to the listed prices.

General hotel-booking websites should be your next port of call; these companies can sometimes get you better rates because of the volume of business they bring in.

BUDGET ACCOMMODATION

If you're on a tight budget, try the so-called 'mini hotels', ie small, often family-run hotels with fairly modern (but modest) facilities. These abound in Hanoi and Ho Chi Minh City, but are also increasingly common these days in the popular resort towns.

There are also smaller family-run guesthouses that offer 'homestay' accommodation. These are mainly found in the Mekong Delta area and offer a more personal touch (you may even be invited to have dinner with the family). In the northern highlands, it's possible to arrange a stay with hill-tribe minority communities. These would have to be booked with a travel agency that specialises in trekking tours. Costs for these homestays vary greatly, from perhaps $10 to $30 per person per night.

There are no official backpacker or youth hostels in Vietnam, although there are a few unofficial guesthouses that try to copy the model. Most budget travellers will find themselves in typical Vietnamese guesthouses known as *nha tro* or *nha nghi*. These have simple but comfortable rooms with one or two beds and their own private bath, and basics such as cable TV, hot water and air conditioning. The general price is $8 to $15, although prices can be higher in downtown Ho Chi Minh City and particularly around Old Town Hanoi. It may be possible to go even cheaper by a dollar if you forgo the air conditioning, hot water and TV, but it hardly seems worth it at these prices. Guesthouses don't normally include breakfast, but occasionally they do serve meals for extra money. Wi-fi may or may not be available. Most do laundry, charged by the kilo. Guesthouses, like hotels, can book most tours and transportation. They can also rent motorbikes and often bicycles.

CAMPING

It isn't legal for foreigners to camp in Vietnam, although it is possible to stay in ranger's stations in national parks, which are booked at the park's front office. This restriction mainly comes down to the desire for Communist authorities to keep tabs on everyone, which they do by forcing accommodation managers to register guests and their passport details with the police at night.

Transport

GETTING TO VIETNAM
By air
The main international airports are in Ho Chi Minh City, Hanoi and Danang. The first is the main gateway to the country, with fewer international flights going to Hanoi. Danang only receives international flights from Singapore, Bangkok and Hong Kong.

Vietnam Airlines still has the largest number of international flights. From Europe, the only direct route is with code-shared flights operated jointly by Air France and Vietnam Airlines via Paris. Flight time is about 12 hours. All other carriers from Europe and the US have to fly through Bangkok, Hong Kong, Kuala Lumpur, Singapore, Seoul, Tokyo or Taipei in order to get to either Ho Chi Minh City or Hanoi. Flight time from the US (via Taipei or Tokyo) to Hanoi or Ho Chi Minh City is around 19 hours, minimum.

Tan Son Nhat Airport, Ho Chi Minh City

Key airline offices in Ho Chi Minh City
Air Asia www.airasia.com
Air France www.airfrance.com.vn
Bangkok Air www.bangkokair.com
British Airways www.ba.com
Cathay Pacific www.cathaypacific.com
Emirates Airlines www.emirates.com
KLM Royal Dutch Airlines www.klm.com
Lufthansa www.lufthansa.com
Malaysia Airlines www.malaysia airlines.com
Qantas www.qantas.com
Singapore Airlines www.singaporeair.com
Thai Airways www.thaiairvn.com
Tiger Airways www.tigerairways.com
United Airlines www.unitedairlines. com.vn
Vietnam Airlines www.vietnam airlines.com

Transport

Tan Son Nhat International Airport (SGN; tel: 08-3844 6662) in Ho Chi Minh City; Da Nang International Airport (DAD; tel: 0511-382 3377); and Noi Bai International Airport (HAN; tel: 04-3827 1513) in Hanoi are all located within their own respective city limits on the northwest side of town.

By road
It is possible to enter Vietnam from China at the Lang Son and Lao Cai border crossings in the north. Travel is disjointed across the Chinese border and travellers must usually make separate arrangements on the Chinese side.

A few people travel overland from Laos to Vietnam by bus via the

Lao Bao border crossing in central Vietnam. Although definitely not common practice, it is becoming more popular among budget travellers. That being said, this can be a miserable ride, lasting 24 hours or more between departure and destination.

Travellers also can enter Vietnam by crossing the border with Cambodia at Moc Bai, only a few hours by road from Ho Chi Minh City, or at Vinh Xuong, located about 30km (18 miles) north of Chau Doc, in southern Vietnam. The ride from Ho Chi Minh City to Phnom Penh is about 6 hours. Buses leave hourly from early morning to mid-afternoon.

To book your cross-border tickets, visit one of the countless tour companies, such as Sinh Café in Hanoi (25 Hong Ha, Ba Dinh District), or Ho Chi Minh City (246–248 De Tham, District 1), contact the call centre (daily 7am–7pm) at tel: 04-3717 1444, or make reservations online at www.sinhcafevn.com.

Heavy traffic on Truong Tien Bridge, Hue

GETTING AROUND VIETNAM

Travel options are limited to what is available; there are only airports in a handful of cities, and several popular destinations have no train access (namely Hoi An, the highlands areas and the Mekong Delta), so the intercity buses are often the best way to get around.

See transport information for Ho Chi Minh City on p.203, Nha Trang on p.164, Hue and Danang on p.136, Dalat on p.185 and Hanoi on p.67.

Domestic flights

Vietnam Airlines (tel: 08-3832 0320; www.vietnamairlines.com) operates domestic flights to Buon Ma Thuot, Cam Ranh, Dalat, Danang, Dien Bien Phu, Haiphong, Hue, Nha Trang, Phu Quoc, Pleiku, Quy Nhon, Tuy Hoa, Vinh, Hanoi and Ho Chi Minh City.

Jetstar Pacific Airlines (tel: 08-3845 0092; www.jetstar.com) is a budget airline that flies to Buon Ma Thuot, Can Tho, Dalat, Danang, Hai Phong, Hanoi, Ho Chi Minh City, Nha Trang and Vinh.

Air Mekong (tel: 08-3846 3666; www.airmekong.com.vn) is the newest airline, covering Ho Chi Minh City, offshore islands and Dalat.

VASCO Airlines (tel: 08-3842 2790; www.vasco.com.vn) connects Ho Chi Minh City with Ca Mau in the deep south and Con Son Island (Con Dao archipelago).

Flying is by far the best way to travel, when you can. A Vietnam Airlines flight from Hanoi to Ho Chi Minh City costs under US$180 return. Flight times are frequent but variable.

Ferry terminal in Ho Chi Minh City

For the lowest prices, buy directly from the airlines.

For more on Lien Khuong International Airport (DLI), also known as Dalat Airport, *see p.185*. For Phu Bai International Airport (HUI), better known as Hue Airport, *see p.136*. (Neither of these airports receive international flights).

Ferries

Most travellers will seldom travel by boat in Vietnam, other than on tours of Halong Bay or the Mekong, or to the Perfume Pagoda (*see Unique Experiences On The Water, p.24*). While Vietnam's boat trips are lovely, they have poor safety records and there have been several very serious accidents in recent years. Be sure your boat has life-jackets.

Hydrofoils operating between Ho Chi Minh City and Vung Tau (around 80 minutes) depart from and terminate at the Passenger Quay of Ho Chi Minh City (Ben Tau Khach Thanh Pho), 2 Ton Duc Thang, District 1. Vina Express (tel: 08-3821 4948; www.vinaexpress.com.vn) and Greenlines (tel: 08-3821 5609; www.greenlines.com.vn) operate six departures daily from both cities, from 6am to 5pm.

The best way to get to Cat Ba Island is by booking a tour through an agency in Hanoi, as it will arrange the rather complicated transportation links. For those doing it on their own, travel from Haiphong or Halong Bay (Bai Chay) to Cat Ba Island via hydrofoil or ferry; the hydrofoil will take an hour and the ferry at least double that. The ferry and hydrofoil schedules change according to the season, but at least one hydrofoil departs from both Haiphong and Halong Bay to Cat Ba daily, and there are at least two ferries.

In the Mekong, small motorboats can be hired from US$5 an hour. A high-speed hydrofoil operates twice daily to Can Tho from the pier at the end of Ham Nghi Street in Ho Chi Minh City for about US$12. Other boat services are available between other towns; enquire locally.

Trains

Train travel, operated by Vietnam Railways (www.vr.com.vn), is very slow. The fastest express train from Hanoi to Ho Chi Minh City (called the Reunification Express), the SE4, covers 1,730km (1,073 miles) in 29 hours, with the slower ones (like the TBN) taking up to 41 hours because of the numerous stops they make. There are five classes of train travel in Vietnam: hard seat, soft seat, hard sleeper, soft sleeper and soft sleeper with air-conditioning. Tickets must be purchased at the train station.

Expect to pay at least US$60 for a berth in a four-person compartment

Transport

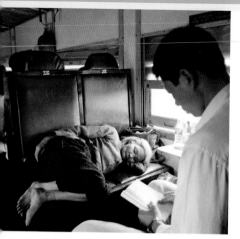
Soft-seat class on the train to Ninh Binh

on the fastest express train from Hanoi to Ho Chi Minh City (or vice versa) via Hue and Nha Trang. There are six trains that make this run every day, and berths are reserved quickly, so try to make reservations early. Lines also run from Hanoi northwest to Lao Cai, east to Haiphong, and north to Lang Son.

From Hanoi, the journey to Sa Pa requires an overnight train trip to Lao Cai, and then a short bus ride from Lao Cai up to Sa Pa. Train tickets and transportation are best arranged through a travel agent in Hanoi as they get discounts on ticket purchases and will also arrange road transport from Lao Cai to Sa Pa. The Hanoi–Lao Cai train runs three times a night and once during the day. The daytime route doesn't have cabins with sleeping berths or air-conditioning, and is not recommended. A soft sleeper with air conditioning costs about US$17.50 if you book tickets yourself at the station.

For more on Vietnam's trains, see p.124–5.

Inter-city buses

If you are planning to travel long distance by bus, it is best to use one of the comfortable 'Open Tour' air-conditioned bus services. Usually departing twice a day, the buses allow you to get on or off anywhere along the route from either Hanoi or Ho Chi Minh City (in places such as Hue, Hoi An, Danang, Nha Trang, Dalat and Mui Ne) with few restrictions. Tickets are purchased at the bus-company office or via resellers. The buses make stops every couple of hours for food and toilet breaks.

With a Ho Chi Minh City–Hanoi ticket costing about US$40, this is certainly one of the cheaper ways to get around. To book your tickets, visit the offices of Sinh Café in Hanoi (25 Hong Ha St, Ba Dinh District), or Ho Chi Minh City (246–248 De Tham, District 1), contact the call centre (daily 7am–7pm) on tel: 04-3717 1444, or go to www.sinhcafevn.com.

Travelling in the Mekong Delta is a little different from the rest of the country. The best place to access the Mekong is from Ho Chi Minh City, and the easiest way to do it is to book an organised tour. Tours will pick up from your hotel and a day trip typically costs from US$17, including lunch.

To blaze your own trail, head to Mai Linh (64–68 Hai Ba Trung; tel: 08-3929 2929) in Ho Chi Minh City, which runs express bus services to the Mekong Delta. Ticket prices vary from US$5–10.

Cycling

Outside the cities, cycling is generally easy, safe and pleasant. The central highlands, national parks and country roads are best for cycling. Bicycles can be rented from hotels and some local travel agents. No equipment is required, but a helmet and pump are advised. There are no official cycle routes or maps available, nor are there any official long-distance tours.

Vehicle hire

It is not generally possible or advisable to rent a car in Vietnam. Road conditions are very poor, many drivers are inadequate, and horrific accidents are an everyday affair. In addition, all foreigners are required to have a Vietnamese driver's licence, and this can take up to five weeks of jumping through hoops to obtain.

The best option is to rent a car with a driver – ask at your hotel for local companies, or try Mai Linh Taxi (telephone numbers differ in each city).

Motorbikes

Motorbikes can be rented for $5–10 per day, but again, by law you should have a Vietnamese driving licence. Many people ignore this and hire a motorbike anyway, but this is not advised.

Another alternative to driving yourself is to use Dalat's Easyriders, a loosely affiliated group of freelance motorcycle guides who wait on corners in central Dalat city and offer tours through the central highlands (*see Highland road trip, p.192–3*) and elsewhere in Vietnam.

Approximate driving times

Most major cities of interest to tourists tend to be spaced about 5–6 hours' driving time apart.

Road conditions

Road surfaces on the main highways in Vietnam are decent, but general driving conditions are very poor. Vietnamese drivers routinely drive on the wrong side of the road, drive while intoxicated and otherwise ignore most traffic rules. Most drivers ignore road signs and traffic lights. Signage is inadequate and the traffic police are generally corrupt. Fuel is readily available at petrol stations, but in rural areas may be sold in glass bottles.

Accessibility

Despite its many disabled citizens, Vietnam makes few allowances for the disabled. Getting around can be difficult but not impossible. Better hotels and restaurants may have wheelchair access but few public buildings provide special facilities for the disabled. Cities can be difficult to navigate due to cluttered pavements and building works blocking paths.

Cyclist near Kenh Ga village, Ninh Binh

Health and safety

INOCULATIONS

Immunisation against hepatitis (A and B), Japanese encephalitis and tetanus are strongly advised. Malaria and dengue fever are prevalent throughout Vietnam, but malaria is rarely seen in tourist areas. Dengue, on the other hand, is very common in both rural and urban areas. The best protection is prevention. Sleep under a mosquito net at night, use potent DEET repellent on exposed skin at all times, and where possible, try to wear long-sleeved tops and trousers. Malaria-carrying mosquitoes are most active at night, but the mosquitoes that spread dengue are most active during the day.

If you are travelling in remote areas, consult with a knowledgeable doctor to determine what anti-malarial drugs are best suited for your travels. For more information, check www.cdc.gov (Centre for Disease Control).

HEALTH CARE AND INSURANCE

Health care in Vietnam is pay-as-you-go. Travellers have been refused medical treatment in dire situations for failure to pay. Foreigners are advised to have comprehensive travel insurance, which includes emergency evacuation.

PHARMACIES AND HOSPITALS

All hospitals have 24-hour pharmacies. Private pharmacies, open late, are also common in cities.

Hanoi
Hanoi French Hospital, 1 Phuong Mai, Dong Da District; tel: 04-3577 1100
Vietnam-Korea Friendship Clinic, 12 Chu Van An, Ba Dinh District; tel: 04-3843 7231

Ho Chi Minh City
Columbia Saigon, 8 Alexandre de Rhodes Street; tel: 08-3829 8520
Ho Chi Minh City Family Medical Practice, Diamond Plaza, 34 Le Duan; tel: 08-3822 7848.

EMERGENCIES

Should you have an accident or an emergency health problem in Vietnam, you may want to consider evacuation to Singapore or Bangkok for treatment. Visitors to Vietnam should therefore have health insurance that includes repatriation (or at least travel to Bangkok or Singapore for emergency treatment).

MEDICATION

Imported pharmaceutical drugs are available throughout the country, but it is best to bring a small supply of medicine to cope with diarrhoea, dysentery, eye infections, insect bites and fungal infections.

NATURAL HAZARDS

The heat of the sun is the most obvious hazard; wear a hat, use sunscreen and carry a water bottle to help to avoid sunstroke.

Pests include venomous snakes such as cobras, as well as scorpions and giant centipedes. Dengue-carrying mosquitoes are common throughout the country, and malarial mosquitoes are common in forested areas. Mosquito repellent is a must.

Vietnam is subject to tropical storms and typhoons in the rainy season between July and November, with the central coastline usually the worst affected. Flooding and landslides are common, particularly in central Vietnam.

FOOD AND DRINK

Food is often prepared in unsanitary conditions. Ice is delivered to restaurants and hotels each day by motorbike and left on the doorsteps. Market produce is doused with canal and river water to keep it looking fresh. Butcher's shops hang meat along dusty streets for hours in the hot sun.

Fruit and vegetables should be peeled before eating. Cooking them is a better idea. Sensitive travellers advise against eating the raw herbs and lettuce served with Vietnamese noodle soup (*pho*) and spring rolls. However, most tourists ignore these recommendations without consequences. It is best to eat in restaurants that are crowded as it's a good sign that they serve freshly cooked food. Because most places do not have refrigeration, food is thrown away at the end of the day.

Do not drink tap water unless it has been boiled properly. It is safest to avoid ice in drinks as well. Imported bottled water is available in most cities, but beware of bottles that are refilled with tap water. Check to make sure the bottle has a seal. And don't forget to drink plenty of liquids to guard against dehydration.

CRIME

Vietnam is a relatively safe country for visitors. That said, tourists present an easy target to unscrupulous locals, and the usual precautions should be taken. Don't carry too much cash with you, use your hotel safe, never leave bags unattended and avoid dark city streets at night. If you hire a motorbike, avoid picking up strangers, particularly in the north – see p.96)

You are most likely to encounter street crime in the big cities; travellers should exercise great caution walking alone in District 1 in Ho Chi Minh City, downtown Hanoi and Beachside Nha Trang. Snatch-and-run thievery is rampant in these areas, especially at night. Do not accept invitations for lunch or coffee from English-speaking Asians you meet on the street in these areas. A foreign mafia runs a common

Sun and rain protection on Waiting Woman Mountain, Lang Son

Health and safety

Soldiers in the Old Quarter, Hanoi

scam starting this way. Victims have complained of being swindled out of thousands of dollars once they arrive at the person's home.

A more common scam to be aware of, especially in Hanoi, is when taxi drivers tell new arrivals that their hotel has closed, then take them to another one where they will earn a hefty commission.

DRUGS

The sale, purchase, transport or use of drugs in Vietnam is illegal. Even small amounts can and do result in lifelong jail sentences or execution for foreigners.

SPOT THE COP

Vietnamese police are easily identified by their olive-green uniforms with red and yellow highlights and Communist emblem on their hats. Traffic police are similarly dressed in tan uniforms. 'Tourist Police' in Ho Chi Minh City and Hanoi are, on the whole, just for show and do not speak English or have much authority. For any incidents, contact your hotel and go through the local police. For serious emergencies you should contact your embassy.

WOMEN TRAVELLERS

Vietnam is relatively safe for women to explore alone, although it's best to respect local customs and avoid skimpy clothing.

POLICE REGISTRATION

By law, all tourists are required to be registered with the local police station. When checking in at hotels and guesthouses at the smaller and more remote towns, the staff will take your passport to the police for registration. They will normally return it to you the next morning, although sometimes they may insist on holding your passport for the duration of your stay.

EMBASSIES AND CONSULATES

See p.18–19.

Emergency contacts

In an emergency, ask your hotel reception or tour guide for assistance. In most cases, police and tourism boards will not offer help. Embassies can make recommendations but will not normally provide direct assistance. Any serious medical emergencies should be evacuated to Bangkok or Singapore. There may or may not be English speakers at the numbers below.

Ambulance: 115
Fire service: 114
Police: 113

Money and budgeting

CURRENCY

Vietnam's unit of currency, the dong (pronounced 'dome', and abbreviated as VND), currently circulates in banknotes of 500,000; 100,000; 50,000; 20,000; 10,000; 5,000; 2,000; 1,000; and now infrequently, 500, 200 and 100. Coins of 5,000; 2,000; 1,000; 500 and 200 denominations are common in cities, but not small towns. Notes from 10,000 to 500,000 dong are now made of polymer plastic, which ensures a longer lifespan and makes them more difficult to counterfeit. The dong's value against the dollar has begun to slide in the past few years: at the time of writing it was about VND20,600 to US$1, or VND32,700 to £1, or VND28,850 to €1.

At present, the dollar is highly desirable in Vietnam and accepted in most transactions. The Vietnamese have an obsession with unblemished US dollars and larger dong notes. They will often refuse notes with tears or handwriting on them, although they can usually be turned in at banks. Counterfeit US dollar notes of $5 and above, as well as VND100,000 notes and higher, are very common.

At present only US$5,000 may be taken out of the country legally.

CASH AND CARDS

ATM machines are now widely available in most cities. There is a withdrawal limit of VND 2,000,000 (just under US$100) per transaction, but the number of transactions is not limited by the ATM. ATM fees are about US$2 per transaction at present. Try always to have some smaller denomination notes on you.

Fairly high commission rates – usually 3 percent – are tacked on to your bill when using credit cards. Cash advances can be withdrawn using major credit cards (again with the 3 percent commission) from a few banks, including branches of Vietcombank and Sacombank. Vietcombank will also provide cash dollars for US-dollar traveller's cheques – for a 2 percent surcharge.

Changing money on the street is never a good idea. Most street moneychangers are scam artists who will try to cheat you by offering ridiculously poor exchange rates or try to slip counterfeit notes into wads of the genuine stuff. It's best to stick to a bank.

Cash machines are widespread in cities

Shoppers at the evening market, Hanoi

In 2011, the government banned currency exchange at gold shops. However, it is still possible to change dollars at some jewellery or gold shops; sometimes the rate is slightly higher than the bank rate. Look for a shop with the sign *hieu vang* (gold shop). They are easily identifiable because the signs usually have bright, gold-coloured letters.

Be prepared to be offered two exchange rates: one for denominations of 50 and 100 US dollars, and a lower rate for smaller denominations. If changing money anywhere other than a bank or gold shop, expect to be scammed.

Budgeting costs

Resort or top hotel: $75–200+ for a double [or per person]
Mid-range hotel: $35–65 for a double [or per person]
Basic hotel: $10–45 for a double [or per person]
Guesthouse: $8–25 for a double [or per person]
Youth hostel: N/A
Motor camp: N/A
Campsite: N/A

Domestic flight: $80–120
Ho Chi Minh City–Hanoi
Inter-city coach ticket: $4–6
Ho Chi Minh City–Mui Ne
Inter-city train ticket: $4–5
Ho Chi Minh City–Mui Ne
Car hire: $80–120 per day
Petrol: $1 a litre
10-minute taxi ride: $2–10
Airport shuttle bus: $2–5

Short bus ride: less than $1
One-day travel pass: N/A

Breakfast: $1–3
Lunch in a café: $1–4
Coffee/tea in a café: $1–3
Main course, budget restaurant: $1–4
Main course, moderate restaurant: $5–10
Main course, expensive restaurant: $25–35
Bottle of wine in a restaurant: $4–50+
Beer in a pub: $1–5

Museum admission: $0–2
Day trip to Cu Chi and Tay Ninh: $10–15
Motorbike rental per day: $5–10
Kiteboarding for an afternoon: $50–100
Foot massage: $5–15 (1 hour)
Theatre/concert ticket: $4–10
Cham woven handbag: $3–10
Nightclub entry: $0–2

Traveller's cheques in US dollars are accepted in most banks and in major hotels, but not in shops, smaller hotels or restaurants. Major credit cards are accepted at upscale hotels, restaurants, shops and many tour offices.

TIPPING

Tipping is not part of traditional Vietnamese culture. However, in venues that commonly serve foreign tourists, it is increasingly becoming expected. For waiters and tour guides, a 10 percent gratuity is adequate. Better restaurants and top hotels may add a 10 percent tax and 5 percent service charge to bills, though whether the money is actually used as designated is doubtful.

TAX

Tax, if collected, is usually included in the price, but better hotels and restaurants may attach an extra 10 percent to bills.

BUDGETING FOR YOUR TRIP

While still inexpensive for most Western travellers, Vietnam is not as cheap as it was just a few years ago. In 2008, inflation sky-rocketed to an all-time high, thanks to the rising price of oil, grains and other commodities around the world. Further political events, natural disasters around the globe, a weakened world economy and plummeting local currency have only caused further uncertainty and rises in prices. Accommodation in Vietnam can be cheap, but is generally more expensive than the rest of Southeast Asia.

For a budget, backpacker-style holiday you will need to set aside $300 per person per week. A standard family holiday for four will cost around $1,000 per week. A luxury, no-expense-spared break can cost over $3,000 per person per week.

Airline prices from the UK and the US vary wildly depending upon the carrier, class, season and city of departure and arrival. Expect a no-frills economy seat from Los Angeles or London, during low season, to be very roughly around US$1,000. A first-class seat in high season, particularly departing from a Midwestern city in the US, can be several thousand dollars.

MONEY-SAVING TIPS

The best way to get a lower price is to shop around and haggle Try to find out the going rate from other travellers or from hotel staff. When you haggle, remain friendly and good-humoured, and remember that you may only be talking about a difference of a few pounds.

Buying vegetables in Phat Diem

Responsible travel

Cuc Phuong National Park tour

GETTING THERE

If you would like to offset the damage caused to the environment by your flight, a number of organisations can do this for you, using online 'carbon calculators', which tell you how much you need to donate. In the UK, visit www.climatecare.org or www.carbon neutral.com; in the US, log on to www.climatefriendly.com or www.sustainabletravelinternational.org.

ECOTOURISM

Environmental issues are not taken seriously in Vietnam. Pollution, deforestation, poaching of wildlife and sanitation are all very serious and ongoing problems. Vietnamese tour operators don't have a clear understanding of the term 'ecotourism'. Quite often, an 'ecotourism destination' is a site of once-natural beauty, where the owners have chopped down all the trees, put wild animals in cages (or on to the dinner table), and erected a hotel complex complete with karaoke and massage parlour. For the most authentic ecotourism experiences, shun the 'ecotourism' theme parks and resorts, and instead head to national parks.

ETHICAL TOURISM

Tourist dollars will rarely go to the local communities. Most hotels, tour companies and ticket fees leave the community and go to government-affiliated 'private' companies.

The best way to help the locals, particularly in hill-tribe villages, is to use a local freelance guide, and to buy souvenirs and snacks from small local vendors along the street and in villages.

CHARITIES

Reputable environmental and conservation organisations operating in Vietnam include: Education for Nature Vietnam (ENV, www.envietnam.org); Wildlife at Risk (WAR, www.wildlifeatrisk.org); WCS (Wildlife Conservation Society, www.wcs.org); and WWF (wwf.panda.org). Respected humanitarian organisations include World Vision (www.worldvision.org.vn) and Save the Children (www.savethechildren.net).

THINGS TO AVOID

Travellers should avoid eating in restaurants that serve wild game or buying souvenirs made from wildlife. Even many exotic-animal farms – some illegally open to tourists – source all their stock from poachers.

Family holidays

PRACTICALITIES

The Vietnamese are very fond of children, so travelling with a family in Vietnam can be a great pleasure. It's common that strangers will want to touch or even pick up young children (especially blond ones), friendly gestures that may become irritating – a polite but firm refusal may become necessary. Always make sure your children carry identification and contact information, perhaps a hotel card. Remember that outside Hanoi and Ho Chi Minh City, health-care facilities are fairly basic.

Supplies for babies such as nappies and baby food are available in supermarkets and pharmacies, common in major shopping centres. Nappy-changing facilities are almost unheard of, but there is no cultural problem with using either male or female lavatories for this purpose. Cleanliness may be an issue, however, so bring your own toilet paper and baby wipes.

You may prefer to leave the buggy at home as footpaths in most Vietnamese cities and towns are not pedestrian-friendly; a papoose or baby-carrier is more practical.

ACCOMMODATION

Vietnamese hotels will usually have no problem accommodating children, though facilities may be basic. Children under 12 generally stay in their parents' room at no extra cost. Child safety may be an issue, particularly around swimming pools or play areas.

FOOD AND DRINK

Vietnamese restaurants welcome children, though may not have high-chairs for babies. Chopsticks come only in adult sizes, but many restaurants can provide cutlery. Typical Vietnamese food may be too spicy for children, though old favourites such as noodles, rice and pancakes should be acceptable. Restaurants will usually be happy to make dishes with less chilli, salt and MSG on request. And of course, there is a fabulous selection of fresh fruit on offer. Most Vietnamese restaurants do not observe a no-smoking policy. Fast-food restaurants such as KFC or Lotteria are common in large cities.

ATTRACTIONS AND ACTIVITIES

Ticketed parks have children's activity areas with simple games and rides. Theme parks have more advanced activities. Safety precautions at scenic sites and sports areas may be lacking, so ensure teenagers are not at risk if they go off on their own.

Family holidays

The Nha Trang Aquarium

History

The early history of Vietnam, like that of all ancient nations, is lost in the mists of time and legend. What is clear beyond doubt is that the ancestors of today's Kinh (as the Vietnamese call themselves) first flourished three to four millennia ago in the fertile floodplains of southernmost China and the Red River Valley of Tonkin. The story of Vietnamese survival and the long fight for freedom and independence is one of southern territorial expansion – defending against China in the north, while systematically extending power over the declining kingdoms of Champa and Cambodia to the south.

LEGENDARY KINGS

Vietnamese legend has it that King De Minh, descendant of a divine Chinese ruler, married an immortal mountain fairy. The product of their union, Kinh Duong, in turn married the daughter of the Dragon Lord of the Sea. Their son, Lac Long Quan or 'Dragon Lord of Lac', is considered to be the first Vietnamese king. To maintain peace with their powerful neighbours, the Chinese – a theme constant throughout Viet history – Lac Long Quan married Au Co, yet another Chinese immortal, who bore him 100 sons. Subsequently, Lac Long Quan's eldest son succeeded him as the first king of the Hung Dynasty.

According to oral tradition, the Hung Dynasty had 18 kings, each of whom ruled for 150 years. This belief alone makes any attempt at accurately dating or even verifying these events pointless. Rather than viewing the Hung Dynasty as historical fact, it should be seen as a heroic legend set in mythical terms to glorify the early establishment of the Vietnamese nation. During this time, the southward territorial imperative of both the Han Chinese and the Vietnamese was established, and thereby a rivalry that has lasted for millennia.

In 258BC, Thuc Pan, ruler of Au Viet, overthrew the 18th Hung king and established a new Vietnamese state called Au Lac, with its capital at Co Loa, just north of present-day Hanoi. Within half a century, in 207BC, a renegade Chinese general, Trieu Da, conquered Au Lac and established power over Nam Viet, a state based in what is now Guangxi in southern China and the Red River

A portrait of Ho Chi Minh in the late 1950s

Delta of northern Vietnam. Chinese dominion over Nam Viet was confirmed in 111BC when the heirs of Trieu Da formally submitted to the Han emperor Wu Ti, establishing Chinese rule as far south as the Hai Van Pass and making Nam Viet the Chinese province of Giao Chau.

A THOUSAND YEARS OF CHINESE RULE

During the 1st century AD, Chinese attempts to 'Sinicise' the people of Giao Chau were partly successful but provoked widespread hostility among the Vietnamese. This resulted, AD40, in the first major Viet rebellion against the Chinese, led by the Trung sisters, two Viet ladies of noble birth who proclaimed themselves joint queens of an independent Vietnam.

The Trung sisters are still honoured as national heroines, but their attempt at breaking away from Chinese rule did not last. Just three years later, General Ma Vien re-established Chinese control over the territory and intensified the process of 'Sinification.' The Vietnamese increasingly came under the Chinese spell, imitating the customs of the great northern neighbour they resented so much.

For the next nine centuries, the Viets remained in thrall to the Chinese, despite a series of major rebellions. In 544 the Viet nationalist Ly Bon led a rising that achieved partial independence under the Early Ly Dynasty, but this was crushed by Chinese armies in 603. The victorious Chinese renamed the country An Nam, or 'Pacified South' – though this would prove to be wishful thinking.

Folk painting showing the Trung sisters (Hai Ba Trung) on a war elephant

In 938 the Viet patriot Ngo Quyen decisively defeated the Chinese at the Battle of the Bach Dang River and reasserted Vietnamese independence after almost 1,000 years of Chinese domination. At last the Viets were free, but by this time they had taken on many Chinese characteriestics, and were the most 'Sinicised' people in Southeast Asia, in marked contrast to their Cham, Tai and Khmer neighbours, all of whom had fallen under the philosophical and religious influence of India.

The Vietnamese had learnt at least one valuable lesson from their centuries of confrontation with China. The Chinese threat wasn't going to go away, and they had to live with their northern neighbours. They achieved this by combining fierce resistance to Chinese aggression with contrite, even humble apologies to the Dragon

Chinese religious influence at Chua Tay Phuong

Throne every time the Chinese were repelled. This rather clever system was formalised in 968 when King Dinh Tien, founder of the Dinh Dynasty, reaffirmed Vietnamese independence but agreed to pay tribute to the Chinese every three years. In a word, it was a matter of saving face.

VIETNAM MOVES SOUTH

From the 11th century on, Vietnam found new ways of imitating China, the neighbour it had learnt both to admire and to fear. Firstly, Buddhism began to make headway as a major religion in Vietnam – though this was the Mahayana faith introduced from China, and not the Theravada system practised elsewhere in Southeast Asia. Confucianism, too, was enthusiastically adopted from the Chinese and established as the basis of state administration.

Secondly, the Vietnamese people, hemmed in by the more populous Chinese to the north and the jagged mountains of the Annamite Cordillera to the west, began to expand in the only direction open to them – southwards. From their new capital at Thanh Long, or 'Ascending Dragon' (later renamed Hanoi), the long subjugation and conquest of the ancient Hindu Kingdom of Champa was begun.

The Viets continued to hold the north with considerable success, defeating a Mongol invasion in 1279 at the Second Battle of the Bach Dang River. By the 14th century, central Vietnam as far as the Hai Van Pass had been secured, with the city of Hue passing under Viet suzerainty. In 1428 yet another Chinese invasion was defeated by the national hero, Le Loi. Meanwhile, to the south, Qui Nhon was seized from Champa in 1471, and the Cham Kingdom was reduced to a near-powerless rump.

By the beginning of the 16th century, everything seemed to be going well for Dai Viet, the Kingdom of the Vietnamese, but new troubles were just around the corner. In 1516 the first Westerners, in the form of Portuguese seafarers, arrived in the country. Moreover, in the distant south, as Champa crumbled, rival claimants to Hanoi's rule were emerging among the Viets themselves. In 1527 the country split in two, with the Mac (and subsequently Trinh) Lords ruling the Red River Delta region from Hanoi, while the Nguyen Lords dominated the south of the country from their capital at Hue.

By the 17th century, the French had replaced the Portuguese as the predominant Westerners in Vietnam, where they paid particular attention to the centre and the south.

The French introduced Catholicism, which gradually spread throughout the country, despite the best efforts of the Confucian and Buddhist establishments. As a consequence, Vietnam was to become the second-most Christian country in Asia, surpassed only by the Philippines. As a corollary of this missionary effort, the French priest Alexandre de Rhodes developed the Quoc Ngu system of Romanised Vietnamese script that is still used throughout the country today.

By 1757, Vietnamese settlers had bypassed the small surviving bastion of Champa between Phan Rang and Phan Thiet and had begun their conquest of the Mekong Delta, until this time, under Cambodian control. The Khmer settlement of Prey Nokor was taken from the Cambodians and renamed Saigon. Finally, in the 19th century, the last vestiges of Champa were snuffed out and Vietnam assumed full control over the territories that it controls today.

THE NGUYEN EMPERORS AND FRENCH CONQUEST

In 1802 the Lord Nguyen Anh defeated his northern rivals and established the Nguyen Dynasty (1802–1945) at Hue, where he proclaimed himself Emperor Gia Long. For the first time in Vietnam's history, power shifted south from the Red River Delta to the centre of the country.

Yet the authority of the Nguyen did not remain unchallenged for long. In 1858 France seized both Danang and Saigon, laying the foundations for its colonies in Annam and Cochinchina. By 1883, supported by modern weapons and an unshakable belief in their 'civilising mission', the French proclaimed Tonkin a colony, too, and Vietnam had become a French protectorate. In 1887 this was formalised and extended with the proclamation of an Indochinese Union of Vietnam, Laos and Cambodia: French Indochina had become a reality.

A depiction of the French-Chinese War, May 1884–June 1885

North Vietnamese troops enter Saigon in 1975

Unsurprisingly, the Vietnamese rejected French imperialism. A proud people who had resisted Chinese domination for two millennia were hardly likely to submit quietly to French rule. Meanwhile, in 1890, at a small hamlet in rural Vinh, Ho Chi Minh, the future leader of Vietnam's struggle for independence, was born.

In 1918 Ho travelled to Paris, and three years later joined the French Communist Party. By 1930 he had visited Moscow, become an agent of the Comintern, and formed the Indochinese Communist Party in Hong Kong. The French didn't know it yet, but the writing was already on the wall.

Ho continued to organise his compatriots for independence throughout the war years and the Japanese occupation, which ended in 1945. Of course, the Communists weren't the only force opposed to French colonialism – Vietnamese of all political colours wanted their freedom – but there can be no doubt that the Communists were the best organised.

Three Indochina wars

Following the Japanese capitulation on 15 August 1945, events moved rapidly towards a series of wars. On 23 August Bao Dai, the last Nguyen Emperor, abdicated. Just 10 days later, on 2 September 1945, Ho Chi Minh declared Vietnamese independence in Hanoi.

This was unacceptable to the French, and in 1946 the First Indochina War began as France sought to reimpose colonial rule. The French fared badly and in 1954 suffered a crushing defeat at the hands of Ho Chi Minh's greatest general, Vo Nguyen Giap, at Dien Bien Phu.

Vietnam was subsequently divided at the 17th parallel, theoretically pending elections. North Vietnam, with its capital Hanoi, was ruled by a Communist regime under Ho Chi

Minh. South Vietnam, with its capital Saigon, was ruled by a pro-Western, Catholic strongman, Ngo Dinh Diem. In 1955 Diem refused to hold elections and, backed by Hanoi, Viet Minh forces began armed attacks in the south. This event led to the start of the Second Indochina War – known to the Vietnamese as the American War, which would ravage the country for almost 20 years.

In a misconceived attempt to contain Communism, the United States first sent advisers to assist the southern regime in 1960. By 1965, the air force had started regular bombing of the north, and US combat troops had landed at Danang in the south. By 1968, US troop strength had risen to more than half-a-million men, but that year's offensive by the Viet Cong sapped Washington's will to fight, and in 1973 the last US combat troops were withdrawn. Within two years, in April 1975, the North Vietnamese Army (NVA) had captured Saigon, and Vietnam was once again unified by force.

Hanoi's victory led to the proclamation of the Socialist Republic of Vietnam. There was no bloodbath, but a sterile command economy was implemented and, for more than a decade, most Vietnamese suffered dire poverty and political oppression. This was compounded by the Third Indochina War (1978–79), when Vietnam invaded Cambodia to oust the murderous Khmer Rouge regime and was in turn invaded as a 'lesson' by Communist China.

ECONOMIC GROWTH

At the Sixth Congress of the Vietnamese Communist Party in 1986, the party leadership launched the country on an ambitious programme of social and economic reform called *doi moi*. Collectivisation of land was rolled back, and a new emphasis was placed on the productivity and personal rights of the people. Consequently, agricultural production increased and Vietnam became a major rice exporter.

More impressively, the economy has grown at an average rate of more than 7 percent over the past decade. Political controls remain strict, however,

Bringing in the rice harvest

Evidence of globalisation in Ho Chi Minh City

and individual rights of expression remain limited.

Globalisation

In 1991 Vietnam officially normalised relations with China. While there is an important trade relationship between the two countries, tension is ever present, particularly over the issue of the Truong Sa archipelago, which both countries claim.

In the mid 1990s a number of key economic milestones were reached, including the lifting of the US embargo and the lifting of restrictions on borrowing from the IMF. In 1995 Vietnam became an official member of ASEAN (the Association of South East Asian Nations), initiating close economic ties with its neighbours and bringing decades of costly international ostracism to an end.

In 2000 Bill Clinton became the first US president to visit Vietnam since the war. He would later be followed by George W. Bush, and then several times by Hillary Clinton, as Secretary of State, in 2010 and 2011.

Recent years have brought an increasing number of international celebrities to Vietnam, including Angelina Jolie (who adopted a son in Vietnam), and a number of British royals – all of which would have seemed unimaginable just twenty years ago. The country's rapid rise as a tourist destination has also contributed to Vietnam's heightened international profile.

Relations with the US have continued to strengthen: the US helped Vietnam to join the World Trade Organization in 2007, and sided with Vietnam against China over the Truong Sa islands in 2010.

Challenges for the future

Despite the impressive economic turnaround, problems remain. Vietnam is predominantly an agricultural country, with over 70 percent of its people engaged in this sector. Income levels nationwide are low and many rural areas are mired in poverty. Unemployment during non-harvest periods routinely hits 25 to 35 percent. The presence of a new urban class of unskilled workers, who have left the countryside and now struggle to survive on low wages in the cities, alongside Vietnam's increasingly visible nouveaux riches, is already a source of social friction.

Corruption and excessive red tape remain endemic in Vietnam, although the government is attempting to trim the fat from the bloated bureaucracy and streamline unwieldy official procedures.

Historical landmarks

258BC
Thuc Pan establishes new Vietnamese state called Au Lac.

207BC
Trieu Da, Chinese general, conquers Au Lac and establishes power over Nam Viet.

AD40
Trung sisters lead first major rebellion against Chinese.

938
Ngo Quyen wins battle at Bach Dang, ending millennium of Chinese rule.

1516
Portuguese seafarers are first Westerners to arrive in Vietnam.

1802–19
Nguyen Anh defeats Tay Sons, proclaiming himself Emperor Gia Long, establishing the Nguyen dynasty.

1861
French forces capture Saigon.

1883
France establishes protectorate over Annam and Tonkin, ruling Cochinchina as a colony.

1890
Birth of Ho Chi Minh.

1930
Ho forms Vietnamese Communist Party.

1940
Japan occupies Vietnam, leaving French administration intact.

1945
Japan defeated; Ho Chi Minh declares independence and Vietnam a Democratic Republic.

1946
First Indochina War begins.

1954
Battle of Dien Bien Phu. Geneva Accord divides Vietnam.

1955
Second Indochina War begins.

1965
First US combat troops land at Danang.

1969
Ho Chi Minh dies aged 79; US begins phased withdrawal of troops.

1973
Washington and Hanoi sign ceasefire.

1975
North Vietnamese Army captures Saigon.

1976
Socialist Republic of Vietnam declared.

1978
Vietnam invades Cambodia, overthrowing Khmer Rouge.

1986
6th Party Congress embraces *doi moi* (economic renovation).

1994
US trade embargo lifted.

2000
Bill Clinton becomes first US President to visit since the war.

2001
US-Vietnam Bilateral Trade Agreement.

2004
Hill tribes protest in Central Highlands.

2007
Vietnam joins World Trade Organization.

2010
The US sides with Vietnam in the territorial dispute with China over East Sea islands.

History

Culture

Vietnam today is trying to balance rapid economic and population growth with a fiercely traditional culture, and all under the watchful eye of a Communist government. The Vietnamese are among the world's most literate and poetic people, and now their contemporary art and crafts are finding favour with collectors around the world.

PEOPLE

Some 3,000 years ago, in the foothills and valleys of the Red River Delta, a distinctive culture emerged that can be traced to the people who now call themselves Vietnamese. This is where, in the 7th century BC, the kingdom of Van Lang came into being. This tiny kingdom is considered the cradle of Vietnamese culture, and the Hung kings the forefathers of the Vietnamese people.

Studies on the origins of the Vietnamese show that the people who settled in the Indochinese Peninsula and its bordering regions most probably came from southern and eastern China, the high plateaux of Central Asia, islands in the South Pacific, and also other parts of the world. Vietnam can thus be considered the proverbial melting pot into which the major Asiatic and Oceanic migrations converged.

Almost 87 percent of Vietnam's 90 million-strong population lists its ethnicity as Kinh (or Viet) – the commonly accepted term for its main indigenous race – but in reality, most Vietnamese have evolved from

a mixture of races and ethnicities over thousands of years. That mixture is the result of repeated invasions from outside Vietnam, particularly from China, along with continual migrations within Vietnam, most commonly from north to south. As a result, you will find in Vietnam today the predominant Kinh as well as distinct ethnic-minority groups, such as the hill tribes *(see p.30–35)* of the northern and central highlands, and pockets of Cham and Khmer people in the south, whose kingdoms were vanquished centuries ago by Vietnamese armies from the north.

The Cham people mainly inhabit the Phan Rang and Phan Thiet regions in southern Vietnam. Today, there is just a small population of Cham – about 100,000 – but the Champa kingdom was once home to

Rural Vietnamese man

Communal exercise in a Hanoi park

a culture that lasted for several centuries. Ethnic Khmers, who are of the same stock as Cambodians, number around 900,000 and mainly live in the Mekong Delta area.

Minority groups have been among the last to reap the rewards of Vietnam's new-found prosperity – with one exception. Ethnic Chinese, who as recently as the late 1970s were ostracised – if not run out of the country – because of tensions arising from the northern border clash with China, have not only benefited from Vietnam's recent economic progress but, in many ways, also fuelled the country's economic growth. This is particularly pronounced in Ho Chi Minh City, the country's main economic hub.

Most of Vietnam's 1.7 million Chinese, known as Hoa, have adopted Vietnamese citizenship. Many Chinese are shopkeepers and businesspeople who settled in Ho Chi Minh City's Cholon district, which has long flourished as the Chinese community's primary commercial centre in southern Vietnam.

SOCIETY

Much of Vietnamese culture has been heavily influenced by the Chinese, who colonised Vietnam over 2,000 years ago. Among their number were the usual tyrants and exploiters, but also administrators and teachers who brought with them religions, philosophies, organisational skills, and a written language, the *chu han*.

In Vietnam, the family is considered to be a small world unto itself. Deeply influenced by Confucian principles, children are taught the importance of *hieu* (filial piety) – respecting one's elders was, in fact, once enshrined by the law. The family, in turn, is duty-bound to pay homage to its ancestors. A traditional family home would typically have as many as three generations under the one roof: grandparents, parents, married sons with wives and children, and unmarried children. In the event that one member needed

Mui Ne harbour

money for an investment or for university studies, the entire family would chip in to help.

Traditionally, having a boy in the family was a 'must' as the eldest son would assume the duties of his father as head of the family when the latter died. Women were generally brought up for domestic duties, and were less educated than men. Despite growing affluence and gender equality today, especially in urban areas, there is still a clear preference for boys, as witnessed by the number of sex-selective abortions in the country.

Today, Vietnam's youthful population – 72 percent of its citizens are under 35 years of age – increasingly dominates Vietnamese society, despite the collective influence of the state and that of older generations raised on Confucian principles during less-privileged times.

Under the table

Corruption is an entrenched part of Vietnamese society. Palms are greased to skip bureaucratic hurdles, win contracts and invite preferential treatment from people in positions of authority. Even teachers frequently receive 'gifts' from parents in the hope that their child might receive extra attention at school. When accidents occur, traffic policemen will skip the paperwork and issue a verbal warning in return for an outright bribe.

The government is trying to root out corruption, but it's an uphill task given the fact that it is deeply ingrained. In the past, the Vietnamese would have blamed the war for the country's poverty; these days, corruption is often cited as the main reason for any perceived ills.

Keep smiling

The Vietnamese often smile when embarrassed, confused or when they're being scolded by an older person or their boss, or when they don't understand what a foreigner is asking. If you lose your temper and this happens, it doesn't mean they are not taking the situation seriously, but rather that he or she is embarrassed for you. Likewise, when a traffic accident is averted, Vietnamese people often crack into a wide smile, especially if you're a foreigner. It means, 'I'm sorry!' or 'Aren't we lucky nothing serious happened!'.

THE ARTS

After decades of obscurity and isolation, Vietnamese artists have started to feature in the international arena. Sold in galleries and exhibited in museums worldwide, Vietnamese paintings are routinely inlcuded in auctions of Southeast Asian art at Christie's and Sotheby's.

Much of the work making waves in the international art scene shares a gentle, lyrical quality – rarely is any self-indulgent anger expressed – with styles ranging from figurative to abstract and surrealist, at other times expressionist or realist. The abundance of this impressionist and figurative art in Vietnam is testament to the tenacious influence of Western culture on art heritage in Vietnam.

The ancient Dong Son bronze drums, which depict dancers performing to the accompaniment of musical instruments, testify to the importance of musical and dance traditions in Vietnam since its early days. For a long time, however, music played an integral part in religious ceremonies, but not as a means of public entertainment. It wasn't until much later that music became part of the cultural landscape in a broader sense and developed further.

Traditional tunes

The majority Kinh or Viet population, and many of Vietnam's 54 ethnic minorities, have a rich musical heritage. Generally, Vietnamese music falls into two basic groups: *dieu bac*, literally 'northern mode', which exhibits more of a Chinese influence, and *dieu nam*, 'southern mode', which features the slower tempo and sentimentality of ancient Cham culture.

The trendy Salon Natasha in Hanoi

Musical performance in Hoi An

Folk music takes the form of tunes sung by villagers illustrating their life in the countryside. There are several broad categories: lullabies, known as *hat ru* in the north, *ru em* in the centre and *au o* in the south; work songs, or *ho*; and mushy love songs, known as *ly*.

Perhaps the most important catalyst in the development of contemporary Vietnamese folk entertainment was the appearance of the call-and-response dialogue song, a genre found widely throughout Southeast Asia. Most ethnic minorities have a version of a flirtatious male-female courting game in which boys and girls engage in sung poetic dialogue that tests each other's skills.

Court music

Despite the establishment of an independent Viet kingdom in the 10th century, successive Vietnamese rulers continued to mimic the courtly traditions of their powerful Chinese neighbour. In subsequent centuries, Confucian music and dance traditions were increasingly appropriated from the Chinese imperial court. Court music was also influenced by the music of the old Hindu kingdom of Champa, in the southern part of present-day Vietnam.

During the Le dynasty, a complicated system of court music was established. A number of categories of music were invented for different religious and social occasions, although the great majority of royal dances functioned as a means to wish the sovereign and his family happiness, prosperity and longevity.

From the turn of the 20th century onwards, the royal court at Hue became increasingly Westernised and, during the reign of French-educated Bao Dai (1926–45), the last of the Nguyen kings, traditional royal music and dances were rarely performed. Since the late 1980s, court music has been revived in the old imperial capital by the Thua Thien Hue Provincial Traditional Arts Company and the Hue Royal Palace Arts Troupe.

Theatre forms

Vietnam's oldest recorded theatrical performance is *tro he*, a farce created during the Tien Le dynasty (980–1009). During the Tran period (1225–1400), two new types of theatre emerged: *hat giau mat*, which means 'masked performances', and *hat coi tran*, 'coatless performances'. These archaic forms of theatre no longer exist today. Today's varieties – *cheo*, *hat tuong* and *cai luong*, are a blend of court theatre and folk performances with some foreign influences.

Puppetry in motion

During the 11th-century Ly dynasty, before a series of dykes were built from soil, the Red River would swell each year, regular as clockwork, bursting its banks and flooding much of the region. This annual flooding of the lowlands inspired a form of entertainment that is found only in Vietnam, namely water puppetry *(mua roi nuoc)*.

The flooded paddies were, of course, the perfect platform in which to conceal both the puppeteer and the long bamboo poles used to control the puppet. Gradually, these theatrical events would have transferred to the small ponds and lakes situated beside the communal houses *(dinh)* found in a typical 11th-century Vietnamese village.

Today, the puppeteers still perform in a chest-deep pool of water but behind a curtain on stage. The water is kept deliberately murky so as to obscure the poles and mechanics used to control the puppets, which are protected from the elements by a layer of lacquer. The puppets usually

White Thai people of Ban Lac and Pom Coong villages put on nightly performances

A water-puppet theatre in Hanoi

The water's surface is also a barometer of the scale of emotion conveyed. Calm and serene when fairies appear to sing and dance, it becomes a heaving tempest when a battle breaks out with fire-spitting dragons.

Water puppetry dropped off the radar during the Vietnam War, until it was revived in the 1980s. While it took time to redevelop the art form due to a lack of numbers and poor facilities, thanks to Vietnam's booming tourism industry, water puppetry has found its way back on to the stage.

Contemporary arts and entertainment

Love it or hate it, it's hard to escape Vietnamese pop music. Long influenced by American music, it is beginning to become overshadowed by the influx of Korean boy-bands that have overtaken much of Southeast Asian pop culture. Vietnamese pop singers, from superstars to lounge singers, all perform at venues in big cities called *phong tra ca nhac* (Music Tea Rooms), as well as at fairgrounds in the provinces.

Domestic films have tended to focus on romantic comedies, Chinese mythology or revolutionary history (all, of course, pro-Communist). The local film industry was neither very serious nor taken seriously until a recent influx of Vietnamese-American actors joined the industry, including Johnny Tri Nguyen (*Spider-Man*, *X-Men: First Class*) and Dustin Nguyen (*21 Jump Street*, *Little Fish*). The two appeared together in the groundbreaking Vietnamese film, *The Rebel* (2007).

range from 30 to 100cm (12 to 39ins) in height and weigh from 1 to 5kg (2 to 11lbs). Larger puppets can weigh up to 20kg (44lbs) and need four people to help manipulate them.

As its origins and themes hark back to farming communities in feudal times, water puppetry is not merely enjoyable theatre, but also a living portrait of Vietnamese culture. A performance will consist of 12 to 18 acts, each telling a mythological story about Vietnam and its history, while a small ensemble of traditional musicians and *cheo* singers provide background music. One story, for example, tells the story of the tortoise that lived in Hanoi's Hoan Kiem Lake and supposedly emerged from the depths to provide King Ly Thai To with the sword he needed to fight off Chinese invaders.

Characters can be heroic, legendary or mythical, but most are ordinary peasants with plot lines that tend to be action-orientated as the puppets are unable to convey emotional conflict.

Food and drink

The essence of Vietnamese cuisine is the pursuit of perfect harmony and balance among the five essential flavours: sweet, sour, savoury, spicy and bitter. This balance may be achieved within a single dish or through an entire banquet, but the experience is always memorable.

Vietnamese cuisine is light, delicious, generally very healthy, and of endless variety. Rice (*com*) is the staple, topped with meat, fish and vegetables. Many Vietnamese believe that a proper meal must always include rice. Thus, one of the most common questions in Vietnamese following a greeting is, '*Ban an com chua* (Have you eaten rice yet)?'. Fresh, raw herbs, subtly spicy broths, separate dipping sauces, and condiments are prevalent in Vietnamese cuisine. Most sauces are made with a base of *nuoc mam* (a pungent fish sauce).

The ubiquitous and delicious *pho*

Modern Vietnamese cuisine borrows heavily from Chinese, but also is significantly influenced by French cuisine, and by some elements introduced by the Portuguese, Khmer and indigenous Cham. The Chinese contributed stir-fries, spring rolls, noodles and soy sauce; the French brought baguettes, pastries, pâté and dairy products. Together with the Portuguese, the French also introduced many of Vietnam's staples, including coffee, black pepper, potatoes and tapioca. Curries and many other spices probably came to Vietnam through the Cham and Khmer (both heavily influenced by Indian culture themselves).

NATIONAL CUISINE

Vietnam has three main culinary regions: the north (Hanoi), south (Saigon) and the centre (Hue and Hoi An), each with differences in both their main dishes and snacks, as well as their use of ingredients and methods of cooking.

The unofficial national dish, *pho* (rice-noodle soup) is the most common street food, especially in Hanoi. Usually eaten for breakfast, it makes a tasty meal at any time of the day. A hot, aromatic broth is poured over noodles topped with either slivers of rare beef (*bo*) or chicken (*ga*). In the south, chillies, lemon, sauces and herbs are added. *See p.37 for more on pho.*

Chao tom is another northern delicacy: finely minced shrimp baked on a stick of sugar cane, eaten with lettuce, cucumber, coriander *(cilantro)* and mint, and dipped in fish sauce. A Hanoi favourite is *bun cha*, charcoal-grilled pork meatballs served in a light broth, accompanied by cold vermicelli noodles, lettuce and herbs.

Hue, a city associated with Buddhism, is famous for its vegetarian cuisine, as well as for the food of the royal court. As the seat of Vietnam's last royal dynasty, many of the local dishes were once reserved for the king. Typical Hue specialities include *bun bo*, or fried beef and noodles served with coriander, onion, garlic, cucumber, chilli peppers and tomato paste; and *banh khoai*, a potato pancake.

As the country's modern commercial capital, Ho Chi Minh City is a place where food from every region can be found in bountiful supply. The city's most celebrated local dish is *banh xeo*, a sizzling crêpe pan-fried with pork, shrimps and bean sprouts, which is folded over and cooked to a crispy golden brown.

Other popular Vietnamese dishes include *cha gio* (known as *nem Saigon* in the north): 'spring rolls' of minced pork, prawn, crabmeat, mushrooms and vegetables wrapped in thin ricepaper and deep fried. These are then rolled in a lettuce leaf with fresh mint and other herbs, and dipped in a sweet fish sauce known as *nuoc cha:* the perfect vehicle for the five essential flavours of Vietnam.

The Mekong Delta is where the bulk of Vietnam's fresh fruit comes from: rambutans, lychees, mangos, bananas, pomelos are all grown there in abundance. Vegetables (particularly artichokes), strawberries and lots of flowers are grown around Dalat. The Central Highlands is the centre of Vietnam's coffee and tea production. Rice is grown in the lowlands, and dragonfruit, cashews, cassava, peanuts and jackfruit tend to be grown in arid coastal zones where soil quality is poor.

The Vietnamese are comfortable eating heavy meals of rice, meat and

Banh xeo is a savoury stuffed pancake

Meal times

Vietnamese eat breakfast between 6 and 8am. Restaurants that serve breakfast may offer it as late as 10am. Lunch is usually 11.30am to 1pm but sit-down restaurants may serve all afternoon. The best dinner offerings are from 5 to 7pm but many venues will stay open until 9pm or later. Dining after 11pm is uncommon but available in the bigger cities with some searching.

Street food in downtown Ho Chi Minh City

vegetables for breakfast, though *pho* is also popular in the morning. Lunch is generally taken at home. Courses come as they are ready, in no particular order. Desserts are light – usually fruit – but may include agar gelatin or *che* (fruit or bean puddings).

WHERE TO EAT
Street food
The most authentic (and best) Vietnamese food is found along streets, down alleys and inside local markets, where stall keepers specialise in just one dish and serve the freshest food. Look out for signs over stalls with steaming cauldrons surrounded by toy-sized plastic chairs. Snack vendors, particularly before and after school hours, sell tasty treats like *xoi* (sticky rice), *banh trang cuon nuong* (stuffed, grilled ricepaper rolls) and *nuoc mia* (sugar-cane juice). Compared with other countries, it's still relatively

inexpensive in Vietnam to dine out, and street food is astoundingly good value. Expect to pay no more than $1–2 per person on the street.

Diners and canteens
Basic indoor eateries, sometimes served in homes or shops, normally offer only one or two house specialities – noodle soups or rice meals with a selection of meat and vegetables. This differs from street food in the slightly higher prices, better seating arrangements, more reliable opening hours and better food hygiene. Usually diners and canteens are open for breakfast and dinner, but most are closed for lunch. Canteens usually have no menus, and often no beverages, other than free ice tea.

Vietnamese restaurants
Typical Vietnamese restaurants have a party atmosphere and are indeed

Dragonfruit in the Mekong Delta

popular for special occasions. The setting is open-air with long folding tables and chairs. Menus offer a large variety of meat and seafood dishes. Vegetarian options are sparse. *Lau* (hotpot eaten family-style) is the most popular dish in these restaurants. Beer is the beverage of choice, usually served by girls in tight-fitting uniforms.

Foreign restaurants

Foreign-owned restaurants and Vietnamese-owned restaurants serving foreign food mostly serve tourists and expats (with the exception of Chinese restaurants). The quality and variety of foreign food has vastly improved in Vietnam over the last decade, and now cuisines from France, Italy, India, Germany, UK, the Middle East and North America are well represented.

Standards range from backpacker lounges to fine, classical French dining. Some of the most notable venues include Sandals and Black Cat in Ho Chi Minh City (see p.225), Le Rabelais at the Dalat Palace (see p.194), the chains of Luna d'Autunno, Good Morning Vietnam and Shree Ganesh that are found nationwide, and Restaurant Bobby Chinn in Hanoi (see p.81), with a sister restaurant coming to Ho Chi Minh City in 2012. Service standards, atmosphere, hygiene and presentation take a much higher priority in foreign restaurants than in their Vietnamese counterparts.

Fast food and foreign coffee

Fast food arrived in Vietnam much later than surrounding countries. A few Western-style fast-food chains and cafés, like Lotteria (a Korean counterpart to McDonald's), Kentucky Fried Chicken and Highlands Coffee (the Vietnamese answer to Starbucks) have been around for a few years.

Newer arrivals include Gloria Jean's, Coffee Bean & Tea Leaf, Pizza Hut, Popeye's and Carl's Jr. Soft-serve ice cream and doughnuts have also recently arrived in force, though no recognisable brands have opened yet.

DRINKS
Fruit shakes

Vietnam cultivates a multitude of tropical fruit, some familiar, some not so familiar – mango, custard apple, durian, pineapple, star fruit, papaya and soursop, to name a few. Found everywhere are *Sinh To* stalls, recognisable by their glass cases displaying piles of fruit and a few vegetables. Point to a selection of fruit and you will receive a thick shake, mixed with sugar *(duong)*, ice and condensed milk. Tourist restaurants serve it as well.

Coffee and tea

The Vietnamese love their coffee. Vietnam is the world's second-largest coffee exporter after Brazil, and domestic coffee is decent but strong. Most coffee is grown in the Central

Western Highlands café in Hanoi

Highlands, in the vicinity of Buon Ma Thuot. Coffee *(ca phe)* comes iced *(da)* or hot *(nong)*; in local establishments, milk *(sua)* is usually sweetened and condensed. When it comes to tea, the Vietnamese prefer green tea, which is grown in the Central and Northern Highlands. *See cultural spread, p.198.*

Wine

Grapes are grown mostly in Ninh Thuan province, and then processed in Dalat. Dalat wine comes in red and white, and while palatable, it's not exciting. Thankfully, better restaurants have a large imported selection.

Rice wine

Rice wine comes in three main varieties: plain distilled alcohol known as *ruou gao*; 'medicinal' distilled alcohol infused with herbs and a range of animal ingredients *(ruou thuoc)*; and *ruou can*, which is a sweet alcohol fermented in large ceramic jars by hill tribes, who drink it on special occasions through long bamboo straws. Rice wine is sold strictly for home use.

Beer

The Vietnamese are avid beer drinkers and virtually any establishment will serve it at any time of the day. Saigon Beer is the popular and inexpensive local brand, with both red and green labels. Tiger and Heineken are also readily available. *Bia hoi*, or fresh (and very cheap) microbrewery beer, is particularly popular in Hanoi. The most popular branded microbreweries are the Louisiane Brewhouse in Nha Trang *(see p.179)*, and the nationwide chain, Hoa Vien.

Food and drink

Phrase book

Vietnamese, the national language, is spoken by nearly the entire population. Significant variations in pronunciation, some vocabulary, and even the tones themselves exist between dialects of the north, centre and south. Through the centuries of Chinese occupation, the Vietnamese adopted the Han characters. In the 13th century, they developed their own written variation – Nom. In the 17th century, missionaries translated the language into its Romanised form, Quoc Ngu. Thankfully, basic English is usually spoken by some people in any given destination or venue, but it is a good idea to learn some basic phrases.

PRONUNCIATION

This section is designed to familiarise you with the sounds of Vietnamese through the use of our simplified phonetic transcription. You'll find the pronunciation of the Vietnamese sounds below with a simple explanation, together with their 'imitated' equivalents in English pronunciation. Every syllable is pronounced with one of six tones (eg level, hanging, sharp, tumbling, asking and heavy), and different tones indicate different meanings, which makes it difficult for non-natives to speak Vietnamese.

TONES

Level tone, as in *ta* (I; we; let's): there is no tone marker for this; the voice stays at a pitch slightly above the normal pitch.

Sharp tone, as in *tá* (dozen): the pitch starts a little lower than at level tone before rising sharply.

Hanging tone, as in *tà* (evil spirit; bad): the pitch starts slightly lower than at level tone and then drops off.

Asking tone, as in *tả* (describe): the pitch starts at the same level as hanging tone. It dips initially and rises back to the starting pitch.

Tumbling tone, as in *tã* (diaper): At the beginning, the pitch starts a little above the hanging tone. It dips and then rises sharply to finish above the starting pitch.

Heavy tone, as in *tạ* (weight): the pitch starts at the same level as the hanging tone before dropping off. In most cases, the final consonant of words bearing a heavy tone is almost inaudible. For example, *đẹp* can sound like 'deh'. Put your lips in the position to say the final consonant, but stop short of actually pronouncing it.

CONSONANTS

Vietnamese consonants are divided into two categories: single consonants and combined consonants (inclusive of some semi-consonants).

Single consonants

Letter	Approximate pronunciation	Example	Pronunciation
b	like b in baby	ba	ba
c	an unaspirated 'k'	cô	ko
d	like z in zombie	dì	zi
đ	like d in dog	đảo	dao
g	like g in go	góa	gwa

h	like h in hotel	**hoa**	*hwa*
k	like k in Pakistan	**kiến**	*ki-uhn*
l	like l in load	**liễu**	*li-yoh*
m	like m in mother	**mưa**	*mur-uh*
n	like n in north	**nắng**	*nag*
p*	like p in pool	**pa nô**	*pa no*
q*	like qu in query	**qua nhiều**	*kwa ni-yoh*
r	like r in rich	**răng**	*rag*
s	like sh in shoot	**sẵn sàng**	*shan shag*
t	like t in stand	**tin tưởng**	*tin tew-ug*
v	like v in very	**vui**	*vui*
x	like s in sea	**xong**	*sog*

* Usually used in a form of combined consonants, with h and u respectively.

Combined consonants

Letter	*Approximate pronunciation*	*Example*	*Pronunciation*
ch	like ch in church	**chính**	*chin*
gh	like g in go	**ghế**	*ge*
kh	like the way Scots say loch	**không**	*kog*
ng	like ng in song	**ngang**	*gag*
ngh	like ng in song	**nghỉ**	*gi*
nh	like ny in canyon	**nhanh**	*nan*
ph	like f in fill	**pha**	*fa*
th	like th in breath	**thanh thoát**	*tan tuwat*
tr	like tr in train	**trà**	*tra*
gi*	like j in jacket	**giảng viên**	*jag vi-uhn*
qu*	like qu in quite	**quản lý**	*kwan li*

* Semi-consonant

VOWELS

Vietnamese vowels can be divided into three catagories: monophthongs (single vowels), diphthongs (double vowels), and triphthongs (triple vowels).

Monophthong

Letter	*Approximate pronunciation*	*Example*	*Pronunciation*
a	like a in father	**cá**	*ka*
ă	like a in jack	**bắc**	*bak*
â	like u in but	**cân**	*kan*
e	like e in red	**xe**	*se*
ê	like ay in say	**mê sảng**	*mei sag*
i*	like i in tin	**mí mắt**	*mi mat*
o	like o in cord	**to**	*to*
ô	like o in hello	**tô vẽ**	*to ve*
ơ	like u in fur	**sợi tơ**	*sur-i tur*
u	like oo in soon	**tu hú**	*too hoo*

| ư | like oo in good, spoken with an American accent | **mừng rỡ** | *moorg rur* |
| y* | like i in sin | **chữ ký** | *choo ki* |

* It is not easy to distinguish the usage of i and y. The position, the combination of the vowels and the consonants determines the usage of i or y in a word.

Diphthong

Letter	*Approximate pronunciation*	*Example*	*Pronunciation*
ai	like ai in Saigon	**mai**	*my*
ao	like ao in Mao	**cao**	*kao*
au	like au in Tau	**mau**	*ma-oo*
âu	like o in oh	**châu chấu**	*choh choh*
ay	like ay in play	**say**	*shay*
eo	ah-ao	**kéo**	*keh-ao*
êu	ay-oo	**mếu máo**	*may-oo mao*
iê	i-uh	**chiến thắng**	*chi-uhn tag*
iu	like ew in few	**tiu nghỉu**	*tew gew*
oa*	wa	**hoa**	*hwa*
oă	wa	**xoăn**	*swan*
oe*	weh	**khỏe**	*kweh*
oi	like oy in boy	**coi**	*koi*
ôi	oi	**tôi**	*toi*
ơi	ur-i	**chơi**	*chur-i*
ua	like our in tour	**thua**	*too-a*
uâ	oo-uh	**tuẩn**	*too-uh*
uê	oo-ei	**hoa huệ**	*hwa hoo-ei*
uô	oor	**cuống**	*koorg*
uy*	oo-i	**uy tín**	*oo-i tin*
ưa	ur-a	**mưa**	*mur-a*
ươ	ew-ur	**sương**	*shew-urg*
ưu	ur-ew	**về hưu**	*ve hur-ew*

* Semi-vowel

Triphthong

Letter	*Approximate pronunciation*	*Example*	*Pronunciation*
aiươi	ew-ur-i	**tươi**	*tew-ur-i*
iêu	like ilk in milky	**tiêu cự**	*ti-yoh kur*
uyên*	oo-in	**nguyên**	*goo-in*
uyêt*	oo-yit	**tuyết**	*too-yit*

* The basic components are 'uyê' but the pronunciation can be different. This depends on the consonant it pairs off with. Here, only the two most common combinations are mentioned.

0	**không** *kog*	100	**một trăm** *mot tram*
1	**một** *mot*	500	**năm trăm** *nam tram*
2	**hai** *haih*	1,000	**một nghìn** *mot gìn*
3	**ba** *ba*	1,000,000	**một triệu** *mot tri-yoh*
4	**bốn** *bón*	Monday	**thứ Hai** *tóor hai*
5	**năm** *nam*	Tuesday	**thứ Ba** *tóor ba*
6	**sáu** *shá-oo*	Wednesday	**thứ Tư** *tóor toor*
7	**bảy** *bảy*	Thursday	**thứ Năm** *tóor nam*
8	**tám** *tám*	Friday	**thứ Sáu** *tóor shá-oo*
9	**chin** *chín*	Saturday	**thứ Bảy** *tóor bảy*
10	**mười** *mèw-ur-i*	Sunday	**Chủ nhật** *chỏo nat*

Hello/Hi. Good morning/Good afternoon.	**Xin chào.** *sin chao*
Goodbye.	**Tạm biệt.** *tam bi-uht*
Good night.	**Chúc ngủ ngon.** *chóok gỏo gon*
Yes. (in response to a yes/no question)	**Có** *ko*
Correct. (to confirm a statement)	**Đúng** *dóog*
No. (in response to a yes/no question)	**Không** *kog*
Incorrect. (to confirm a statement)	**Sai** *shai*
OK.	**Vâng** *vag*
Excuse me! (to get attention)	**Xin chú ý!** *sin chóo í*
Excuse me. (to get past) Excuse me!/Sorry!	**Xin lỗi** *sin lõi*
How are you?	**Bạn khỏe không?** *ban kwẻh ko*
Fine, thanks. And you?	**Vẫn khỏe, cám ơn. Còn bạn?** *vãn kwẻh kám urn kòn ban*
I'd like…	**Tôi muốn…** *toi móorn…*
How much is that?	**Bao nhiêu tiền?** *Bao ni-yoh tì-uhn?*
Where is the…?	**…ở đâu?** *…ửr doh*
Please.	**Vui lòng** *voo-i lòg*
Thank you.	**Cám ơn** *kám urn*
Thank you very much.	**Cám ơn rất nhiều** *kám urn rát nì-yoh*
Please speak slowly.	**Bạn có thể nói chậm hơn không?** *ban kó tẻ nói cham hurn kog*
Can you repeat that?	**Bạn có thể nhắc lại không?** *ban kó tẻ nák lai kog*
I don't understand.	**Tôi không hiểu.** *Toi kog hỉ-yoh*
Do you speak English?	**Bạn nói tiếng Anh được không?** *ban nói tí-uhg an dew-urk kog*
My name is…	**Tên tôi là…** *ten toi là…*

Arrival and Departure

I'm on holiday [vacation]/business.	**Tôi đến đây để nghỉ mát/kinh doanh.** *toi dén day dé gỉ mát/kin zwan*
I'm going to…	**Tôi đang đi…** *toi dag di…*
How do I get to the… Hotel	**Tôi đến khách sạn… như thế nào?** *toi dén kák shan… noor té nà-o*

Money and banking

Where's the nearest…?	**…gần nhất ở đâu?** *…gàn nát ử r doh*
– bank	**– ngân hàng** *gan hàg*
– currency exchange office	**– phòng đổi tiền** *fòg dỏi ti-uhn*
Where are the ATMs [cash machines]?	**Máy ATM ở đâu?** *máy ei-ti-em ử doh*
I'd like to change pounds/dollars into Vietnamese dong	**Tôi muốn đổi đồng bảng/đôla Anh sang đồng Việt Nam.** *toi móorn dỏi dòg dola/bảg an shag dòg vi-uht nam*

Transport

1/2/3 for…	**Một/hai/ba vé đến…** *Mot/hai/ba vé dén…*
To… please	**Vui lòng đến…** *Voo-i lòg dén…*
single/one-way	**một chiều** *mot chì-yoh*
return/round-trip	**khứ hồi** *kóor hò-i*
When is the… flight to… Da Nang	**Khi nào có chuyến bay… đến Đà Nẵng?** *ki nà-o kó choo-ín bay… dén Dà Nãg*
First/next/last	**đầu tiên/tiếp theo/cuối cùng** *dòh ti-uhn/tí-uhp teh-ao/kóori kùg*
What time will we arrive?	**Chúng ta sẽ đến nơi lúc mấy giờ?** *chóog ta shẽ dén nur-i lóok máy jùr*
Is there a bus into town?	**Có xe buýt vào thành phố không?** *kó se boo-ít và-o tàn fó kog*
How do I get to the train station?	**Tôi đến nhà ga bằng cách nào?** *toi dén nà ga bàg kák nào*
How far is it?	**Bao xa?** *bao sa*
I'd like to reserve a seat.	**Tôi muốn đặt một vé.** *toi móorn dat mot ve.*
Which platform does the train to… leave from?	**Tàu đi… rời ga ở đường sắt số mấy?** *tà-oo di… rùr-i ga ử dèw-urg shát shó máy*
Is this the train to…?	**Đây là chuyến tàu đến…?** *day là choo-ín tà-oo dén…*
Where is the bus/coach station?	**Bến xe liên tỉnh ở đâu?** *bén se li-uhn tỉn ử r doh*
How long does the journey take?	**Chuyến đi mất bao lâu?** *choo-ín di mát bao loh*
Is this the right bus/tram to…?	**Có phải đây đúng là chuyến xe buýt đến…?** *kó fải day dóog là choo-ín se boo-ít dén…*
Where can I get a taxi?	**Tôi có thể gọi tắc xi ở đâu?** *toi kó tẻ gọi ták si ử r doh*
Please take me to the…	**Vui lòng cho tôi đến…** *voo-i lòg cho toi dén…*
– airport/train station	**– sân bay/nhà ga** *shan bay/nà ga*
– this address	**– địa chỉ này** *dia chỉ này*
How much will it cost?	**Giá sẽ là bao nhiêu?** *zá shẽ là bao ni-yoh?*

Accommodation

Can you recommend a hotel in…?	**Bạn có thể giới thiệu một khách sạn ở…?** *ban kó tẻ júr-i ti-yoh mot kak shan ử…*
How much is it per night?	**Giá mỗi đêm bao nhiêu?** *zá mõi dem bao ni-yoh*
I'd like a room with…?	**Tôi muốn phòng có…** *toi móorn fòg kó…òg kog*
– twin beds	– **hai giường đơn** *hai jèw-urg dur*
– a double bed	– **giường đôi** *jèw-urg doi*
– a bath/shower	– **phòng tắm** *fòg tam*
We'll be staying…	**Chúng tôi sẽ ở…** *chóog toi shẽ ử…*
– one night only	– **chỉ một đêm** *chỉ mot dem*
– a few days	– **vài ngày** *và-i gày*
– a week (at least)	– **(ít nhất) một tuần** *(ít nát) mot tòo-uhn*
How much is it…?	**Giá… là bao nhiêu?** *zá… là bao ni-yoh*
– per night/week?	– **mỗi đêm/tuần** *mõ-i dem/tòo-uhn*
– for bed and breakfast?	– **phòng và bữa sáng** *fòg và bữr-a shág*
What time do we have to check out by?	**Chúng ta thanh toán phòng lúc nào?** *chóog ta tan twán fòg lóok nà-o*
Can I have my bill please?	**Vui lòng cho tôi hóa đơn?** *voo-i lòg cho toi hwá durn*

Internet and communication

Can I access the internet here?	**Tôi có thể truy cập Internet ở đây không?** *toi kó tẻ troo-i kap internet ửr day kog*
How do I connect/log on?	**Tôi đăng nhập như thế nào?** *oi dag nap noor té nà-o*
I'd like a phone card please.	**Vui lòng cho tôi một thẻ điện thoại.** *voo-i lòg cho toi mot tẻ di-uhn twai*
Where's the post office?	**Bưu điện ở đâu?** *bur-ew di-uhn ửr doh*
What time does the post office open/close?	**Mấy giờ bưu điện mở/đóng cửa?** *máy jừr bur-ew di-uhn mửr/dóg kửr-a*

Sightseeing

Where's the tourist information office?	**Văn phòng du lịch ở đâu?** *van fòg zoo lik ửr doh*
What are the main attractions?	**Những điểm du lịch chính là gì?** *nõorg die-uhm zoo lik chín là gì*
Is there an English-speaking guide?	**Có hướng dẫn viên tiếng Anh không?** *kó héw-urg zãn vi-uhn tí-uhg an kog*
Do you have any information on…?	**Bạn có thông tin gì về… không?** *ban kó tog tin gì vè… kog*

Shopping

Where's the main shopping centre [mall]?	**Trung tâm thương mại chính ở đâu?** *troog tam tew-urg mai chín ửr doh*
How do I get there?	**Tôi đến đó như thế nào?** *toi dén dó noor té nà-o*
How much is this/that?	**Giá cái này/kia bao nhiêu?** *zá ká-i này/kia bao ni-yoh*
Can you help me?	**Bạn có thể giúp tôi không?** *ban kó tẻ jóop toi kog*

I'm looking for…	**Tôi đang tìm…** *toi dag tìm…*
I'd like…	**Tôi muốn…** *toi móorn…*
Where is the cashier [cash desk]?	**Thu ngân ở đâu?** *too gan ửr doh*
Thank you	**Cám ơn** *kám urn*

Culture and nightlife

What's there to do in the evenings?	**Vào buổi tối có thể làm gì?** *và-o bỏori tói kó tẻ làm gì*
Do you have a programme of events?	**Bạn có chương trình sự kiện không?** *ban kó chew-urg trìn shoor ki-uhn kog*
Can you recommend a good…?	**Bạn có thể giới thiệu một… hay không?** *ban kó tẻ júr-i ti-yoh mot… hay kog*
- concert	**– buổi hòa nhạc** *bỏor-i hwà nak*
- opera/ballet	**– buổi nhạc kịch/vở ba-lê** *bỏor-i nak kik/vửr ba-le*
- disco/nightclub	**– sàn nhảy/câu lạc bộ đêm** *shàn nẩy/koh lak bo dem*
Where can I get tickets?	**Tôi có thể mua vé ở đâu?** *toi kó tẻ moo-a vé ửr doh*

Emergencies

Help!	**Giúp với!** *jóop vứr-i*
Get a doctor!	**Gọi bác sĩ!** *goi bák shĩ*
Call the police!	**Gọi cảnh sát!** *goi kản shát*
Where's the nearest police station?	**Đồn công an gần nhất ở đâu?** *dòn kog an gàn nát ửr doh*

Health

Where can I find an English-speaking doctor/dentist?	**Ở đâu có bác sĩ/nha sĩ nói biết tiếng Anh?** *ửr doh kó bák shĩ/na shĩ bí-uht tí-uhg an*
It hurts here.	**Nó đau ở đây.** *nó da-oo ửr day*
I feel feverish.	**Tôi thấy nóng sốt.** *toi táy nóg shót*
Where's the nearest chemist [pharmacy]?	**Nhà thuốc gần nhất ở đâu?** *nà tóork gàn nát ửr doh*
What would you recommend for…?	**Bạn khuyên tôi làm gì với…** *ban koo-in toi làm gì vứr-i…*
- insect bites	**– vết côn trùng cắn** *vét kon tròog kán*
- diarrhoea	**– tiêu chảy** *ti-yoh chẩy*
- sunburn	**– cháy nắng** *cháy nág*

Eating out

Can you recommend a good restaurant?	**Bạn có thể giới thiệu một nhà hàng ngon không?** *ban kó tẻ júr-i ti-yoh mot nà hàg gon kog?*
Is there a… near here?	**Có… gần đây không?** *kó… gàn day kog*
- Vietnamese restaurant	**– nhà hàng Việt Nam** *nà hàg Vi-uht Nam*
- vegetarian restaurant	**– tiệm ăn chay** *ti-uhm an chay*
Can you recommend some typical local dishes?	**Bạn có thể giới thiệu một số món ăn địa phương đặc trưng không?** *ban kó tẻ júr-i ti-yoh mot shó món an dia few-urg dak troorg kog*
I'd like…	**Tôi muốn…** *toi móorn…*
The bill [check] please.	**Vui lòng cho xem hóa đơn.** *voo-i lòg cho sem hwá durn*

Meat, fish and poultry

thịt *tit*	meat (general)	**ga** *gà*	chicken
thịt bo *tit bò*	beef	**vịt** *vit*	duck
thịt lợn *tit lurn*	pork	**cá** *ká*	fish
thịt bê *tit be*	veal	**hải sản** *hả-i shản*	seafood

Vegetables

rau *rau*	vegetable(s)	**ớt (xanh)** *ửrt (san)*	peppers (green)
măng tây *mag tay*	asparagus	**đậu Hà Lan** *doh-u hà lan*	mangetouts
măng *mag*	bamboo shoots	**rau muống** *ra-oo móorg*	spinach
đậu *doh*	beans	**hành tươi** *hàn tew-ur-i*	spring onions
giá *zá*	bean sprouts	**cà chua** *kà choo-a*	tomatoes
nấm *nám*	mushrooms	**rau cải xoong** *ra-oo kả-i so-og*	watercress

Fruit

hoa quả *hwa kwả*	fruit (general)	**vải** *vả-i*	lychee
táo *tá-o*	apple	**xoài** *swài*	mango
chuối *chóor-i*	banana	**cam** *kam*	orange
nho *no*	grapes	**đào** *dà-oo*	peach
ổi *ổ-i*	guava	**dứa** *zéw-ur*	pineapple
mít *mít*	jackfruit	**dâu tây** *dâu tây*	strawberries
nhãn *nãn*	longan	**dưa hấu** *zew-ur hó-uh*	watermelon

Noodles, Rice, Bread

cơm trắng *kurm trág*	cooked white rice	**bún** *bóon*	soft noodles
cơm chiên/cơm rang *kurm chi-uhn/kurm rag*	fried rice	**mì sợi** *mì shur-i*	wheat/egg noodles
gạo nếp *gao nép*	sticky rice	**bánh mì** *bán mì*	bread
mì sợi/bánh đa *mì shur-i/bán da*	rice noodles	**bánh bao/bánh bao hấp** *bán bao/bán bao háp*	dumplings/ steamed buns

Dairy Products and Desserts

phó mát *fó mát*	cheese
sữa chua *sữr-a koo-a*	yoghurt
kem *kem*	cream
bơ *bo*	butter
sữa *sữr-a*	milk
kem *kem*	ice cream

Seasonings

muối *móori*	salt
tiêu *ti-yoh*	pepper
xì dầu *sì dòh*	soy sauce
nước mắm *néw-urk mám*	fish sauce

Drinks, Soups and Snacks

cà phê *kà fe*	coffee
trà xanh/đen *trà san/den*	green/black tea
rượu vang *rew-uru vag*	wine (grape)
rượu gạo *rew-uru gao*	rice wine
bia *bi-a*	beer
nước *new-úrk*	water
nước ép *new-úrk ép*	juice (fruit)
Khoai tây rán *kwai tay rán*	chips
bánh kếp *bán kép*	spring rolls
canh nóng *kan nóg*	hot soup
canh gà với ngô *kan gà vur-i go*	chicken and sweet corn soup

Index

Accommodation Index

Credits for Berlitz Handbook Vietnam

Written by: Adam Bray
Series Editor: Tom Stainer
Commissioning Editor: Tom Le Bas
Map Production: Stephen Ramsay and Apa Cartography Department
Production: Linton Donaldson, Rebeka Ellam
Picture Manager Steven Lawrence
Picture & Design Editor Tom Smyth
Photography:
All photography Peter Stuckings/APA except: akg images 271; Alamy 5BR, 58, 211, 246; The Cargo Club Restaurant 162; Corbis 15, 42, 59, 95, 163, 197, 238, 239T; CPA Media 199T, 268, 269; Georges Erhard/Rainbow Divers 6; Fotolia 7TR, 273; Getty Images 48, 272; Hilton Hotels & Resorts 88; iStockphoto.com 28, 255; Chien Lee/Minden Pictures/FLPA 44; Leonardo 157; Mark Newman/FLPA 47; OnAsia 199B, 239B, 247; Photolibrary 43, 125B; Andrea Pistolesi 198; La Résidence Hôtel & Spa 156, 252; Gaby Salas 9BL; Six Senses Resorts & Spas 178; Starwood Hotels & Resorts Worldwide 90, 224, 250; Tam Dao Golf Course 94; Victoria Hotels & Resorts 29, 113, 125T, 244; Werner Forman Archive 54

Cover: front: Corbis; back middle: Peter Stuckings/APA; back left: iStockphoto; back right: Corbis

Printed by: CTPS-China

Contacting Us

At Berlitz we strive to keep our guides as accurate and up to date as possible, but if you find anything that has changed, or if you have any suggestions on ways to improve this guide, then we would be delighted to hear from you. Write to Berlitz Publishing, PO Box 7910, London SE1 1WE, UK or email: berlitz@apaguide.co.uk

Worldwide: APA Publications GmbH & Co. Verlag KG (Singapore branch), 7030 Ang Mo Kio Ave 5, 08-65 Northstar @ AMK, Singapore 569880; tel: (65) 570 1051; email: apasin@singnet.com.sg
UK and Ireland: Dorling Kindersley Ltd, a Penguin Group company 80 Strand, London, WC2R 0RL, UK; email: customerservice@dk.com
United States: Ingram Publisher Services, 1 Ingram Boulevard, PO Box 3006, La Vergne, TN 37086-1986; email: customer.service@ingrampublisherservices.com
Australia: Universal Publishers, 1 Waterloo Road, Macquarie Park, NSW 2113; tel: (61) 2-9857 3700; email: sales@universalpublishers.com.au

www.berlitzpublishing.com